1867

1867

How the Fathers Made a Deal

~

CHRISTOPHER MOORE

National Library of Canada Cataloguing in Publication

Moore, Christopher
    1867 : how the Fathers made a deal / Christopher Moore.

Includes bibliographical references and index.
ISBN 0-7710-6094-7 (bound).—ISBN 0-7710-6096-3 (pbk.)

1. Canada–History–Confederation, 1867. 2. Fathers of Confederation.
I. Title.

FC474.M66 1997   971.04'9   C97-931484-4

We acknowledge the financial support of the Government of Canada through the Book Publishing Industry Development Program and that of the Government of Ontario through the Ontario Media Development Corporation's Ontario Book Initiative. We further acknowledge the support of the Canada Council for the Arts and the Ontario Arts Council for our publishing program.

Set in Minion by M&S, Toronto
Printed and bound in Canada

McClelland & Stewart Ltd.
The Canadian Publishers
481 University Avenue
Toronto, Ontario
M5G 2E9
www.mcclelland.com

3 4 5 6   08 09 10 11 12

"On all great subjects, much remains to be said."

–Walter Bagehot

CONTENTS

PREFACE

As If Confederation Mattered

~

Uring the collapse of the Meech Lake constitutional accord
– a collapse I watched with some regret but with a surprisingly
strong blend of contempt and anger – I took up Donald Creighton's
thirty-year-old *The Road to Confederation*. I had never worked
seriously on nineteenth-century political history, and much of
Creighton's story was, frankly, news to me. One detail about the way
the deal was made became stuck in my mind. Creighton mentioned
in passing that Nova Scotia's premier, Charles Tupper, was invited
to the constitutional conference at Charlottetown in 1864 – and
Tupper refused to go unless the leader of the opposition would go
with him.

This astonished me. I could not imagine any of today's imperial
first ministers ever considering such a proposal. I could not help
wondering what might have happened if they had. But Creighton
offered no explanation for Tupper's odd gesture, and when I asked
some of Canada's leading historians about it, none had any coherent explanation.

As I read further, it began to seem that the nineteenth-century makers of confederation worked with constitutional machinery rather similar to what exists today. Yet actions like Tupper's suggested they operated the machine differently. George Bernard Shaw once said that English and Americans are divided by a common language, and we have the same problem with our nineteenth-century constitution-makers. I began to wonder if a translation was possible, and if there were comparisons for our time in the processes for constitutional deal-making that the confederation-makers employed in the 1860s. This book is the product of that wondering.

As I tried to grasp the constitutional deal of the 1860s, I grew aware of how deeply unfashionable an exercise it was. If we have had one element of consensus amid our present constitutional wrangles, it lies in the agreement that we are wholly superior to those dead white males, the "fathers" of confederation. We probably know that John A. Macdonald was witty and a drunk, but we are unlikely to think his ideas on constitution-making have anything to do with us. "When the boys went down to Charlottetown," said Brian Mulroney disdainfully in 1990, "they spent a lot of time in places other than the library. There was no public participation." "The constitution of Canada must be a modern document," began one of Pierre Elliott Trudeau's constitutional proposals, with all the confidence of a platitude, as if our modern industriousness enables us to dismiss tradition and change our constitutions like hemlines.

Our experts take the same view. Peter H. Russell, to take one of the most accomplished of our political scientists, is massively learned in constitutional law and has been deeply involved in the recent decades of constitutional struggle. In the historical sketch with which this wise and humane observer of our national difficulties opens his book *Constitutional Odyssey* – its revealing subtitle is *Can Canadians Become a Sovereign People?* – Professor Russell allows only that the constitution-makers of the 1860s did not act "in a totally undemocratic matter," before dismissing their beliefs and processes out of hand. His book, which is indeed hugely informed and deeply thought-out, proceeds on the understanding that our inheritance from 1867 is worthless, that we are compelled to begin afresh to become what we have never been.

Professor Russell gets no argument from our historians. In the years before the Centennial celebrations of 1967, Canada's leading historians filled a shelf with books about confederation. And then they stopped. In the last thirty years, there has scarcely been a single new book about how confederation was made in the 1860s. Nineteenth-century high politics has vanished almost entirely from the agenda of the Canadian historical profession and the historical popularizers. The books are out of print, the documents almost unavailable, and the issues undebated. The historians of thirty and forty years ago became supremely unfashionable, and no one has begun to take a fresh look at their subjects.

Meanwhile, all the questions about constitution-making have changed. On the eve of the Centennial, there was inevitably a triumphal and celebratory mood in even the most scholarly treatises. Confederation had endured, and Donald Creighton read out the lesson: The fathers had decreed that a tightly centralized Canada was both the right answer and the inevitable one. Evidence to the contrary hardly seemed worth examining, and minor issues of just who had been in the room could be neglected. Today, when we have no such confidence about confederation, we find that the histories of the 1960s do not address the issues that seem most important.

The more I looked into the histories of confederation that languished on the shelf, the more contemporary analogies I wanted to pursue. I wanted to explore Charles Tupper's odd stance in 1864 – and what might have happened if contemporary premiers had responded similarly when invited to Meech Lake in\1987. I found myself comparing today's assumptions about leadership against the tactics that worked for John A. Macdonald. What did it imply for our pursuit of unanimity that about one in four of the men honoured as the "fathers of confederation" dissented from the confederation proposals of 1864 – or that four of their five legislatures at first refused to ratify a deal endorsed by premiers and opposition leaders alike? What did Hector Langevin, arguing *in favour* of the confederation settlement, mean when he declared that French Canadians were a separate people? Reading such questions into the 1860s, I found myself trying to take seriously the way their constitutional deal was made, and made to seem legitimate – not because they had all the answers, but because they help us to think differently about the way these matters are attempted today.

This book does not presume that the makers of confederation were heroes. Even on the discreet testimony of the triumphal histories and biographies, some seem to have been quite appalling human beings. Some of their strongest shared beliefs – that women must not vote, to cite only one – have no place in our world. Many of the accommodations they made to the circumstances of the 1860s need neither be justified nor imitated today.

Still, the political world of the citizens of the 1860s was not a separate universe from ours. In the midst of our repeated constitutional failures, we should not be so quick to condescend to their successes. Amidst the endless efforts to strike a constitutional "deal" that would become legitimate and lasting, I thought it might be worthwhile to interrogate the deal-makers of the 1860s about the deal-making processes that seemed to work then.

Considering historical analogies for present circumstances went against my habits as an historian. I have constantly preferred history's potential to offer examples of how gloriously foreign the past is, rather than to present didactic lessons. Nevertheless, the 1860s experience with constitution-making might enlighten us on several points:

• Constitution-making is divisive.
   The constitution-makers of the 1860s seem to have accepted that unanimity was not to be expected and disagreement had to be allowed for.

- Representative democracy has its uses.

  Much more than our counterparts of the 1860s, we have made access to voting nearly universal. They, however, were much more aware that a voting population is represented in legislatures, not in any particular first minister or party leader. Constitution-making in the 1860s was ultimately a legislative, rather than an executive, responsibility, and could not have succeeded otherwise.

- All legitimate political opinion deserves a place at the table.

  In the 1860s, government members and opposition members took each other "not by the hand but by the throat," (as the historian Ged Martin put it) and accepted each other's presence in constitution-making as essential. The practicality of this continues to elude our leaders.

- Constitution-making takes time.

  In the 1860s, for a union of just five small provinces and three and a half million people, thirty-six parliamentary delegates from several rival parties spent about seven weeks in face-to-face negotiating sessions spread over three conferences and two years. Even then, they would have done better to take longer and include more delegates.

This book considers how these lessons took hold in the politics of the 1860s. It is not by any means a complete account of confederation. Because I was interested mostly in the process by which a deal was made, and made to seem legitimate, I neglected a host of conditions specific to the 1860s: railway economics, the American civil war, tariffs and taxes, rivalries of region and class and religion, to name just a few. All these were vital in their time, but it was the processes of deal-making I was trying to follow.

Process mattered to me as an observer of Canada's seemingly endless struggles to reach and ratify a new constitutional deal. After twenty-five years of unsuccessful wrangles, I took for granted that a legitimate process was what was lacking. In his book *Meech Lake: The Inside Story*, Professor Patrick Monahan has argued otherwise, insisting that complaints about "process" were merely a "rallying cry for those who objected to Meech for other reasons." As an unelected adviser, Professor Monahan was virtually "in the room" at Meech Lake, and I claim none of his expertise about the content of that accord. But this book grew out of the sense that how the deals were made was far and away the most important obstacle to successful and persuasive constitutional reform in Canada in the 1980s and 1990s; indeed, that if there were a legitimate process, it might be possible to make and ratify a constitution.

It was on questions of that sort that the experience of the original confederation-makers seemed worth re-examining. This book is a reading of some political history as if confederation mattered.

ACKNOWLEDGEMENTS

I gratefully acknowledge the support of the Ontario Arts Council through a Work-in-Progress grant awarded to this work.

I would also like to thank executive producer Bernie Lucht and producers Alison Moss and Jill Eisen of CBC-Radio's "Ideas," where some of these ideas germinated. Alec Fiorentino and Ivan Chorney of Excelsior Collectors Guild in Ottawa helped turn my interest to the makers of confederation. Christopher Dafoe of *The Beaver: Exploring Canada's History* solicited an article on the subject. Beth MacAulay and Kristopher Churchill assisted me with research at different stages.

I hold that a writer ought to be able to leave work on the desk and lead a normal life outside working hours, but this book sometimes impinged on that schedule. I am deeply grateful to my wife, Louise Brophy, and my children, Elizabeth and Kate, for their tolerance in this and their support in so many other ways.

CHAPTER ONE

George Brown and Impossibility

∾

IN THE 1860s, western alienation began at Yonge Street, and George Brown was the Preston Manning of the day.

In the 1860s George Brown led a feisty, crusading regional party named Reform, and he expressed grievances that were more than regional. Like their late-twentieth-century counterparts, Brown's reformers wanted to change political life in Canada. Stubbornly, a perpetual minority, they insisted on their own particular program. They persisted even though the political establishment agreed that adopting reform's principles would shatter the compromises on which the fragile national consensus depended. Brown's ideas, said the men of the political centre, were fanatical and bigoted. They would sow dissension among the founding peoples and divide the regions one from another. Pushed to their logical consequences, they would destroy the union. For the sake of unity, there could be no place for George Brown or his radical ideas in the governing of the country.

The longer Brown was excluded from the ruling consensus, the more fiercely his regional supporters backed him. His faction grew stronger in what was then the West. He was marginal, prickly, alienated, and his only moment of power had been a fiasco – and yet he held a kind of veto over political development in the country. By the 1860s, George Brown was the impossible man. A "governmental impossibility," one of his former allies, now estranged, had called him, and his enemies took it up like a chant. But Brown could make government by his rivals nearly impossible, too. They could barely keep him out, but they couldn't imagine letting him in, either.

From this awkward position, George Brown became one of the architects of the most successful round of constitutional negotiations ever held in this country. He did it in partnership with men whom he hated and who despised him. And he did it on the policy of federalism, which seemed almost as much an impossibility as he was. The idea of a federal union of all of Britain's North American colonies had been around forever. Politicians of every stripe had trotted it out again and again, and they had never moved it one inch toward reality. When Brown began to promote federalism in 1859, even his supporters took it for a diversionary tactic more than a declaration of principle. As the 1860s began, constitutional change seemed simply not feasible.

Blockages, deadlocks, impossibilities – familiar aspects of late-twentieth-century Canadian politics – were the very stuff of political life in British North America in the years before confederation. George Brown, both a headstrong cause and a frustrated victim of the great political deadlocks of the mid-nineteenth century, is worth considering for more than merely antiquarian reasons. Fortunately, we have the means to consider his experience; a century after his immersion into impossibility, George Brown had the happy fate of becoming the subject of one of the most readable, engrossing histories written in Canada, J. M. S. Careless's remarkable biography *Brown of the Globe*.[1]

Encountered as a labelled spine on the library shelf, "Careless Brown of the Globe" may produce only a joke and a turning away. The two thick volumes, now more than thirty years old, seem to promise another respectful tombstone biography of another Victorian worthy, the kind of history book that is saluted more than read – and not even saluted very often. As the masterwork of a skilled historian inspired to a peak performance by the right subject, they deserve better. Sadly, however, they now need the same defence Careless once gave Brown himself. In his preface, Careless laments that George Brown "is generally envisaged among the 'fathers' of confederation as a stern, white-headed Old Testament patriarch – instead of the vigorous, exuberant man of forty-five that he was at the time." Brown, urges Careless, "deserves rescuing from the indifference and near-ignorance that Canadians so often display about their past."

So indeed do confederation and all its makers, for Brown is hardly unique. Except for John A. Macdonald, who everyone knows was a drunk, the men whom we call the fathers of confederation blur together, a single stultifying mass of white-haired patriarchy. The confederation they made seems boring because it seems irrelevant, and it seems irrelevant because it seems to have been so easy, indeed inevitable. Professor Russell speaks for a consensus when he gives us a group that was like-minded in its ruling assumptions, unanimous in its agreements, and unencumbered by the constraints of democracy. So it is useful to rediscover that Canadian politics in the 1860s was as full of hatreds, conflicts, suspicions, and impossibilities as it was in the late twentieth. George Brown is a wonderful guide to all those conflicts and obstacles, and he even offers a clue as to how to overcome them.

Careless's vigorous, exuberant man in his forties was already a political veteran in the 1860s – he had held a seat in the colonial assembly since 1851. He was also influential and becoming wealthy. As the editor and publisher of the most important newspaper in British North America, the *Globe*, he made his opinions heard throughout the colonies. Most people who heard them might have agreed with Careless's "vigorous" and "exuberant," but they used other terms too: hothead, smasher, extremist, bigot.

Brown talked of union, but his career had flourished amid poisonous hatreds. For all his talk of building a nation, he was a fervent southern-Ontario patriot, and the fierce pride he took in his own fast-growing, prosperous region dismayed all the other regions. He resented French-Canadian and Roman Catholic influence over the union that already existed between the future Ontario, then Canada West, and the future Quebec, then Canada East. Catholic Canada East mostly loathed him as a bigot. He talked of federation with the Maritime colonies and expansion to the West, but he hardly knew the East, and his interest in the prairie West was frankly imperial. He talked of co-operation – but he had helped provoke endless splits in his own reform coalition. With his great conservative rival, John A. Macdonald, he nursed a venomous mutual hatred. The two men had not spoken in years, unless they were hurling invective at each other in the legislature.

Brown was good at invective. He liked polemics, and he was always ready to assume he knew just what Canada West required. That kind of thing had made him a success in the newspaper business almost from the moment he founded the *Globe* in March 1844. Young Brown, not yet twenty-five and an immigrant newcomer when he started the paper, quickly proved himself as a publisher and as a hard-headed businessman. The *Globe* began as a weekly, moved to two, and then three, issues a week, and became a daily in its tenth year. Brown marketed his paper energetically, taking advantage of the new railroads to offer same-day delivery in Hamilton and London and other centres all over the province. As circulation grew, he poured money into better presses, larger premises, new wire services, and a widening network of correspondents.

It was a good time for Brown to offer himself as the tribune of Canada West, a good time for a vigorous, useful newspaper. What had been Upper Canada was putting aside the homespun days of being Montreal's up-country frontier dependency. It was beginning to display the strengths that would make it the powerhouse of the new confederation. The population, swelled by constant immigration from Britain, was surging past a million. The farmlands were filling up. The commercial towns were prospering. Railroads now linked them to each other and to their markets.

The busy, prosperous, proud people of Canada West read the *Globe* for its news, its advertising, and its features – in its second year it ran a new Dickens novel as a serial – and many who abhorred Brown's politics read the *Globe* for those qualities. But Brown's *Globe* was above all pungently political. Its creed was the political faith Brown had absorbed and made his own in his family's literate, well-informed, politically active milieu in Scotland. That faith was classical British constitutionalism, which rooted the liberties of Englishmen (and Scotsmen, and potentially colonials, too) in parliamentary government under the Crown. British constitutionalism had seemed backward and out-of-touch in the republican climate of New York City, where Brown and his father lived for five years after they first crossed the Atlantic in 1837. In Canada, however, such views put Brown firmly on the progressive side of the key political battles. It is difficult, at this remove, to imagine that parliamentary government could be controversial and could make Brown hated or loved or dismissed as impossible, but it is worth the effort.

The first controversial cause Brown championed in the *Globe* was the thing called responsible government. To state Brown's position today is to provoke wonder as to what could have been controversial. Simply, Brown believed that politicians elected by the voters, not a governor appointed from Britain, must control the making of domestic policy. Specifically, the governor should defer in policy matters to his executive committee – the cabinet, as it was already being called. And the cabinet in turn should be selected from, and responsible to, the elected legislature. It is now hard to imagine the Canadian governor general being descended from powerful, policy-making autocrats. But in 1845 there were such governors, and the curbing of their authority was the hottest of political issues.

The British North American colonies of 1845 were emphatically not self-governing. Most men, though no women, voted, and they had been electing assemblies since 1792 in "the Canadas," as far back as 1758 in Nova Scotia. The assemblies they elected had some real power, including powers of taxation. But the governor in each colony had powers too, including control of revenues that often left him in little need of the tax monies that only the legislature could provide.

The governor answered to Britain's government, not to the colony's voters. He was usually an aristocrat experienced in colonial administration or in service in the British cabinet itself, and the British government intended him to carry out its colonial policy. He also represented, at least in theory, a firm personal authority. Buttressed by the prestige of Britain and his own aristocratic standing, he could expect to be honoured as a figure worthy of respect and deference from all, immune to the factional strife of petty locals. In 1845, the governor in each British North American colony still appointed his own cabinet (it was then called his council) to run the departments of government under his direction.

This system had worked badly. For all the governor's personal authority, his broad powers seemed arbitrary instead of dignified – and the elected assembly had enough sense of its own importance to resent the limitations upon it. So governors and assemblies fought, and in the Canadas the fight veered outside the confines of legitimate government. In 1837, rebellions against arbitrary government had exploded in both Upper and Lower Canada. When the rebellions were crushed, the governors emerged stronger than ever. When the two troublesome colonies were stuck together in the united Province of Canada, the intention was as much to buttress British authority as to yield power to either of them.

After the rebellions, however, the governors – and the British government – wanted to avoid the confrontations between assemblies and governors that had plagued the 1830s. Governors tried to find supportive assemblymen, and they sought cabinet members acceptable to the assembly. In effect, governors found themselves trying to win elective support without actually becoming bound to any party line. They proposed a compromise: they would co-operate with elected representatives without entirely yielding to them.

Many politicians and voters were ready to accept the governors' olive branch – and the governors' patronage, since they remained the font of honours, favours, and jobs. The governors' common-sense request to be allowed to run administrations composed of the best-qualified men, "above mere faction," convinced many British North Americans. It was, after all, an appeal to good will, a plea for accommodation among reasonable men who shared the goal of good government.

George Brown was among those who would have nothing to do with this half-measure. Characteristically, it was for him a matter of absolute principle. As long as the governor preserved the power to "take steps" on his own, parliamentary government was compromised. Brown would tolerate no compromise of a fundamental rule: "The executive cannot take a step without the advice of his council – his council must be chosen from the representatives of the people and have their confidence."[2] This was the nub of responsible government: an executive constantly answerable as a group to the people's elected representatives. A cabinet would be put into office by the legislature whether the governor liked its members or not, and the cabinet would be bounced from office the moment a majority of the legislators turned against it, even if it held the governor's confidence. Brown insisted on parliamentary government. British North Americans in their internal affairs must have all the powers of British citizens.

Indeed, Brown was more radical than the British example he constantly cited. Giving power to parliamentarians meant empowering those who elected them. In British North America as in Britain in the 1840s, property owners alone could vote. But in the colonies (unlike Britain), property ownership was widespread, and most Canadian men voted. Not only would a properly constituted Canadian government be controlled by the representatives of the people, trumpeted Brown in the *Globe*, but "in the election of those representatives, so low is the qualification that no man need be without a vote if he chooses to have one."[3] Brown's government would be not only responsible, but also representative. In the British North America of the early 1840s, Brown's position was controversial, reformist, and democratic. He never deviated from it.*[4]

In 1845, just after George Brown launched the *Globe* in Toronto, Governor General Lord Metcalfe, architect of the "governor-above-party" line, retired home to Britain. Metcalfe had recently helped to bring about the defeat of the reformers in a general election, but he was battered from the endless political strife. Metcalfe was also dying; facial cancer had already blinded and disfigured him. Yet, when his retirement was announced, Brown showed no sympathy. He promptly produced a special celebratory issue of the *Globe*. "We heartily congratulate the country on the departure of Lord Metcalfe," he wrote.

Brown abominated the policies Metcalfe had pursued; everyone knew that. Still, the attack suggested why many would see George Brown as a political "impossibility." His attack on the aging, sickly governor could seem not only vindictive, but also tinged with disloyalty. Metcalfe, after all, represented the natural authority of the British aristocracy, the majesty of the Queen, and all the glory of Britain and its Empire. These had no small attraction in Britain's North American colonies. The colonies needed Britain, and loyalty meant a lot. Criticism of a governor, even when voiced in constitutional terms by a loyal Briton, still smacked of *lèse-majesté*.

Yet the principle championed by the reformers whom Brown supported in his paper (and would soon join in the legislature) triumphed. The Metcalfe policy, which had obliged the governor's picked team to win every election and every legislative vote, never

---

* The electoral franchise and its exclusions are considered in more detail in Chapter Six.

was feasible. In 1847, after a change in government in Britain itself, the Colonial Office accepted that its governors in British North America must appoint as their ministers whomever could command support in the elected legislature – and no one else.

No act of Parliament, no notable ceremony, marked the transition, and in the various colonies it took effect over several years. But it was momentous. Henceforth British North America's internal affairs would be directed by politicians who could command the support of its elected legislatures. Canadian politics assumed a form still familiar at the end of the twentieth century. Lieutenant-governors and governors general suddenly became ceremonial. They would entrust the government to the leaders of the dominant party. They would appoint friends of that party to all the jobs and posts that had previously been the governor's patronage, and they would sign into law whatever bills the governing party could get through the elected legislature.

"Under British responsible government as now in operation in Canada," wrote George Brown a couple of years later, "the people of Canada have entire control over their public affairs."[5] Within about a decade, the British government would acknowledge that the British North American colonies had the right even to decide whether they would remain part of the British Empire. In effect, the Canadian colonies had secured sovereign authority over their own affairs. Responsible government had created the conditions under which confederation would be made and ratified less than twenty years later. All the makers of confederation were children of that moment.

Brown had been on the winning side on responsible government in the late 1840s, though he was only a fledgling journalist and held no elective office. By the 1860s, responsible government was no longer controversial. Its former opponents had adapted to the new facts of political power so successfully that they had defeated and replaced the reform ministries in several of the British North American provinces. Ironically, another of George Brown's great principles had

helped doom the reformers to minority status in the united Canadas
– and had made him the voice of western alienation and anger.

George Brown believed fiercely in the separation of church and
state. Not because he was irreligious or anti-religious. Brown was
a devout, God-fearing Scots Presbyterian, an heir to those early
Protestants who had first condemned the worldly power and worldly
corruption of the Church of Rome. His "voluntaryism" – the conviction that churches should be supported by their believers, not
by the state – was deeply rooted in his family. An invitation to his
father to edit a Toronto Presbyterian newspaper "on the voluntary
principle" had helped bring the Browns to Canada. As true Scots
Presbyterians, the Browns would have no bishops, no popes, and no
elaborate worldly institutions standing between a man and his God.

Today, separation of church and state seems as much a political
platitude as responsible government. Even in the 1860s, church and
state were separate; there were no longer any "established" churches
in the colonies. But it was an age of faith, and everywhere religion
impinged on politics. The split between tories and reformers over
responsible government could still be found mirrored in tension
between high-church Anglicans and evangelical-minded dissenters
like the Presbyterians. It was Catholics, however, not Protestants, who
felt most threatened by the voluntaryism that was part of George
Brown's religion and his politics. And in the union of the Canadas,
what threatened Catholics threatened the union itself, for Canada East
was as staunchly Catholic as Canada West was Protestant.

As a Scotsman, a Briton, and a Protestant, Brown had been
brought up to cherish deep suspicions of the Roman Catholic Church.
Any Presbyterian minister could thunder for hours about the
Church of Rome's worldly pomp, its idolatry, its support for super-
stition and ignorance, and its malevolent efforts to inject popish
power into civil society. The historical pageant of British liberty and
parliamentary government, which Brown loved and sought to extend
to British North America, was also a story of English resistance to

the pope, to absolutist and Catholic powers in Spain and France, and to the Catholic Stuarts, who had been deposed from the English throne in 1688. Brown could not help but look with scepticism and alarm at the Catholic Church, wherever it was found. And in British North America, Catholicism was as fundamental as the French language to the identity of the majority population of Canada East.

Brown respected the right of all people to worship as they pleased. Individual liberties and freedom of conscience were touchstones of his politics, amply demonstrated in his support of anti-slavery movements and of American slaves who had escaped to Upper Canada. He believed in economic freedom too: freedom of trade, freedom of contract, unfettered competition of the kind the *Globe* had with many rival newspapers. But the kind of religious freedom Brown ringingly defended was not the kind most Roman Catholics wanted.

In the 1850s, the Catholic Church was on the move. In Lower Canada, dynamic bishops, supported by energetic priests from newly founded seminaries, had shored up the church's institutions and extended its moral influence. The church no longer needed to curry the support or tolerance of powerful governors. As political power shifted from royal governors to elected parliamentarians, bishops and priests could influence Catholic voters directly, and they did so openly and willingly. Few politicians seeking election in Catholic communities cared to provoke the disapproval of the church.

The church's social role and political power were most evident in francophone Lower Canada. But as Irish Catholics poured into Upper Canada, the church was eager to acquire the same place there for its bishops, its separate schools, and its social message. No admirer of the church's social and political sway in Lower Canada, George Brown was all the more alarmed to sense Catholicism on the march in Upper Canada.

Brown's opposition to separate schools, to the extension of Catholic dioceses, to the political influence of priests and bishops –

to what he called "priestcraft and statechurchism" – all flowed from his voluntaryist principles. And they tended to alienate every Catholic who heard them. It made little difference to faithful Catholics whether Brown was in his heart a principled voluntaryist or simply an anti-Catholic fanatic. They understood he was no friend to them or to their religion as it was practised.

Whether voluntaryism or bigotry, Brown's campaign to separate church from state was no friend to his own political ambitions either. In the union of Canada East and Canada West, where the East was heavily Catholic and the West mostly Protestant, anything that raised Catholic–Protestant tensions was hotly political. Catholic legislators wanted nothing to do with Brown, and voluntaryism as Brown espoused it played a vital role in keeping his reform cause out of power for a generation. Voluntaryism cemented his reputation as an anti-French politician at a time when the first requirement for political success was the building of French–English alliances.

Britain had forged the Province of Canada in 1841 amidst ringing declarations that its purpose was to absorb and assimilate French Canada into a properly British colony. In renaming Lower and Upper Canada as Canada East and Canada West and fusing them together under a single parliament, the Colonial Office hoped to see the anglophone majority take firm control. It did not happen. Under responsible government, the provincial Parliament became the forum in which the political power of the francophone minority of what is now Canada was permanently established. In retrospect, the reason seemed obvious to anyone who could count votes: Canada East had half the seats in the assembly of the new union, and most of those depended on francophone votes. Minority status encouraged the francophones, much more than their anglophone neighbours, to vote as a cohesive bloc. As a result, Canada East was never much more than one vote away from a working majority.

As soon as the union of the Canadas was formed in 1841, reform strategists in Canada West grasped that an alliance with Canada East was their sure and only route to power, and the man they had to talk to was Louis-Hippolyte LaFontaine. LaFontaine had seen in the assembly a forum in which to defend the French-Canadian community – *if* the assembly achieved its potential through responsible government. On that basis, he secured massive support from the francophone electorate for the policy of responsible government. In the 1840s, responsible government produced an alliance between Catholic francophones (otherwise suspicious of English Protestant power) and Protestant anglophones (otherwise rather anti-Catholic and anti-French). That alliance put the reformers in power in 1848, under the joint leadership of LaFontaine and his partner from Canada West, Robert Baldwin.

Once responsible government (and francophone influence) was assured, however, the voters of Canada East had what they needed from that reformist alliance. They drifted toward more-conservative concerns – notably the preservation of their language, faith, and traditions against English Protestant onslaughts. Reformers in Canada West also moved on – to issues such as separation of church and state. Since French Canadians understood these as code for an assault upon their religion, indeed upon their whole society, the alliance of English and French reformers soon fell apart. As long as George Brown's newspaper was raising the alarm about "papal aggression" and proclaiming "no permanent peace in Canada until every vestige of church domination is swept away," there was not much likelihood of restoring an Anglo–French reform coalition. A new and longer-lasting partnership between French and English leaders of the union was forged. It was conservative rather than reform-minded. Its great names were George-Étienne Cartier, who was LaFontaine's political heir, and John A. Macdonald, who was Brown's nemesis.

By the 1850s, when George Brown took a seat in the legislature, Canada West's reformers had detached themselves from those of Lower Canada – and put themselves out of power. Brown seemed to have imprisoned himself in the role of regional spokesman, eyed with suspicion and hostility by most of Lower Canada and by advocates of Anglo–French co-operation. The third great principle Brown came to advocate during the 1850s solidified his regional power, even as it seemed to preclude him from any larger role. This was the principle most of all that made Brown a governmental impossibility. He called it "rep-by-pop."

Representation by population is another apparently uncontroversial proposition.* It proposes that all votes should be of the same weight, and that communities of equal size should have equal representation in the legislature. In the union of the Canadas, however, representation by population had been overruled by a competing principle, sectional equality.

When the union was made in 1841, sectional equality had been an essential part of Britain's plan to control and assimilate the French-speaking population. Francophone Lower Canada, despite its larger population, had been compelled to accept only the same number of assembly seats as Upper Canada, instead of the clear majority that "rep-by-pop" would have given it. But within a decade, constant immigration to Upper Canada – the Brown family was part of that migration – had reversed the proportions. Suddenly sectional equality became a protection for the French Canadians against their shrinking relative numbers. At just that point, Upper Canadian reformers began to campaign for rep-by-pop – more seats for Upper Canada, in effect, and probably more seats for Upper Canadian reformers.

It is easy – it was easy in the 1850s – to make sectional equality seem little more than cynical gerrymandering. Each section of the united Canadas, after all, had denounced sectional equality when its numbers were larger and embraced it when outnumbered. But the defence of sectional equality was, in its way, as principled as

---

* Maybe not. The "provincial equality" proposed by advocates of the Triple-E Senate has been criticized on rep-by-pop grounds. And when the Charlottetown accord proposed to guarantee Quebec one-quarter of the seats in Parliament, rep-by-pop did indeed become controversial again.

rep-by-pop. One of its great defenders was an old reform ally of George Brown, Francis Hincks.

Francis Hincks is mostly known to historians as a master financier. He could work out deals of astounding complexity, which usually proved to be of substantial benefit to his friends. The most notorious of these was "The Ten Thousand Pounds Job" of 1852, when his government guaranteed some previously risky private bonds. The bonds naturally jumped in value, enriching Hincks himself, at the expense of much of his reputation, and obliging his withdrawal from Canadian politics for more than a decade.

But deal-maker Hincks was also one of the architects of the politics of the union of the Canadas. He moved easily between Montreal and Toronto, and his legwork had fused the mutually suspicious blocs led by Robert Baldwin and Louis-Hippolyte LaFontaine into the reform majority that had secured responsible government. When reformers like Brown endangered that French-English alliance, Hincks stood by it. "The truth was," said Hincks in 1853, as he demolished George Brown's arguments for rep-by-pop, "that the people occupying Upper and Lower Canada were not homogeneous; but they differed in feelings, language, laws, religion and institutions, and therefore the union must be considered as between two distinct peoples, each returning an equal number of representatives." [6]

Hincks understood – as all the really successful politicians of the union eventually did – that so long as Canada East and Canada West were joined together, Anglo–French alliances were the key to power. Alliances had to be built on trust, and trust was founded on an equality that would outlast any particular election or census. To give either side predominant influence over the politics of both could only destroy the other side's trust in the union itself. Sectional equality had become the *raison d'être* of a state originally intended as a machine for assimilation. That was why reformer Hincks, the sectional-equality man, dismissed fellow reformer Brown, the apostle of rep-by-pop, as a governmental impossibility.

Yet it was not hard, at least in Canada West, to find justice in Brown's principle, too. The *Globe* and George Brown exulted in Canada West's size and prosperity, and at the same time they seethed with indignation that their region lacked the political clout to which its size and wealth and confidence made it feel entitled. It was no abstract indignation, either. Sectional equality meant that the cohesive bloc of French-Canadian legislators needed only a few supporters from Canada West to impose policies most of Canada West's voters and their representatives might oppose. During the 1850s, George Brown had conceived a passion for rep-by-pop, and it was shared by masses of Upper Canadian voters.

Francis Hincks the reformer – apostate reformer, in Brown's eyes – was not the only Upper Canadian ready to defend the union, even in the face of such consequences. Canada West's conservatives, including John A. Macdonald, who was rising to leadership among them, were also willing to forsake Protestant solidarity for the sake of the French–English sectional alliance. Macdonald could justify that alliance as essential to racial harmony and to the preservation of the union, but it also put him and his tory colleagues into power for much of the 1850s and 1860s. As LaFontaine's heir, Cartier led the big bloc of francophone legislators. As long as each section was equal in parliament, Macdonald needed only to deliver a handful of anglophone seats in order to give the Macdonald–Cartier partnership something close to a permanent majority.

Macdonald and his supporters saw themselves as adroit politicians, building the coalitions of interests that union politics demanded. Brown's reformers drew a different lesson: "sectional equality" meant the imposition of French Canada's agenda, no matter how unpopular, upon Canada West whenever Canada East got the support of a few western collaborationists, who would sacrifice western interests for the sake of the alliance that kept them in power. Brown concluded that "sectional equality" was a high-sounding phrase that masked an unscrupulous advantage for Canada East over Canada

West. He had his own ugly phrase for it: "French domination," and later simply "French Canadianism."

The fight between sectional equality and rep-by-pop lasted for a decade, and the survival of the union was always at stake. If French Canada would not accept rep-by-pop, would Canada West's reformers tolerate sectional equality for the sake of the union? Some would, to Brown's fury and frustration. John A. Macdonald, embattled-but-ever-resourceful leader of the small band of Upper Canadian conservatives, gleefully built his "Liberal–Conservative" party by drawing union-minded reformers, like Francis Hincks, into his coalitions with Cartier's Lower Canadian conservative *bleus*.

But other reformers were actually more radical than Brown in their attack on sectional equality and on other institutions of the union. Brown himself had dubbed them the "Clear Grits." If the union itself had to be sacrificed in order to bring in the rep-by-pop principle, the Clear Grits were ready to kill the union.

Even more than George Brown and his fierce parliamentary liberalism, the Clear Grits constitute a demolition of the legend that "democracy" was unknown to mid-nineteenth-century Canadians. Even today, enacting their platform would constitute a radical remaking of Canadian politics. In the 1850s, their victory would have produced a constitutional earthquake. The Clear Grits – "all sand and no gravel, clear grit all the way through" – intended to scrape away all the undemocratic and unegalitarian elements of their society to produce a pure democracy in Upper Canada. Like George Brown, they were eager to sweep away religious privilege and the injustices suffered by Canada West in the union. But they went much farther than Brown.

The Clear Grits attacked privilege of every other kind, too. Brown wanted the Queen to be a symbolic ruler, but still a revered one. The Clear Grits would replace the monarchy with a directly elected head of government. Brown had extolled parliamentary rule. Clear Grits proposed that every public official, from the governor down to local judges and officials, should be directly elected and wield power directly. They believed public institutions must be cheap, simple, efficient, and as local as possible: every man should be his own lawyer as well as his own political representative. They wanted legislators limited to fixed two-year terms. They had not brought themselves to admit the equality of women, but they would give a vote (and a secret ballot) to every adult male.

Of course, Clear Grits were rep-by-pop campaigners, for they were fierce partisans of the unfettered rule of the majority. Indeed, they were ready to be western separatists rather than compromise with the French Canadians of Canada East. Ready to junk British parliamentary traditions, they were also willing to consider annexation to the United States more favourably than dependence upon Catholic Quebec. But the radicalism of the Clear Grits did not mean they were fanciful, impractical theorists. They drew on close-by examples from the United States, but they also reflected British radicalism. Many British emigrants who had gladly left behind a Britain of privilege and inequality were ready to listen.

Clear Grits celebrated the sturdy self-reliance and innate egalitarianism of the farmers who had been the main supporters of rebellion in 1837, and the romance of 1837's lost cause became part of Clear Grit appeal. Upper Canada was a land of farmers, and farmers' votes were the essential source of electoral success. If the farmers of Upper Canada drifted into Clear Grit thinking, reform-minded politicians would have to consider drifting with them.

Brown had a moment when the constitutional dynamite of the Clear Grits – "organic change" was his shorthand for it – did attract him. His temptation began when the parliamentary system he had always extolled delivered him his most humiliating setback. George Brown tasted power in 1858 – for two days. Then he fell victim to the double shuffle.

The double shuffle of August 1858 is the kind of event that persuades historians not to write about nineteenth-century politics. It depends on such an accumulation of period detail and constitutional arcana that making it plausible is like trying to explain the notwithstanding clause to a visiting Martian. Nevertheless, the effort may be worthwhile. The obscurities of the double shuffle can help to suggest constitutional choices of the 1860s that echoed in the 1990s.

The fundamental fact of union politics was the diversity of political faiths and factions. The split between reformers and conservatives, compounded by regional and linguistic divisions, resulted in two sets of reform and tory caucuses, one each for Canada West and Canada East. Those blocs often divided into the alliance-minded (Hincks, the reformer, for instance) and the no-compromisers (the Clear Grits, for example). In addition, there were independents, who joined parties or followed leaders only on their own terms and schedules. Such diversity made for lively politics, frequent crises, and endless jockeying (sometimes subtle, sometimes startlingly ruthless) to make parliamentary coalitions and to build voter loyalties. If deal-making is the essence of politics, then the politics of the union of the Canadas was second to none in the world.

Brown's moment of power in the summer of 1858 began with the fall of one coalition ministry and the fight to build another. Macdonald and Cartier's government, caught in a compromise that had managed to alienate supporters on both edges of the coalition, had lost its majority and decided to resign. Barely six months had passed since a general election, and Brown seized his chance by offering to avert an election. He offered to see if he could assemble a legislative majority where Macdonald and Cartier had just failed. In association with Antoine-Aimé Dorion, leader of the French-Canadian reformers called the *rouges*, Brown went to see the governor general, a scholarly Englishman named Sir Edmund Walker Head.

We will see more of Antoine-Aimé Dorion and the *rouges* in another chapter. Suffice it here to acknowledge that French-Canadian politics was not monolithic. George-Étienne Cartier, secure in the approval of the church, a spokesman for conservative French-Canadian opinion, and approved by the tycoons of English Montreal's

Square Mile, might dominate politics in Canada East, but the *rouges* had inherited a minority tradition that was reformist and frequently secular-minded, if not actually anti-clerical, when such positions exposed them to fiercer attack in Catholic Canada East than Brown's voluntaryism had to endure in Protestant Canada West.

As reformers, the *rouges* had some common ground with the western reformers, but only some. The *rouges* expressed anti-English grievances as vigorously as the reformers expressed anti-French ones, and the coalition was risky for both partners. Dorion and his group were to join George Brown, universally condemned in Canada East as a bigot, an anti-Catholic, and an Upper Canadian imperialist. For his part, Brown, the scourge of French domination and sectional equality, was proposing to lead his reformers into a government as dependent on the votes of Canada East as any of John A. Macdonald's.

Brown saw this as his moment to show he was not merely a sectional protest leader – or a bigot either. He and Dorion promised a government that would prove reform ideas were not impossible, and that they could save the union rather than destroy it. Brown and Dorion promised to introduce rep-by-pop while safeguarding the position of Canada East, to build a secular education policy without threatening Catholic education, and generally to advance Canada West's interests without damaging Canada East's.

Governor Head seems to have shared the widespread suspicion that both Brown and Dorion were dangerously radical and their principles a threat to the union, but they were entitled to form a government. They assembled a cabinet and thrashed out the basis of an agreement between their parties.

Brown and Dorion never had a chance to flesh out their promises or test them in action. Their new government had to meet the legislature and win a vote of confidence. Under the custom then still prevailing, politicians who accepted public office were obliged to resign their seats and seek the approval of their constituents for their decision to serve in the Crown's administration. So Brown, Dorion, and all the members who had become cabinet ministers had to resign and watch from the gallery as their government faced its first legislative test one day after they took office.* Their absence ensured the defeat of their government.

At this point, Brown and Dorion wanted a general election, in which they could run as a government seeking a mandate rather than as a collection of opposition members. They asked Governor Head to dissolve the legislature. But Sir Edmund refused. In the 1850s, as in the 1990s, granting or refusing dissolution of the legislature was one of the few enduring powers of a governor general. Head used his authority to snub Brown and Dorion's advice about a new election. Already he had an alternative government at hand.

The ever-inventive Macdonald and Cartier had put their problems behind them, rebuilt their coalition, and recruited some new supporters. They were ready to try again, and Governor Head was ready to let them. He invited Macdonald and Cartier back into power. In just three days, Macdonald and Cartier had resigned, been replaced, defeated their successors in the House, built a new coalition, and regained office. Once again they were in and Brown was out.

Even after going back through the revolving door on the cabinet room, Macdonald and Cartier had to pull one more rabbit from their top hat of parliamentary skills, for they had to evade the problem that had beaten Brown and Dorion: the need to resign their seats and

---

* There was an ancient logic to this odd requirement. When kings actually ruled, parliaments existed not to govern but as a check upon the government of the Crown. Hence a parliamentarian who agreed to become an adviser to the Crown – a cabinet minister, in other words – was about to serve two masters: the king and the people. It was thought proper that he should secure the consent of his electors before doing so. As the parliament took control of government, and the king ceased to rule, the two-masters problem became moot. But constitutional usages die hard. The obligation on a new cabinet minister to seek re-election survived past confederation.

seek personal re-election upon accepting office. Macdonald and Cartier proved equal to the challenge by inventing the double shuffle.

Ministers who merely changed cabinet posts did not need to be re-elected. So, as if they had never left office, Macdonald and Cartier and their ministers solemnly shuffled the cabinet offices amongst themselves, and then after a day reshuffled them. Each minister recovered his old position, and Macdonald blithely told the House the law had been satisfied. While the Brown–Dorion team was still out seeking re-election to validate its members' right to offices that had already been taken away from them, the Cartier–Macdonald team reoccupied its old cabinet posts and held on to its legislative seats. After two days in opposition, Cartier and Macdonald would stay in office for two more years – an eternity in the union's lively politics.

Those two days were the only days George Brown would ever run a government. (Dorion had another brief stint in power in 1863-4.) His "short administration" was a humiliating failure. Opponents rejoiced that the disaster of a Brown government had been avoided, and happily denounced his greedy, short-sighted lust for power. They mocked him for abandoning his principles for office and then losing the office as well, proving he was not merely unworthy of political office, but also too inept to get it. More than ever, they said, George Brown had proved himself a governmental impossibility.

Locked once again in opposition, his causes and ambitions further than ever from becoming realized, Brown went from fury to a kind of despair. Brown's newspaper poured abuse on the governor general who had hobbled Brown and assisted Macdonald, and the reformers launched a court challenge to the double shuffle. When they lost, Brown observed bitterly that the presiding judge was William Draper, Macdonald's mentor and himself a tory premier from the bad old days before responsible government. But Brown's condemnations began to go beyond personalities. He began to condemn not just Macdonald, Cartier, the judges, and Sir Edmund Head, but the constitutional system that had made possible his humiliation.

Over the next months, the *Globe* began to sound steadily more like the Clear Grits. "Responsible government," said the paper in February 1859, "has not realized the expectations of its promoters. Men begin to pronounce it a failure." Brown spoke the same epitaph in a political speech. Given the enduring existence of two incompatible popular wills – French Canada's and English Canada's – he said sadly, "responsible government could only end in failure." And with the union and parliamentary government simultaneously discredited, the *Globe* began to proclaim that dissolution of the union and a presidential constitution for Canada West were the likely choices to replace them. Sir Edmund Head's tampering with the usages of the constitution, said the *Globe*, had done more to Americanize Canadian institutions than all other influences combined. Brown began to consider the case for a written constitution on the American model, for separating the executive branch of government from the legislative, and for abandoning the attempt to govern Protestant, English Canada West and Catholic, French Canada East within one state.[7]

We need not grieve much for George Brown and his expulsion from office in 1858, any more than Careless, his mostly admiring biographer, did. The abrupt fall and sudden realignment of coalition ministries was a normal part of public life in a state like the Province of Canada, and Brown's rivals should hardly be condemned for employing all the stratagems the laws provided. Even if Sir Edmund Head seemed partisan in his preference for Macdonald over Brown, the outcome seemed to confirm the governor's *realpolitik* judgement that Brown's rivals offered a better prospect of political stability. The double shuffle is hardly an edifying part of Canadian political history, but the mere question of who deserved to get in and who deserved to go out in the summer of 1858 need hardly disturb us now.

If, however, the disasters and embarrassments of the double shuffle had permanently soured George Brown on parliamentary government, the consequences might have been momentous.

Brown's aspirations and grievances were attuned to those of Canada West voters. As both its leading politician and its dominant newspaperman, he was superbly placed to guide and channel its political choices. Had he repudiated the union with Canada East and the British parliamentary tradition, he would have given an enormous boost to Clear Grit radicalism. A Clear Grit Brown, harnessing the West's powerful sense of destiny, its impatience with compromise, and its anger at the French, would have pointed the way toward an Ontario without Quebec, and to a presidential system of government that aspired toward direct, rather than representative, democracy.

Such was not to be. John A. Macdonald would have been delighted to raise the loyalty cry and to campaign against George Brown as an annexationist and a traitor, and all the benefits of union, notably the skyrocketing growth and prosperity of Canada West, would have been marshalled on Macdonald's side. Brown himself, whatever his frustration and his anger, was in the end too astute a campaigner and too much a patriotic British constitutionalist to plump wholeheartedly for such radical change. All his life he had been devoted to reform, but he had always insisted that true reform was the cause of representative, parliamentary democracy. In the wake of the double shuffle, he may have been tempted by the Clear Grit vision of an Upper Canadian paradise and vengeance on his tormentors. But only briefly. Before long, George Brown returned to the parliamentary system.

He remained the governmental impossibility. He was less likely than ever to form a government. In many ways, he was too zealous for the compromises that union politics required. Yet he returned to the parliamentary process. He seems to have returned to a root belief: that even a parliamentarian permanently in opposition had a role to play and a contribution to make. His return insured that, no matter how vigorously the Canadians debated union, disunion, and federalism in the 1860s, they would do so within the forms of the parliamentary system.

The analogy between George Brown and Preston Manning with which this chapter began is real enough. Manning acknowledged it when he named his modern party "Reform" and listed George Brown among its patron saints. But nineteenth- and twentieth-century Reformers part company at the point where Brown rededicated himself to parliamentary struggle. Preston Manning's late-twentieth-century Reform Party promised to change the process of Canadian politics, not merely to exchange the Outs for the Ins. "To give effect to the common sense of the common people," the platform of the modern Reform Party endorsed "direct consultation, constitutional conventions, constituent assemblies, national referenda, and citizens' initiatives" to involve citizens directly in government. Its leader mused about impeaching unpopular prime ministers, and endorsed the recall of members of Parliament who followed their own judgement over their constituents' wishes.[8]

The views of the modern Reformers were ones the Clear Grits would have understood. Like the Clear Grits, they expressed a scepticism about representative democracy far deeper than anything George Brown permitted his party to embrace. In its impatience with representation, however, the Reform Party was not nearly so radical in the twentieth century as the Clear Grits were in the mid-nineteenth. All twentieth-century parties from right to left had grown impatient with representative democracy. Radical, threatening, even "impossible" in other ways, the modern Reform Party was close to the centre of Canadian political culture in its belief that direct democracy and democracy itself were synonyms. All parties had ceased to see themselves as caucuses of representatives. They all sought to present a single message, marketed to a mass audience by a single leader. Inevitably, their efforts to forge a direct bond between leaders and the people downgraded legislatures and those who sat in them – except as election-night tally sticks to determine which leader achieved power. As one result, the role of legislatures in twentieth-century constitutional discussions was minuscule, by apparently unanimous consent.

George Brown, on the other hand, returned to the representative democracy that was the central faith of nineteenth-century politics in British North America. In his biography, Maurice Careless located Brown's return to the parliamentary faith in a single event, the great reform convention at St. Lawrence Hall in Toronto in November 1859. Because of Brown's choices, St. Lawrence Hall, still standing on Toronto's King Street East, deserves to rank among the sites where confederation was made. Careless recreated the drama of the convention and its climax, "when even the gods and goddesses disporting on the ceiling of St. Lawrence Hall seemed to hang still and breathless in the yellow gaslight, far over the tall figure that now strode to the front of the platform." George Brown was about to call for a federal union between Canada West and Canada East.[9]

Brown's task in the convention he had organized was not to deny Canada West's anger and ambitions, but to channel them into a renewed parliamentary campaign. His solution was federalism. To end Canada East's interference in Canada West's affairs, they would split the union into "two or more local governments" for Canada East and West. In 1859, western alienation still pointed toward separation, and when Clear Grit calls for a pure-and-simple dissolution roused cheers, Brown went far to accommodate them. The convention's final resolution declared there would only be "some joint authority" to regulate matters of mutual interest between what would be two largely autonomous provinces.

In 1859, George Brown professed himself satisfied with only a restricted and inexpensive central government. But he talked no more of "organic change," of abandoning British political traditions to pursue a presidential constitution. With a platform of federalism to propose, Brown no longer wanted to demand new political processes. The convention would leave it to the legislature to decide on the details of federal union. After the St. Lawrence Hall convention, Brown's was still a minority party excluded from power. He was still derided or made a bogey by both conservatives and rival reformers. Yet Brown had accepted that, even as a minority politician, perhaps condemned to perpetual opposition, he could do something useful, could perhaps see his causes brought to attention and to fruition.

In 1864, Brown was proven right. In the interim, he had struggled against both radical reformers impatient for "organic change" and moderate reformers still reluctant to change the union at all. Sandfield Macdonald, the most moderate of reformers and the union's warmest champion, had put aside the rep-by-pop principle and formed a government, in alliance for a time with Antoine-Aimé Dorion. Brown, meanwhile, had taken a break from politics and made his first return visit in Britain. The visit mostly confirmed his commitment to Canada, but while in Edinburgh, Brown, then forty-three, fell suddenly in love. Within five weeks he was married. Anne Nelson at once became his steadiest and most secure commitment. Friends declared that her influence made Brown less impetuous, more thoughtful and tranquil. Better educated and more widely cultured than he was, she could hold her own in discussion with him. Maurice Careless pointed to her, through her influence on Brown, as a plausible "mother of confederation."

By the spring of 1864, Sandfield Macdonald was out of power, and Macdonald and Cartier had returned once more to the cabinet room. The constant effort to construct a government without the impossible man, who commanded the largest bloc of Canada West's representatives but would only enter government if he could change the union to a federation, was coming to an end. Brown's instinct that Parliament could provide a solution finally bore fruit in May 1864. Even though Macdonald and Cartier were in power, the legislature approved Brown's resolution to create an all-party legislative committee on constitutional matters. Even John A. Macdonald voted in favour, and Brown himself was appointed chairman. Power eluded Brown as much as ever, but Parliament would listen to his ideas.

In the House committee, parliamentarians of all shades of opinion discussed the constitutional deadlock: Canada West's insistence on

voting power to match its population; Canada East's refusal to surrender to an English and Protestant majority; the widespread reluctance to abandon the union; the persistent ambitions to unite all the
British provinces of North America. When the committee reported
to the legislature (just as the Macdonald–Cartier government collapsed), Brown got the chance to make his historic offer. On June 17,
Brown stood up in the hot, crowded legislative chamber in Quebec
City and broke the mould of union politics.

He offered to go into coalition with his hated rivals. He accepted
the impossibility of forming a government of his own choosing, and
offered to sustain Macdonald and Cartier in office. They had only
to accept the constitutional solutions that his parliamentary committee had recently endorsed: either federation – a federal union of
Canada East and West – or confederation, which would include the
Maritime colonies and potentially the North-West as well. Macdonald
and Cartier swiftly agreed to make the pursuit of these alternatives
into government policy. Amid cheers and handshakes, politicians
who had been at each other's throats for a decade told each other
they had broken the political deadlock.

From the perspective of the 1990s, what was most striking about
Brown's offer is how much it was a *parliamentary* negotiation and
a parliamentary accommodation. No single party could impose a
solution to the problems of governing the united Canadas. No party
commanded enough support to command the legislature, and no
one-party policy would have been accepted in good faith by the
others. Brown, however, had been proven right in his trust that, in a
flourishing parliamentary system, where the voters' elected representatives had real power to make both governments and policy,
even a "governmental impossibility" could have a decisive impact.

The united Province of Canada has had an historical reputation,
above all else, for political deadlock and for squalid deal-making.
Professor Russell spoke for the late-twentieth-century mainstream
when he dismissed parliamentary government at the time of confederation as a top-down form of democracy, obeying traditional

élitist theories that are no longer tolerable today. But the union's parliamentary government had defenders. In a heterodox study of Ontario's political traditions, Professor S. J. R. Noel wrote that "in the United Canadas, the combination of responsible government and brokerage politics produced a system in which practically all the important areas of public policy . . . were dealt with through the processes of bargaining, dealmaking and compromise: in other words, almost everything was legitimate grist to the political mill. . . . At its best it was innovative, practical, and wonderfully civilized." Professor Noel declared that the political system of the Canadas in the 1860s "was in some respects in advance of any other in the world at that time."[10]

Professor Russell – and presumably Preston Manning – would dismiss all this civilized parliamentary bargaining because it was done by "élites." Certainly most politicians of the confederation era were wealthier, more prominent, and more successful than the mass of their supporters – much as politicians were in the late twentieth century. But they hardly enjoyed the kind of quasi-feudal authority suggested by "top-down democracy." Politicians like George Brown and John A. Macdonald (essentially self-made successes, neither of whom received leadership as a birthright) were close to their electors. Macdonald is said to have known by name everyone who voted for him in Kingston, and (since voting was mostly done in public) everyone who opposed him, too. He and his rivals were elected on electoral franchises as broad as any then existing in the world, and they frequently staked their seats upon the support of an active, confident, well-informed, and changeable electorate. When they brokered the deal that broke the deadlock in June 1864, Macdonald, Brown, and Cartier had every right to believe that they represented the broad mass of the electorate which had recently put them into the legislature.

George Brown's moment in government was brief. In the two vital conferences where confederation was negotiated, and in the parliamentary debates that followed, he was a powerful force. But he was not in the end a government man, and not all the elements of the new Canadian constitution pleased him. Once confederation was settled, Brown no longer had any wish to sit in cabinet with his old rivals. He left the coalition in the summer of 1866, eager to see traditional party lines restored.

He never did become quite the white-haired patriarch that Careless says we have made him. In 1880, not entirely weaned from irascibility and impulse, he got into a struggle with a dismissed employee who came into his *Globe* office to complain. The employee had a gun, and it went off. Shot in the leg, Brown minimized the extent of the wound, but it became infected and he died. He was sixty-two.

It remains striking that a man so stiff-necked about his own principles and so ready to denounce those of others, above all so uneasy about co-operation and compromise, was also a parliamentary man. George Brown's career suggests the strengths of nineteenth-century parliamentary politics. Even Brown – in the mainstream view a dangerous fanatic who preferred his principles to power and didn't much care whom he offended – hewed to the conventions of parliamentary process and parliamentary authority.

In the deal-making of the late twentieth century, by contrast, Canadian politicians acted as if they felt trapped in parliamentary forms, which they tried as much as possible to circumvent. By general consent, and certainly without a murmur of protest from parliamentarians, the legislatures played no significant part in the patriation of 1982, the Meech Lake accord of 1987, or the Charlottetown accord of 1992. (Rarely, they could play a negative role, as in 1990, when procedural rules enabled a single Manitoba legislator to disrupt the careful ratification schedule that the triumphant first ministers had decreed.) In the late twentieth century, only leaders of parties in power had any place in constitutional deal-making. There was no place for the ideas of a party that could not hold power. In the 1990s, a sectional party could not represent its region in constitution-making unless it achieved power, and it could only achieve power in Ottawa by ceasing to speak for one section.

Had the rules of the 1990s applied in the 1860s, George Brown's persistent inability to form a government would have precluded him (and his party) from any role in settling the constitutional crisis of the Province of Canada. In the 1860s, however, when parliaments were powerful, a seat in Parliament promised influence at the constitutional table. Even a governmental impossibility like George Brown preserved his faith in parliamentary government out of a belief that the people were represented by legislatures, not by first ministers alone. And that belief was ultimately rewarded. Brown was able, as a fiercely sectional partisan, to be a vital participant in brokering a deal acceptable to many rival sections.

To see how a sectionalized political society sincerely dedicated to parliamentary process handled constitutional challenges in the midst of deadlock, we have only the 1860s to observe. We can follow George Brown and his rivals-turned-partners to Charlottetown, where another parliamentary accommodation had brought a diverse collection of politicians from the Atlantic provinces together to meet them.

CHAPTER TWO

Charles Tupper Goes to Charlottetown

~

SIR CHARLES TUPPER died in 1915, in his ninety-fifth year. In his final years, he made periodic excursions to the Vancouver home of his son Charles Hibbert Tupper, but his residence at the end was an English country estate with the Wodehousian name of Bexleyheath. It is an enormous leap – almost too much for one life to contain – from the young political scrapper who entered Nova Scotia's colonial assembly in 1855 to this ancient baronet of Bexley. It seems odd to us, now, how so many Canadian nation-builders, even those born and raised in Canada, took themselves off to Britain in retirement, preferring to die in the "old country," even if, like Tupper, they had never been young there. The last Canadian political leader to choose a British deathbed was R. B. Bennett, child of Hopewell Hill, New Brunswick, who in 1938 removed himself to an English village called Mickleham, wangled himself a viscountcy, and died impersonating an English gentleman. Today, of course, Tupper and Bennett would be more apt to die in Palm Beach or Lyford Cay, which at least have weather to commend them. As the natural refuge of superannuated Canadian leaders, Britain has become unimaginable.

So Tupper at the end of his life cuts an incomprehensible figure. The last of the thirty-six fathers of confederation, all his contemporaries long dead, sits, a huge old ruin in a fur collar with a blanket over his knees, chauffeured about the damp English countryside in some clanking black motor car, doubtless trying to comprehend the horribly modern slaughter of young Canadians at Ypres and Festhubert, gradually letting it go.

That unedifying twilight makes it hard to recapture the energetic nation-building young Tupper of the 1860s. And Tupper himself does not help us. He left two volumes of memoirs and an authorized *Life and Letters* – all so bland, superficial, and sanitized that they tell us little of his achievements and almost nothing about him. His personal papers were, in historian Peter Waite's phrase, "not so much laundered as starched." The destruction of most of what was worthwhile in them has made it almost impossible to flesh out the stiff cardboard of his public image with anything human and tangible.

He had his admirers. There are many reports of the Tupper who always overflowed with energy and enthusiasm, who kept his black medical bag under his parliamentary desk and would offer medical help at any time. Those who liked him said he was bluff and foursquare and immovable in his determination. He was full of "a characteristic which may be defined in a favourable sense as audacity," as one journalist put it. "In repose, even, he looked as if he had a blizzard secreted somewhere about his person," said a fellow MP. With the wives of his friends and colleagues, he was said to be gallant and flirtatious, never too busy to hear some medical confidence, organize an outing, or simply present a flower from the garden.[1]

Those who liked him said he was dogged in adversity. Actually he was a bully. When he had power, he was constantly eager not merely to defeat but to humiliate his rivals. Historian Waite, who made a wonderful biography from the well-preserved papers of Tupper's fellow Nova Scotian John Thompson, notes in it the legend that "Tupper" arose from the French *tu perds*, "you lose." For the weak or dependent, Tupper was hardly the trusted companion his more secure friends imagined. He was married for sixty-five years, and friends insisted the marriage was happy and close, but letters – vanished from Tupper's papers but preserved in Thompson's – suggest a Tupper who was aggressively sexual. Waite reports how Tupper, a Baptist and a minister's son, once bullied Thompson into taking him to mass, simply to pursue a young Catholic woman he was attracted to. That and a hundred other incidents might have been simply flirtatious, but Waite also cites the Washington typist who alleged in a legal action that Tupper got her pregnant, talked her into an abortion, and vanished. Her complaint was unproven, and her court case, denounced as a blackmail, was either abandoned or privately settled. Still, such stray details give an unpleasant inkling of the kind of bullying endured, if half the rumours are true, by vulnerable citizens upon whom Tupper forced his attentions.[2]

Tupper's public record was long and distinguished. After the great editor and statesman Joseph Howe brought Nova Scotia responsible government in 1847 by welding supporters of reform into a disciplined party with broad electoral support, Tupper helped bring the conservative party back into contention by transforming it from an aristocratic Anglican clique into a broad coalition of middle-class Protestants and Catholics. He personally came to public attention by unseating Howe himself in a head-to-head contest. Howe acknowledged Tupper as a worthy foe, both as a campaigner and a strategist – though he regretted that young Tupper, for all his talents, could never simply argue a principle; he had to attack the good name of his opponents, too. As premier of Nova Scotia, Tupper led the confederation negotiations, and against deep opposition he brought his province into confederation. Moving to the federal stage, he became an indefatigable cabinet minister, ambassador, and political fixer, and finally prime minister of Canada.

Two deep scars flaw the record of nearly fifty years in public life. The more visible of the two was inflicted in 1896, after Tupper returned from nearly a decade as Canadian High Commissioner to Britain to become party leader and prime minister. He had to face the voters at once, and was swept from office. Defeat left him the shortest-serving prime minister ever. With fewer days in office than Kim Campbell or John Turner, Tupper the prime minister ranks merely as one of the four hapless Conservatives – Waite's Thompson was another – who briefly held the office after the death of Sir John A. All have been totally eclipsed by Macdonald's halo and by the bright light of Wilfrid Laurier's sunny ways, which flared out upon Tupper's rout and outshone all rivals for fifteen years. Tupper, the last of the futile four and the only one to face election, seems now diminished rather than elevated by having held the office, an asterisk prime minister, a trivia question.

The other deep flaw in Tupper's record is the nasty business of Nova Scotia's entry into confederation in 1867. At the very end of his term of office, Premier Tupper got confederation through without an electoral mandate and over the protests of many Nova Scotians. The unwilling province responded with fury, driving his party from office provincially and electing anti-confederates to eighteen of Nova Scotia's nineteen seats in the first Canadian House of Commons. Tupper's bullying of his province remains a complaint in Nova Scotia, part of the black legend of Maritime grievance against the Canadian union. Neither 1896 nor 1867 lends lustre to Charles Tupper's political reputation.

But something Tupper did in 1864 deserves to loom large. Eighteen sixty-four was, like 1992, a summer of constitutional accord at Charlottetown. But the first constitutional Charlottetown was as much a success as the second was an embarrassment and a failure. The 1864 conference at Charlottetown transformed the pious, impractical ideal of confederation into a political program to be taken seriously. Charles Tupper more than anyone put in place the crucial factor that made success at Charlottetown possible in 1864. So it is worth giving some attention to how Charlottetown came to be and how Charles Tupper came to Charlottetown.

"It was the enthusiasm of Gordon of New Brunswick that gave the movement its real start," reads the opening sentence of *The Road to Confederation*, Donald Creighton's 1964 book about the shaping of the nation. Creighton was the pre-eminent Canadian historian of the 1950s and 1960s. His *Road to Confederation*, written just after his magisterial biography of John A. Macdonald, is a marvellous book, with wonderful detailing, strong ideas, and an unrelenting narrative drive to catch and carry the reader along. It's much the most readable account of the confederation process. A reader comes away thinking that Creighton knew a lot about his subjects, and wondering why historians don't often write like that.

For all the authority and readability of his work, however, historians began to react against Creighton even before his long life ended in 1979. His late-in-life role as a national scold, inveighing against bilingualism, liberals, women, the American empire, and the modern world in general, certainly diminished his stature. His dismissive contempt for anyone who resisted or questioned John A. Macdonald's view of Canada (or was it Creighton's own) provoked resistance as confederation itself ran into trouble. But historians were also made suspicious by his wonderful prose. Creighton's narratives are so rhetorical, so persuasive, so dismissive of even the possibility of any other interpretation of events, that any critically attuned reader must suspect that many noteworthy alternates are being buried and denied. "The prince of pattern makers," an historian recently called him, with just a hint that the pattern was as much imposed as discovered.

The sceptics are right enough. Much of Creighton's steamroller version of confederation urgently needs to be reconsidered. Still, giving the storyteller his due, we have to inquire: who was this "Gordon of New Brunswick" to be honoured with the master storyteller's first line? What could he have done to have given confederation "its real start"?

Gordon of New Brunswick was Arthur Gordon, lieutenant-governor of the province. Obviously we *have* come a long way, if an office now so wrapped and bound in absolute irrelevance could be the springboard of confederation. Creighton opened with Gordon for one reason. Gordon had provoked the Charlottetown conference into being.

Creighton, however, was not out to make Arthur Gordon a hero. He wanted Gordon for comic relief, a foil for his real heroes. In Creighton's sketch, Gordon was the Bertie Woosterish son of an earl, just thirty-five in 1864 and unshakeably certain that he was meant to rule New Brunswick as an Imperial potentate. He had taken the job on the assumption that New Brunswick was meant to be ruled by expatriate autocrats, like any other corner of the British Empire, and he found responsible government a rude shock. Gordon thought it beneath his dignity to do anything but dictate to colonial politicians, whom he characterized as the "ignorant lumberer," the "petty attorney," and the "keeper of a village grog shop."[3]

Gordon proposed a conference at Charlottetown because he wanted to unite Nova Scotia, New Brunswick, and Prince Edward Island, not British North America at large. Given his high opinion of the importance his office should have, he naturally assumed that the governors of the three provinces would take the lead in securing the union, and that he would govern it. He could not entirely ignore the people's elected representatives, but what he proposed was an executive conference, a meeting of the three governors and their premiers. When that cosy conclave had approved the union, the dutiful premiers would be sent to secure the consent of their legislatures, while the governors arranged with the Colonial Office to have the change made. Gordon set about organizing a meeting of six, the three governors and their three premiers.

Charles Tupper killed that. He was not even premier when Gordon's proposal for an intercolonial conference reached Halifax in the fall of 1863. After eight years in politics, Tupper still deferred to his party's titular leader, his father's old Baptist colleague, James Johnston, who had brought him into politics. The recent elections had made Johnston premier, at least in name; Tupper did not succeed him until May 1864. But Tupper's influence on party policy was already substantial. When Gordon's proposal came to Nova Scotia, Tupper declared that the government of Nova Scotia would not attend the conference unless delegates from the opposition went with them.

In March 1864, the Nova Scotia legislature approved a resolution by Tupper for an all-party delegation to attend the conference on Maritime union. When the premiers of New Brunswick and Prince Edward Island followed Tupper's lead, Arthur Gordon found, to his fury, that the small executive conclave he had planned had become a much larger legislative conference, and politicians from all parties would participate. Tupper had hijacked his plan, cutting out the governors and handing the conference over to the politicians Gordon despised. Gordon promptly denounced him as a man of limited ability "and considerable obstinacy."[4]

From the perspective of the 1990s, Tupper's position was riveting, for it was almost inexplicable. A premier who insisted on taking members of the opposition to a first ministers' conference confounded everything the late twentieth century knew of politics. Through all the constitutional discussions from the Confederation of Tomorrow conference of 1967, through the Victoria conference of 1971, the patriation round of 1981-2, the Meech Lake talks of 1987-90, and the Charlottetown accord of 1992, participation was exclusively an executive prerogative. In the late twentieth century, six successive prime ministers and scores of provincial premiers preferred Arthur Gordon's executive model to Charles Tupper's representative one. Premiers and political analysts alike declared that to let anyone else participate in constitution-drafting would be an insult to government as it was practised in the 1990s.

Rivers of historical ink have flowed over the forces that persuaded George Brown, John A. Macdonald, and George-Étienne Cartier to sink their deep animosities and form the Canadian coalition of June 1864. By comparison, the constitutional armistice into which the politicians of the Maritime colonies entered voluntarily, shortly *before* their Canadian counterparts, has interested hardly anyone. Donald Creighton and his fellow historians made little of the reasons why the politicians transformed Gordon's autocratic plan into an all-party parliamentary conference. Writing of triumphal nation-building, they had little incentive to dwell on such arcana as the proper quorum for constitutional meetings. Yet, in its way, the Maritimers' choice to co-operate on the constitution was even more extraordinary than the Canadian coalition, since no political deadlock forced co-existence upon them.

Tupper's sanitized memoirs are useless on this point, and the testimony of other contemporaries is not much more enlightening. D'Arcy McGee mentioned the inter-party consensus on confederation as "an extraordinary armistice in political warfare," but did not dwell on its causes. John Hamilton Gray, who was one of New Brunswick's delegates at Charlottetown and Quebec, said blandly that it was done to remove "the question of the union . . . beyond the pale of party conflict," but he did not inquire why there should have been such a dispensation from the fierce partisanship that had long been the norm.[5]

The man who initiated this armistice was "Tu perds." Charles Tupper was never magnanimous towards his rivals or gentle with those in weaker positions. His ruthlessness in the use of patronage would shock even John A. Macdonald, and he never lightly threw away the advantages of office. And Tupper's partisanship typified mid-Victorian politics in Canada. The conservative and reform tendencies were generations old by the 1860s. Both parties understood the value of party loyalty and the uses of power and patronage. Each side had its talismans and its martyrs, and passionate hatreds had long been nursed on both sides. Tupper himself had done much to build Nova Scotia's conservatives into a disciplined party, and he had not done it by kindness to his rivals. This sudden outbreak of bipartisan courtesy was something rare and strange.

The power of Gordon and the other governors may provide some explanation for it. After the great change of 1847, governors of

British North American colonies had to accept the advice (at least on local matters) that they received from ministers chosen by elected legislatures. But in the 1860s, governors were still powerful men, not to be disdained by any politician. If they were not earls' sons, the governors were often generals or ex-cabinet ministers. In the era when being a "gentleman" signified much more than merely polite behaviour, they were all British gentlemen, imbued with an easy, instinctive sense of natural superiority over the colonials they ruled. Even with their powers curtailed by responsible government, governors remained intimidating.

In Gordon's small conclave of governors and premiers, the three governors, wrapped in the mantle of social precedence as well as the delegated authority of the British Crown and cabinet, would have been in the best possible position to compel consent from three over-awed colonial premiers. Invited into Gordon's web, then, Tupper may have recruited his fellow legislators, even those from the opposition benches, as allies against the dangerous coercive power of the governors.

But that cannot be the whole explanation. Gordon had been right to complain of Tupper's special obstinacy, but colonial politicians had to be able to stand up to even the most august governors if they hoped to prosper. Indeed, for the country lawyers, small-town journalists, and local merchants who won office in the Canada of the 1860s, the governors' *obligation* to take advice must have been one of the pleasures of responsible government. Politicians now made policy, and some dignified baron or imperious general, fresh from the British court or cabinet room, had to dignify it with his approval and signature, no matter what his personal opinion of it or of the people who gave it to him as their "advice." From Baldwin's and LaFontaine's government in the 1840s to Mackenzie King's in the 1940s, a century of Canadian politicians loved to wrap themselves and their policies in all the pomp and prestige an aristocratic governor could provide, combining fawning deference to the viceregal office with a cold determination to ensure that it served their own will and purpose. Arthur Gordon found himself helpless – "and that helplessness felt to be a triumph over the past by the people," as he wailed to the colonial secretary in London. Tupper could not afford to be trapped by Gordon on the union issue, but he had never been trapped before, and he had not previously needed the opposition members to save him.[6]

If fear of being bullied by powerful governors provided only slight reason for premiers to welcome their political rivals into constitutional meetings, the state of parliamentary government in the 1860s gave a stronger one.

Parliamentary government, at least the full-fledged version that had been ushered in with responsible government after 1847, was still new and shiny in the British North American colonies in the 1860s. British North Americans of the day were proud, not merely of their victory over autocratic rule, but of inheriting the thousand-year mythology of Parliament. They claimed to be equal and rightful heirs, not merely colonial beneficiaries, of that tradition. Reformers raised in the struggle for responsible government were particularly given to setting out the virtues of parliamentary government, but conservatives were not far behind. Orators on the hustings effortlessly celebrated their share in "the rights of Englishmen," guaranteed by the English Parliament's victory over autocratic royal power in the "Glorious Revolution" of 1688. If they were journalists, they paraphrased Edmund Burke on the glories of representative government. If they were lawyers, they quoted the justifications of parliamentary rule they had imbibed from the Blackstone they read as law students.

Politically active Canadians in the 1860s unashamedly and confidently declared parliamentary government the best of all possible political systems. They were plagued by no sneaking doubt that some other system was better because it was "more democratic." They certainly feared the tyranny unfettered majorities could wield, but they did not concede that the system they preferred made them less than free citizens. When they condemned democracy, they usually meant mob rule, and when they extolled constitutional liberty, they meant something close to what we call parliamentary democracy.

Being proud of parliamentary democracy, the politicians of the 1860s worked all the harder to be masters of it. They learned the subtleties, both of its high ideals and of its low practices. They tinkered with the valves and levers of parliamentary government like the engineers who were tinkering with the powerful, temperamental steam engines then transforming society. In the process, mid-nineteenth-century politicians achieved a mastery of parliamentary practice hardly possible in another age with little respect for merely parliamentary skills.

Charles Tupper, who would practise parliamentary politics for more than fifty years, was already an adept of the art even before he assumed the premiership of Nova Scotia in 1864. And it seems to have been his practical understanding of parliamentary democracy that led him to seek inter-party participation in constitutional discussion, even without the spur of necessity that influenced the Canadians.

Tupper saw, surely, that constitutional politics were almost certain to be divisive, unpredictable, and dangerous. Constitutional proposals, particularly those focused on new colonial unions, provided a leader with few obvious favours to dispense and no clear ideological cry to hold a party together. To go alone to a constitutional conference – particularly one where he was likely to be bullied by the governors – probably meant getting into some commitment. Any commitment Tupper made might not be welcomed by his own party, let alone by the legislature, or the voters. To commit himself to any particular change might simply expose a weakness which political rivals would exploit, first to woo away doubtful back-benchers, then to attack the weakened government in elections. As Tupper knew better than Gordon, support for Maritime union was barely an inch deep in the spring of 1864. It would be better, Tupper understood, to share the credit than risk taking the blame.

Tupper's instinctive wish to bring along the opposition – and to transform the meeting at Charlottetown from an executive conclave into a parliamentary conference – was not some magnanimous gesture from a gentler age. It recognized that power lay ultimately in the legislature, not in the cabinet room. It reflected a skilled tactician's calculation, based on long experience of parliamentary risks and benefits. As the perceptive British historian Ged Martin put it, the fathers of confederation took each other "not by the hand but rather by the throat."*[7]

In the late twentieth century, politicians had much less sense of Parliament as a potential source of risk and danger – because such dangers had indeed largely vanished. With disciplined, obsequious parliamentary caucuses, modern party leaders had become virtual presidents when they commanded a majority. Premiers, so skilled at striking the postures of leadership that became the essence of television politics, were inexperienced in the work that was meat and drink to mid-nineteenth-century politicians – namely building and holding together parliamentary consensuses. Lacking any experience of situations where they might need to *seek* parliamentary support or to defuse parliamentary resistance, modern premiers and prime ministers saw no advantage in letting members of the opposition participate in constitutional deal-making.

Nevertheless, even in the debased parliamentary system of the 1990s, it is intriguing to consider the long list of premiers who went home from Meech Lake or Charlottetown to proclaim themselves new fathers of confederation – only to be chopped down brutally by the voters after opposition leaders accused them of having gotten too little and given too much at the constitutional table. The opposition leaders, excluded from the negotiations, were free to claim they could have done better. The modern presidential-style premiers, never having had reason to grasp the benefits of sharing the

---

* Ged Martin used this phrase to me in an interview in 1991, when I was beginning to look into confederation. It crystallized the process for me instantly and has stayed with me ever since. I am glad to have a chance to acknowledge Ged Martin's perception and enthusiasm for his subject.

credit as Tupper did, repeatedly reaped the disastrous consequences Tupper skilfully avoided. Neither more noble nor more devious than his modern counterparts, Tupper simply enjoyed the benefits of superior experience in adapting parliamentary process to his political needs – a by-product of living in a time that put its trust in parliamentary processes.

The Nova Scotia legislature had voted to send five delegates to Charlottetown "for the purpose of arranging a preliminary plan for the union of the three provinces under one government and legislature." Tupper, now premier in his own right, was the dominant figure in the delegation, and the one earliest inclined to favour a union. Tupper had a Victorian faith in railways and economic growth, and a rather less Victorian eagerness to draw new groups into his coalitions. Tupper favoured throwing railroads across the colonies, doing away with their separate postages, coinages, and customs tariffs, and finding new political supporters among their disparate populations. Any union that could do these would have Tupper's instinctive support.

To complete the government side of the Charlottetown delegation, Tupper took with him two lawyers: his attorney-general, William Henry, and Robert Dickey from Nova Scotia's appointive upper house. From the opposition he did not want merely token representatives. He first tried to recruit his great rival, Joseph Howe. Howe, like most colonial politicians, had often mused about a union of the colonies. Just two weeks before the Charlottetown meeting, he rhetorically asked a boozy, sociable dinner organized to welcome Canadian visitors to Halifax: "Why should union not be brought about? Was it because we wish to live and die in our insignificance?" Howe was formally out of elective politics in 1864, but his prestige was enormous and his campaigning skills legendary. Had Tupper recruited Howe to Charlottetown and the union cause, he would have had few concerns about political risks at home. But a year earlier, Howe, eager to prove that colonials could help to run the

Empire in which he considered them equals, not subjects, had accepted an Imperial commission to report on the Atlantic fishery. He could not go to Charlottetown.[8]

Replacing Howe in the delegation to Charlottetown were Adams Archibald, who had succeeded Howe as leader of the liberal opposition, and Jonathan McCully, who faced Robert Dickey in Nova Scotia's upper house. When the matchless Howe had retired from journalism, McCully had become the most successful political journalist in the province. Both he and Archibald had dismissed colonial union as an impractical fancy. Weeks before Charlottetown, McCully had hooted at confederation as "a new, untried, and more than doubtful expediency adapted to the exigencies of Canadian necessities."[9]

Tupper had not sought yes-men; his four fellow delegates were strong figures in Nova Scotia's two houses. But the delegation consisted of four lawyers and a doctor. There were no financiers from the Halifax banking houses who might crack open the details of a complicated financial proposal, no one from the seafaring towns of western Nova Scotia, no Scots Catholics, no one from Cape Breton. Tupper had reached far by inviting leading opposition figures, but each constituency left out of the delegation would view its work with deep suspicion.

New Brunswick's politicians were even more cautious than Nova Scotia's about the Maritime union conference. Nova Scotia was the largest, richest, oldest of the three provinces, with 350,000 people to New Brunswick's 270,000. For all its doubts, it could expect to dominate any union of the three provinces, and its resolution appointing delegates was the one most optimistic about the outcome. New Brunswick's legislature appointed delegates, not to "arrange," but only to "consider," this idea about Maritime union. In New Brunswick, the premier was reformer Leonard Tilley, a businessman who, at forty-six, was a fifteen-year veteran of colonial politics. Union, particularly a union which might reduce New Brunswick to subservience to Halifax, had produced no wave of enthusiasm in New Brunswick, but it could appeal to Tilley's hard-headed appreciation of such progressive virtues as tariff reductions, improved communications, expanded trading units, and governmental efficiency.

Tilley took with him his attorney-general, John Mercer Johnson, and the reform leader in the upper house, William Steeves, a lumberer and shipbuilder. From the opposition came Edward Chandler, a lawyer and a scion of the old loyalist gentry of the province. An old-fashioned politician from before the days of responsible government, Chandler had a touch of tory *noblesse oblige* about him; he was considered sympathetic to the Acadian and Catholic interests of north-shore New Brunswick. The other conservative delegate was lawyer John Hamilton Gray, who at different times had been both an ally and a rival of Tilley's, and who was himself a former premier. Formidable as a courtroom lawyer, Gray was considered a weathercock politician, likely to follow the prevailing trends.

Notably absent from New Brunswick's delegation were spokesmen for two large New Brunswick minorities, the Irish Catholics and the Acadian French. Both groups had representatives in the legislature, but none was appointed. Tilley, an evangelical Protestant, had never had much Catholic support. Absent by their own choice were two powerful figures who wanted no part of Maritime union: Albert Smith, a fiery reform lawyer, and Timothy Anglin, a Saint John journalist who would have spoken for New Brunswick's Irish Catholics. Smith and Anglin would become confederation's implacable foes in New Brunswick. They would use it to drive Tilley, nominally a fellow reformer, from office.

In Prince Edward Island, neither party saw much advantage in having Prince Edward Island joined to the larger colonies across Northumberland Strait. Prince Edward Island was not all bucolic charm and hayseed amusements. Even the farmers among the Island's 80,000 people were hardly lost in rural contentment. Most were tenants on lands owned by great absentee landlords, and in

1864 a new mass movement, the Tenant League, was launching a campaign of non-payment of rents that would sweep the Island during the summer of Charlottetown. Island people were also timber-cutters, shipbuilders, and cargo-traders, and the Island's merchant fleet linked Charlottetown's harbour to all the seaports of the world. As the collector of customs reported with calm pride, sea trades had become "the means of introducing into our colony a large amount of gold or its equivalent in exchange." Why, many asked, should the Island yield its independence and its customs revenues to become a small unit in a large union?[10]

"If the provinces of Nova Scotia and New Brunswick were to be annexed to Prince Edward Island, great benefits might result to our people," said Colonel John Hamilton Gray, the retired Imperial soldier who was premier, "but if this colony were to be annexed to these provinces, the opposite might be the effect." * Gray's government agreed to participate in the conference, it was said, only because the other colonies proposed to meet at Charlottetown, making it seem churlish for the Islanders not to take part. Prince Edward Island appointed delegates only to "discuss the expediency" of a union, and it took a party vote by the government side to see even that half-hearted measure adopted. Premier Gray was joined in the delegation by Attorney-General Edward Palmer, an ultra-tory who even then was working to undermine Gray's leadership of the party, and by William Henry Pope, who was almost the only strong enthusiast for union in the government.[11]

The opposition had voted against appointing delegates, but the bipartisan principle prevailed here as well, and reformers filled two of the five places in the Island's delegation. Opposition leader George

---

* It is one of the oddities of confederation history that two of the thirty-six fathers of confederation were fiftyish gentlemen of conservative views named John Gray, and both of them had the middle name Hamilton. Colonel Gray, a retired soldier, was premier of Prince Edward Island; Mr. Gray, a lawyer, was ex-premier of New Brunswick.

Coles, a successful brewer and the Island's former premier, had denounced the whole notion of Maritime union as "bogus," but he accepted a place in the delegation along with Andrew Macdonald, reform leader in the elected upper house, who was a shipbuilder and merchant from an established Island family and the only Catholic among the Maritime delegates.

The fifteen Maritime delegates who gathered at Charlottetown on the last day of August 1864 were joined the next day by eight Canadians, all ministers in the coalition cabinet. Macdonald, Cartier, and Brown, the leaders of the three main parties in the governing coalition, had each brought one additional member from their own parties. Macdonald and Cartier were each supported by former law students turned political protégés. Macdonald's colleague, Alexander Campbell, would remain mostly a backroom fixer until Macdonald made him lieutenant-governor of Ontario. The public career of Cartier's supporter, Hector Langevin, still a relative novice in 1864, would be much longer and more prominent. George Brown brought William McDougall, a Toronto lawyer and journalist with a Clear Grit background and an independent streak that irritated all the party leaders he served. Two other Canadian delegates spoke for the powerful, uneasy, English minorities in Quebec. Businessman and railway promoter Alexander Tilloch Galt was an early advocate of confederation and an expert on its finances. Thomas D'Arcy McGee was an Irish Catholic journalist who dreamed that ethnic and religious tribalism would soon be submerged in a new Canadian nation.

Striking by their absence from the Canadian delegation were men such as Antoine-Aimé Dorion, Brown's ill-fated ally of 1858 and former premier of the united Canadas in his own right. His *rouge* party remained powerful in Quebec, but the Canadian delegation was a governmental one, and the *rouges* were not partners in the coalition. Cartier, unlike Tupper and the other Maritime leaders, had seen no reason to bring his strongest political rivals into the constitutional discussions. The *rouges* were the only substantial political party in any of the colonies not to be included in the confederation bargaining. The confederation movement would suffer for having excluded them.

The twenty-three delegates to the Charlottetown conference illustrated the weaknesses *and* the strengths of political representation in that time. There were no women and only a handful of Catholics from a population that was half female and almost half Catholic.* The two French Quebeckers could hope to wield a veto through their power in the Canadian cabinet, but there were no Acadians or Irish from New Brunswick, no Scots from Nova Scotia. There were no workers or farmers in a society where almost everyone lived by manual labour and most people lived in the countryside. The confederation-makers never imagined seeking participation from the native nations. In the mid-nineteenth century, British North Americans looked ahead to the rapid extinction or assimilation of native society. Native peoples were seen as foreigners, and they would be dealt with through treaties rather than by inclusion in colonial politics. The nineteenth-century treaties would at least underline the separate and independent status of the native nations, but they would also reflect the vast disparity in power between the contracting parties.

On the other hand, the delegates were hardly so unrepresentative as has routinely been presumed. Coming from two parties in each of the Maritime provinces and three in the Canadas, the delegates spoke for almost the whole of their legislatures. Legislatures in the 1860s were elected by all adult males in some provinces and most of them in the rest, so the delegates had a legitimate claim to represent a large part of the political class of their society. Strongly middle-class and professional, they typified political representation then as today. A few were holdovers from the old days of *noblesse oblige*, but as many had made political careers as advocates for the common farmer against élite interests.

---

* I take up the political status of women in Chapter Six.

Increasingly, colonial politicians were brokers, well-placed inter-
mediaries rather than authority figures in their own right. It was no
longer necessary to have inherited wealth and position to succeed
in politics, but it did help to have the skills that gentlemen and
lawyers and successful businessmen tended to possess. Members of
Parliament were paid (in Britain they would not be until 1911), but it
helped to be well-to-do, or at least to be able to carry off the lifestyle
of the independently wealthy. In all these ways, mid-nineteenth-
century politicians were not much different from late-twentieth-
century ones.

As the delegates gathered at Charlottetown in 1864, constitutional discussions of the sort they were about to launch were something new in British North American politics. All previous British
North American constitutions, down to the most recent – the union
imposed upon Upper and Lower Canada in 1841 – had been made
in London to serve Imperial objectives. Responsible government, the
sea-change of 1847, had changed that, too. In 1862, in response to
union talk, Britain's colonial secretary declared that the British
government "do not think it their duty to initiate any movement
towards such union, but they have no wish to impede any well-
considered scheme which may have the concurrence of the people
of the provinces through their legislatures, assuming of course that
it does not interfere with Imperial interests." The Colonial Office
suggested "consultation on the subject among the leading members
of the governments concerned" without much consideration of the
details, beyond the need for ratification in the colonial legislatures.
The bipartisan form of the mid-nineteenth-century constitutional
talks was a Canadian innovation.[12]

The Charlottetown conference gave a uniquely carnivalesque air to
the sober world of Canadian political history. George Brown, sailing
to Charlottetown with the Canadian delegation, rose at four for a
saltwater shower and saw dawn revealing the rich green shores of
Prince Edward Island, "as pretty a country as you could ever put

your eye upon." Everyone going to Charlottetown seems to have been similarly inspired. The charms of the Island and the glorious high summer weather that prevailed throughout the conference soon enveloped all the potentially quarrelsome participants in a festive, party mood.[13]

No one has evoked this mood better than Peter Waite. Waite's 1962 book *The Life and Times of Confederation* was the first of the great 1960s histories of confederation to appear; its opening sentence notes that no book had been published on the subject since 1924. When he researched *The Life and Times*, Waite was determined that its themes would grow out of the "raucous voices" of the "vast and multifarious native sources" in the newspapers of the time. Later, he would describe himself as "driven to the newspapers, to the Parliamentary Library, to the St. John's library, to the hot little sheds on Pinnacle Street, Belleville, Ont., not by the exigencies of a Ph.D. but by adrenalin." He was caught, he said, "as the newspapermen of the time were, by the sheer magnitude of confederation, of colonials meeting and greeting for the first time, a bit star-struck some of them, the way the writer was, who'd caught it too."[14]

Waite's quarryings from those newspapers yielded the details of the Charlottetown conference that historians have relied on ever since. Charlottetown in 1864 was a town of just seven thousand people, with red dirt streets running in parallel lines down to the spacious, sheltered harbour. Its landmark was Province House, the Georgian legislative building built with Island stone and Island craftsmanship in 1847, and still central in the modern city of Charlottetown.

In late August 1864, Waite tells us, the great excitement in the town was caused not by the hastily scheduled political conference, but by Slaymaker's and Nichol's Olympic Circus, the first circus seen on the Island in twenty years. Charlottetown's twenty small hotels were crowded with excursion visitors drawn by this sensation. As one of the newspapers noted, even Island politicians could not be deprived of their chance to see the elephants, and in his book Waite has fun with the casual reception given to the arriving delegations.

When the spit-and-polish steamship *Queen Victoria*, carrying the Canadian delegation, the last to arrive, anchored in the harbour on September 1, the Island's provincial secretary William Pope had to have himself rowed out to her in an oyster boat "with a barrel of flour in the bow and two jars of molasses in the stern." Once Pope had welcomed the visitors, the *Queen Victoria*'s boats were lowered, "man-of-war" fashion. In Brown's amused phrase, "we landed like Mr Christopher Columbus, who had the precedence of us in taking possession of portions of the American continent."[15]

That same day, the conference opened in Province House. For all its giddy improvisation and champagne-fuelled sociability, the delegates to the Charlottetown conference also spent quite a few hours grinding out constitutional details around a conference table – more hours, in fact, than late-twentieth-century first ministers usually devoted to constitutional accords. Today, half-legislature and half-museum, Province House still preserves that serious side. Visitors to "the Confederation Room," which in 1864 was the chamber where the Island's upper house met, still lean over the barrier to see the long table and leather chairs where the business of the conference was conducted.

The Charlottetown conference began with its original mandate of Maritime union, and no Canadians. The Maritimers, veterans of parliamentary business, set about electing Colonel Gray, their host, as chairman, and the visiting premiers, Tupper and Tilley, as joint secretaries, and hearing the enabling resolutions from their three legislatures. Despite some dissent, they soon decided they would have no observers and no transcripts. "Buncombe speeches will be out of place, and politicians will for once deal with naked facts," wrote a surprisingly sympathetic journalist. While no transcript was made, the shape of the discussions was soon widely known and widely reported.[16]

Having organized the formalities, the Maritimers decided almost at once to bring in the Canadians and hear their proposal.

Charlottetown thereupon became two conferences proceeding in tandem – the Maritimers' sessions on Maritime union, interspersed with much longer meetings to discuss confederation with the Canadian guests. The Charlottetown conference would continue all week, and the delegates would hold further sessions in Halifax and Saint John before adjourning the Charlottetown conference indefinitely (in fact, permanently) in Montreal in October. The vital sessions, however, were those with the Canadians in the upstairs room at Charlottetown.

With the entry of the Canadians, Maritime union was effectively marginalized. Begun as a whim of Arthur Gordon, it was not a vital interest of any of the three governments. None of them had done the preparatory planning the governors might have ordered had they retained control. Gordon, who disapproved of both the confederation idea and the representative form the conference had taken, spent only a couple of days at Charlottetown before returning to Fredericton to draft a scathing report for his masters in London. The elected politicians of the Maritimes, however, were eager to learn more of the larger union before making any decision on the smaller one. So the Canadians, straight from the boat and many of them quite unknown to their Maritime colleagues, were ushered in for what Brown called "the shake elbow and the how-d'ye-do and the fine weather." Charlottetown had been permanently redirected.

For the next three business days, Friday, Saturday, and Monday, September 2, 3, and 5, the Canadians led the conference through a long presentation on the ways and means of a federal union of British North America. They had done their homework. George Brown, Alexander Galt, and others in the Canadian delegation had been thinking hard about such a union for half a decade, and the parliamentary committee led by Brown had given the concept a rigorous examination in May and June 1864. After the Brown–Cartier–Macdonald coalition was formed in June, federal union had dominated the Canadian cabinet's agenda, and the last-minute opportunity to join the Maritimers at Charlottetown had provoked furious preparation of position papers and background documents. The Canadians' scripts were ready, and they knew their lines.

John A. Macdonald and George-Étienne Cartier introduced the confederation proposal. Macdonald spoke more than Cartier, who to the end of his life was never entirely comfortable speaking formally in English. "Federalism" was a large part of Macdonald's presentation. A federal union, one that divided power between central and provincial governments, was the basis on which the Canadian coalition had formed, and any proposal that did not guarantee the survival of local legislatures would be hard to sell in the Maritime provinces. But federalism provoked doubts, too. None of the colonials had ever lived under a federal regime. The United Kingdom, to which they all looked, was a unitary state, not a federal union, and the collapse of the United States into secession and civil war was no recommendation for the federal principle. Macdonald, both an instinctive centralizer and an adroit politician, must have spent much of the day threading his way between the centralized authority he would have preferred and the local autonomy he had to accept, eagerly seizing any hint of what leeway the delegates would tolerate.

The next day was devoted to Alexander Galt's exposition on the finances of a federal union. Galt also inclined to a strong central government, and his presentation may have begun to bring home to the Maritimers just how much power the Canadians expected the national government to wield in confederation. Big, energetic, dogmatic George Brown took all of the third day to outline the Canadians' proposals on constitutional mechanics: the divisions of powers, the relations of the provinces to the central government, the harmonization of laws, the judiciary. Back in 1859, at the great reform convention in Toronto's St. Lawrence Hall, Brown had sold federal union to the restive, separatist-minded delegates by describing its central government merely as "some joint authority" between powerful provinces. Memories of that stand, and of Brown's long fight to free Canada West from the union, may have reassured local patriots that their provincial prerogatives would endure. But by 1864 Brown's views on federalism were changing. He too foresaw a central government with broad powers, and he would soon be describing the provinces as "mere municipal institutions." [17]

After three days of detailed proposals, the next day, not surprisingly, was for questions, answers, and discussion. Hector Langevin of the *bleus*, D'Arcy McGee, and the old Clear Grit reformer William McDougall gave speeches, perhaps to suggest all-party support for the leaders' views within the Canadian delegation. But the Maritimers also probed and tested the broad concept. Setting out their concerns and interests, they gave the Canadians a sense of where to push hard, where to pull back.

Only on the sixth day, Wednesday, September 7, did the Maritimers hold a substantial session on Maritime union, the formal business their legislatures had authorized them to discuss. The return to formal session required a resolution to drive the business, and Tupper moved Charlottetown's first substantial motion: "Whereas in the opinion of this conference a Union of Nova Scotia, New Brunswick, and Prince Edward Island under one government and legislature would elevate the status, enhance the credit, enlarge the influence, improve the social, commercial, and political condition, increase the development, and promote the interests generally of all these provinces, RESOLVED that the time has arrived when such Union should be effected." [18]

For all the confidence of the preamble, this was a resolution of principle only. Tupper, who would have been happy to see its passage as a first step in the rebuilding of greater Nova Scotia, spoke forcefully of the benefits of union. But he had no details comparable to those the Canadians had been providing about the federal union, no suggestions for where the capital of a united Maritime province would be, nothing to say how distinct (and politically explosive) schools systems would be integrated, nothing about how the delicate ethnic, religious, and class coalitions of each province would be reordered in a united province.

Tupper's notes confirm that debate on his motion quickly exposed deep divisions amongst the delegations. The tactless suggestion of New Brunswick attorney-general Johnson that it would be good for Prince Edward Island to become "a partner in the land of New Brunswick" invited retaliation. Colonel Gray soon replied that Nova Scotia and New Brunswick were already as good as united, but the disadvantages to the Island would be great. Edward Palmer reminded the room that the Islanders were there only to listen. Their legislature, he said coldly, had given them no authority to endorse a union – or even to express an opinion. Chandler, the loyalist aristocrat from New Brunswick, perhaps offended by Colonel Gray's dismissal of his province's individuality and aware that Halifax was the most likely capital of a united Maritimes, noted that New Brunswick was going to have difficulty with the seat-of-government problem.

The more these issues loomed, the more eagerly the Maritimers brought confederation back into the Maritime-union debate. The Canadians were eager to see the Maritimes become one province, suggested Tilley darkly, because Canada might have to offer better terms to the three provinces separately than to one united province. William Pope of Prince Edward Island took the same view. George Coles said eagerly that a federal government would have the authority – and the money – to settle the Island's vexed problem of absentee estates, a tempting carrot for the Islanders. (Indeed, withdrawal of this carrot would make Coles a vigorous anti-confederate who would help keep Prince Edward Island out of confederation in 1867.)

Finally, Leonard Tilley voiced a gathering consensus about Maritime union and confederation. Confederation seemed possible, he said, but Maritime union would not help confederation and, given its difficulties, would probably delay it. "If we get the confederation now," Tilley said breezily, "we could easily unite the Maritime provinces . . . afterwards." If we want to, some of his audience perhaps added silently.

With that settled, Maritime union was disposed of as a serious alternative. The Maritimers adjourned their discussion of Tupper's motion and invited the Canadians back in. Brown summed up in a phrase. "The conference gave the Canadian delegates their answer – that they were unanimous in regarding federation of all the provinces to be highly desirable, *if the terms of union could be made satisfactory* – and that they were prepared to waive their own more limited question until the details of our scheme could be more fully considered and matured."[19]

The delegates took the next day off. Though there would be further sessions, that agreement on Wednesday, September 7, marked the effective end of the Charlottetown conference. Simultaneously, it had launched the Quebec conference. Maritime union had been shelved; substantive discussions of the terms of a federal union were now required. The Canadians had already planned to invite the Maritimers to Quebec if the Charlottetown sessions succeeded, and within a few weeks new delegations were being appointed to gather there on October 10.

Charlottetown had done more than dispose of Maritime union, however. The conference had endorsed the principle of a federal union of the British North American provinces – a union in which the central government would be supreme, but in which local legislatures would retain significant powers. This was the principle of the British North America Act in a nutshell. This was Canada in a nutshell, in fact.

Not all, or even half, of that agreement had been achieved at the conference table in what is now the Confederation Room at Province House. Around the business sessions developed an extraordinary social whirl. The politicians of the united Canadas and those of the Maritime provinces hardly knew each other, and their occasional previous dealings had most often led to acrimonious failure. On the delicate and momentous matters that had come to dominate the Charlottetown conference, they needed to sound out each other's sense of what was essential and what was unacceptable, what each might offer and what each would demand. For the business to succeed, they needed to know something about each other, and that was where Charlottetown had its great and memorable success.

Charlottetown hospitality was constant and exhausting. The first night, the Island's lieutenant-governor held a lavish dinner at his waterfront residence. The next day, after the conference adjourned at three, William Pope invited delegates to his home for an elaborate "luncheon" of Island delicacies: oysters, lobsters, and champagne. "This killed the day," reported George Brown, "and we spent the beautiful moonlight evening in walking, driving, or boating, as the mood was on us."[20]

The social calendar remained crowded for the rest of the week, even as the business sessions ground through their agenda. After Galt's financial presentation, a late lunch aboard the *Queen Victoria* was followed by a grand dinner at Colonel Gray's country estate, "Inkerman." On the Monday, George Coles, the Island opposition leader, gave *his* luncheon. Next day, it was the turn of Edward Palmer to offer the late luncheon. That night Lieutenant-Governor George Dundas and his wife hosted a grand ball at Government House – "a very nice affair, but a great bore for old fellows like me," wrote Brown to his wife, Anne, who was visiting Scotland. On the following days, there would be another reception aboard the *Queen Victoria*, excursions to the country and the north-shore beaches, and yet another ball at Province House.

For Peter Waite, "the beginning of confederation" could be precisely dated. It happened when the Canadians began pouring from their plentiful stores of champagne aboard the *Queen Victoria* on Saturday, September 3, after the second day of their presentation. They were celebrating, he wrote, "the heady discovery of a national destiny." Waite had Brown's evidence to back up his claim. "Cartier and I made eloquent speeches," said Brown about that shipboard party, "and whether as the result of our eloquence or of the goodness of our champagne, the ice became completely broken, the tongues of the delegates wagged merrily, and the banns of matrimony between all the provinces of BNA having been formally proclaimed . . . the union was formally proclaimed and completed." Champagne flowed like water, commented Waite, "and union talk with it. The occasion took hold of everyone. Champagne and union. . . . Here was a metamorphosis indeed: this transformation of the dross of reality into the gold of personal conviction." [21]

Champagne and union inspired a lot of cynical comment, to the effect that confederation was made when a conspiracy of politicians got drunk together at the public expense. But confederation at Charlottetown had two requirements. Men who had good reason to consider themselves legitimate representatives of the electorates of five future provinces had to be persuaded that confederation was both worthy and feasible. In the business sessions, the politicians confronted serious issues and fundamental principles. In the sunshine and the dinners and the country excursions, they established the trust that helped the business sessions go forward. Charlottetown's social sessions and business sessions worked in tandem.

At the closing ball, the most lavish yet, the delegates tried blending business and sociability. George Brown heard that at 2:00 a.m, after the dancing and the dinner, "the Goths commenced speechmaking and actually kept it up for two hours and three-quarters, the poor girls being condemned to listen to it all." Brown himself had gone to bed early and avoided such horrors. The next morning, as the delegations left for Halifax, one newspaper correspondent noted that most of the statesmen were as befogged as the harbour.[22]

Charles Tupper was surely there to the end, and his attention to the poor girls, though unrecorded, may well have been more assiduous than Brown's. Charlottetown had been a triumph for Tupper. As the leader of the largest Maritime province and the most bullish enthusiast among them, both for Maritime union and for confederation, he was crucial in forging Atlantic Canada's welcome to the Canadian proposal. John A. Macdonald told Joseph Pope, his official biographer, that he had concluded on the first day of Charlottetown that Tupper was exactly the man needed for the accomplishment of confederation. While this smacks of Macdonaldian bonhomie, it strikes the right note about Tupper's influence at Charlottetown, and the two men did forge a political alliance that lasted almost thirty more years. In time, their sons would become law partners and cabinet colleagues. Tupper was enamoured of big opportunities and had the personality to dominate most gatherings. Charlottetown must have been glory to him.

After Charlottetown, Tupper never doubted the feasibility or the worth of confederation. He took ruthless measures to get it through, and in the following decades confederation carried him to Ottawa, to Washington, to London, to the prime minister's office, and to a baronetcy. It opened the way for his sons and daughters to move from Nova Scotia to Ottawa, Winnipeg, Vancouver, and London, to political honours, legal prominence, and social eminence. Confederation opened to the Tuppers all the larger horizons that the delegates toasted as the champagne flowed and the ice broke aboard the *Queen Victoria* in Charlottetown harbour.

Yet Tupper had done his vital work before the conference started, when he made Charlottetown an all-party conference. Whether it was in the business sessions, or in the champagne-fuelled sociability aboard ship, or in the great houses, the politicians had let down their guard precisely because their rivals were beside them. At Charlottetown, Tupper abandoned once and for all his previous concerns that confederation might be an impractical dream. But for him and all the politicians in the room, practicality meant political practicality as much as anything. As Tupper began to make up his mind to support confederation, the leader of the Nova Scotia opposition, Adams Archibald, and Halifax's most powerful newspaperman, Jonathan McCully, were in the room making the same decision. Leaders of government and opposition from the other provinces were making the same simultaneous commitment. Even Island rivals like Edward Palmer and George Coles, who days earlier had been competing over which would be most determinedly hostile to any

threat to Island independence, were joining the gathering consensus
that the thing was possible.

The explosion of enthusiasm and ambition at Charlottetown was
possible because of the diversity of participation – Tupper's gift to
the process. Multi-party participation was the *sine qua non* that
enabled the politicians to consider endorsing the new ideas without
worrying about being blindsided back home. Tupper, the hard-
edged, high-stakes political battler, would never have made the large
commitments he made at Charlottetown if he had anticipated that
what seemed so enticing in the sunshine of Charlottetown would be
turned into a partisan fight at home. Given the pre-Charlottetown
views of McCully and Archibald, they surely would have opposed it,
had they not been there.

The men of Charlottetown could be converted by union and
champagne because they saw their rivals being converted at the same
time. That Joseph Howe, Timothy Anglin, Antoine-Aimé Dorion,
and other political leaders who did not attend soon became confederation's fiercest critics confirms how essential broad participation
was – and how confederation might actually have been achieved
more easily had participation in the conferences been even broader.

The bipartisanship of Charlottetown started a brief constitutional
tradition. The Charlottetown delegations would be joined at Quebec
in October 1864 by a two-party delegation from Newfoundland.
Bipartisanship prevailed immediately after confederation as well.
Even during the Red River uprising of 1869-70, the delegation which
negotiated Manitoba's entry into confederation represented a broad
cross-section of anglophone and francophone Métis and recent set-
tlers. When British Columbia negotiated its entry to confederation
in 1871, its autocratic lieutenant-governor would have nothing to do
with those who advocated responsible government such as Amor de
Cosmos and John Robson. Parliamentary government came to
British Columbia only with confederation (and both de Cosmos
and Robson became premiers). Nevertheless, the B.C. delegation

that settled terms with Ottawa did include representatives of both Vancouver Island and the mainland, as well as both advocates and sceptics about confederation.

Prince Edward Island broke the bipartisan tradition. When it decided to enter confederation in 1873, it did so amidst a partisan squabble over which side could get most and give up least in the deal-making. A Conservative government, with better ties to John A. Macdonald in Ottawa, displaced a Liberal one, and brought Prince Edward Island into confederation without the participation of its rivals, initiating a long and mostly counter-productive tradition of partisan constitutional deals. But even in the twentieth century, some sense of the value of bipartisan constitution-making endured: an all-party constitutional assembly preceded Newfoundland's decision to seek terms with Canada in 1949. Only with the new initiatives of the 1960s did executive federalism come to be taken for granted.

At Canada's late-twentieth-century constitutional conferences, at Meech Lake in 1987 and Charlottetown in 1992, the first ministers in their executive conclaves quickly reached unanimity – by excluding all their rivals. They meant well and they worked hard, only to find themselves assaulted and finally defeated by partisan attack and local resentment. Eager to float above the political landscape as fathers of the new confederation, they made themselves irresistibly juicy targets for every opposition leader who lined up to declare that *he* would have gotten more and given up less.

Charles Tupper, a political brawler and not a man to shed tears for losers, would surely have sneered at the defeated makers of the Meech Lake accord, the would-be confederation-makers who failed to get their deal through. Bringing his rivals to Charlottetown had been no act of kindness. Tupper did it as much to protect his hide as to ensure success. But it did both. Bipartisanship gave the results a legitimacy no modern constitutional initiative has achieved. The premiers of Meech Lake failed where he succeeded, because they followed their presidential egos when he followed his parliamentary guile. In its strategic calculation and in its understanding of parliamentary necessities, it demonstrated in Tupper and his confrères a parliamentary sagacity never matched in the constitutional efforts of the late twentieth century.

CHAPTER THREE

Ned Whelan and Edmund Burke
on the Ramparts of Quebec

~

T HE CANADIAN steamship *Queen Victoria*, which had carried the Canadian delegation down to Charlottetown in August 1864, sailed again in October. This time, she collected Maritime delegates at Pictou, Charlottetown, and Shediac, and carried them up the St. Lawrence, bucking headwinds and snow squalls all the way. Among the passengers eager to get to Quebec and the second confederation conference was Edward Whelan, who had recently been added to Prince Edward Island's delegation.

Whelan makes an odd figure among the makers of confederation, at least among the anti-democratic, élitist fathers we take for granted. He was of working-class origins, raised by his mother and largely self-educated. He never had money or any security beyond what an Island printing office provided, and he had built his political career as a troublemaker and an agent of change. He once declared that all of history was an endless battle of aristocratic power against "the humbler classes of society, the men of small means and limited education." In the cause of the humbler classes, he was capable of calling loyalty to the Empire "old rubbish" and the British constitution "a mockery, a sham, and a delusion." Smashing the exist-ing state of property relations on Prince Edward Island was the foundation of his twenty-year political career there.[1]

In the tributes given him after his early death, everyone said Ned Whelan was "convivial." There are just hints that he ate and drank too much and neglected his family. His power base lay with the Island's Irish Catholic minority, but he was a backsliding Catholic and occasionally a thorn in the bishop's side. Yet neither his con-frontational politics nor his private life made him an outcast. He was generally acknowledged as Prince Edward Island's liveliest orator on any subject from Shakespeare to educational reform. He ran the Island's best newspaper, the *Examiner*, and filled it with his perceptive and wide-ranging writing. Though he was just forty in 1864, Whelan had been in Island politics since 1846 and he had never lost an election. In 1864, he was in opposition, but he had been a cabinet minister during most of the 1850s.

A perceptive political tactician, Whelan understood why he had been invited to join the delegation going to Quebec. As an opposi-tion member who favoured union, he was doubly useful to provin-cial secretary (and confederation advocate) William Henry Pope, usually his bitter foe, who seems to have secured his appointment, along with that of an establishment tory, Heath Haviland. Whelan and Haviland would become Pope's strongest pro-confederation allies among the increasingly sceptical delegates from the Island.

Whelan was the only confederation delegate to note the political calculation behind the recruiting of opposition members to the con-ferences. "Politicians are generally cunning fellows, and those in the several Maritime governments showed this quality to great advantage when they appointed members of the opposition," he told a Montreal banquet in October, "because if the people of the several provinces should be so unwise as to complain, . . . the opposition would have to bear the censure as well as those in the administration."[2]

Whelan, so clear-eyed about why he had been invited, was none the less happy to participate. No apolitical ambassador, he saw himself "representing the opinions of the liberal party" at the conference, and he had his own political agenda to pursue. Whelan had endorsed confederation mostly for its promise to bring the changes he wanted for the Island, and he wanted his views on this confederation heard, whatever the political risk. He boarded the *Queen Victoria* in high enthusiasm. From shipboard he sent back a promise to his readers to report on "the ancient and historic city" and its "mazy, crooked, narrow, and bewildering streets," as well as "the great question of inter-colonial union." He had never been to Quebec – or any part of the united Canadas – before.[3]

Whelan had a magpie curiosity about people and places, but he was also temperamentally inclined to argue all his political stances back to principles. This makes him doubly curious, for historians have been at pains to insist that the makers of confederation were plain-speaking pragmatists, not philosophers. It was a point of pride, almost, for the historians of the 1960s to declare that the makers of confederation, as Donald Creighton put it in his forthright way, "saw no merit in setting out on a highly unreal voyage of discovery for first principles." In the pragmatic, end-of-ideology 1950s and early 1960s, historians preferred to see the constitution-makers as politicians to their fingertips, manoeuvring their way with one eye on the voters and the other on Westminster toward any deal that seemed possible.[4]

Since then, Creighton's praise has often been turned into a rebuke to the delegates, used to characterize them – and their confederation – as unintellectual, reactionary, and incapable of assimilating big ideas. Professor Russell backhands the Canadian constitution as "a practical, though not philosophical accord." Writer George Woodcock, less restrained, sneers at it as "a makeshift document cobbled together by colonial politicians."[5]

If historians and political scientists do challenge this aphilosophical view of confederation, they do so by invoking the name of Edmund Burke. This is no compliment. In the twentieth century, Burke has become perhaps the most spectacularly out-of-fashion political philosopher in the canon. Few who point to Burke's influences on the makers of confederation mean to honour them by the identification.

Edward Whelan would not admit being a disciple of Edmund Burke. An Irish Catholic immigrant with more than a little sympathy for Irish nationalism and Irish rebels, he preferred as his role model Henry Grattan, who, as the founder of a short-lived Irish parliament in the late 1700s, was a hero to mid-nineteenth-century Irish nationalists. Edmund Burke was Irish, but he had made his career in London and had opposed Grattan's plans for Ireland. To Whelan, he seemed entirely too English and too conservative. Whelan ranked Grattan far above Burke both as orator and thinker.[6]

As an ink-stained newspaperman in a small town in a small colony where politics were mostly known for their petty viciousness, Whelan wrote to meet deadlines rather than out of philosophical contemplation. He had gone to work at Joseph Howe's newspaper office at the age of eight, and his further education, at a modest Catholic institute in Halifax, ended at nineteen when he moved to Charlottetown to launch his own newspaper. He had none of the cultivated leisure of Burke in England or Madison and Jefferson among the American founding fathers. No philosophical giant, simply someone who had absorbed Howe's – and the age's – love for wide reading, debate, and self-improvement, Whelan was never intimidated by ideas. He cited English political writer "Junius" for the motto of one of his Charlottetown papers and Euripides for another, and he studded his speeches with literary and historical references in the best Victorian fashion.[7]

Whelan expressed and acted on a philosophy of government virtually extinct today, easily caricatured and easily misunderstood, but characteristic of his era and shared by many of his fellow makers of the Canadian constitution. Despite Whelan's urge to make government an engine of social change in Prince Edward Island, that philosophy was indeed best exemplified and argued out by Edmund Burke. And so, arriving at Quebec in October 1864, Whelan brought

with him the ghost of Edmund Burke to haunt the proceedings of
the conference. We cannot take that conference's measure without
measuring Burke's shadow on it.

In life, Edmund Burke never walked the ramparts of Quebec. Born
in Ireland in 1729, he went to London as a student, and remained
near there as a writer, a political adviser, and a member of Parliament,
mostly in opposition, until his death in 1797. He went once to
France, but rarely anywhere else. He did not visit North America,
even when he was the London agent for the colony of New York in
the years before the American Revolution, and he made few substantial references to Canadian matters.

In Whelan's day as in ours, Edmund Burke was most famous as
the author of *Reflections on the Revolution in France*, a spectacular
polemic, one of the greatest in the language. Published in 1790,
Reflections condemned every part of the French Revolution, even
its rights-of-man, *Liberté-Égalité-Fraternité* phase, before the Terror
and the rise of Napoleon soured many of Burke's fellow citizens on
it. Burke called ceaselessly not merely for resistance to revolutionary France but for war, "a long war," to confront, contain, and overthrow the revolution abroad and to repress its admirers in England.

The uncompromising force and rhetorical brilliance of *Reflections*
made it an inspiration for every counter-revolutionary tract for the
next two centuries. *Reflections* was also an impassioned declaration
of the sacredness of the Bourbon monarchy, with a paean to the
glories of Marie Antoinette that today is incomprehensible. "The
unbought grace of life, the cheap defence of nations, the nurse of
manly sentiment and heroic enterprise is gone!" was the lesson Burke
drew from the queen's fall from the elevated sphere where he had
once worshipped her, "glittering like the morningstar, full of life and
splendor and joy."[8]

More deeply, *Reflections* was an argument against abstract theories of government and in favour of tradition – seemingly, in favour
of any tradition, no matter how unjust (or actually *because* of its

injustice, in the view of those who saw Burke as the paid apologist of the ruling class). While its subject was France, *Reflections* was addressed to Burke's British compatriots. It was an argument against political change in Britain.

Reflections has remained Burke's most famous work, the one most often anthologized and reprinted. It is frequently taken as the essence of Burke's political philosophy. As disciples of Burke, therefore, the confederation-makers are often declared to be not merely averse to change, but positively hostile to it and to democracy, national autonomy, and most of the values that have held sway in the twentieth century. Ned Whelan's case suggests, however, that the lessons they drew from Burke were hardly so simple.

As a counter-revolutionary monarchist and impassioned defender of the British constitution, Burke might be expected to be a blimpish Imperialist, celebrating the blessings of British rule worldwide. Yet, during the American Revolution, Burke consistently supported the cause of the American colonists, even when he was a member of the Parliament that was waging war against the Thirteen Colonies. He devoted decades to a probing criticism of Britain's empire in India, going so far as to argue that, in ruling India, Britain's goal should be "studying the genius, the temper, and the manners of the people, and adapting to them the laws that we establish" – an incomprehensible and subversive notion to most of the builders of the British Raj. The Irish writer Conor Cruise O'Brien has discovered inside Burke the tribune of Protestant England an Irishman with deep sympathies for oppressed Catholic Ireland. Burke opposed Whelan's hero Grattan because Grattan's Irish Parliament, despite the rhetoric of national independence that attracted Whelan, had mostly empowered Irish Protestants to oppress Irish Catholics more effectively.[9]

Burke was hardly more favourable to Imperial power in his comments about British North America. Canada, a minor appendage to the more consequential Thirteen Colonies, was mostly beneath his notice, but his few remarks about it were strikingly unsympathetic to the cause of Empire. Burke had condemned Britain's deportation of the Acadians as both evil and self-defeating. "We did, in my opinion, most inhumanly, and upon pretenses that in the eye of an honest man are not worth a farthing, root out this poor, innocent, deserving people, whom our utter inability to govern, or to reconcile, gave us no sort of right to extirpate."[10] In 1780 he attacked Acadia's successor colony, Nova Scotia – then serving as a vital bulwark in Britain's war against the Americans – as an "ill-thriven, hard-visaged, and ill-favoured brat," and an endless, useless drain on the British taxpayer.[11] In 1774, just a decade after the conquest of New France, he made a proposal to empower the conquered French Canadians that would have been startling in Lord Durham's day – and long after. "Give them English liberty, give them an English constitution," he told Parliament about the Canadians, "and then, whether they speak French or English, whether they go to mass or attend our own communion, you will render them valuable and useful subjects of Great Britain."[12]

Why did Burke consistently dismiss the whole basis of British Imperial rule in Canada? Burke was an anti-imperialist at the heart of the Empire, and his anti-imperialism grew from the same roots as his counter-revolutionary fervour. He believed British political usages were best for Britain because they had evolved in Britain for British needs, and he believed all governments should, in effect, be grown rather than invented according to a theory. Against the theoretical Enlightenment philosophy of the rights of man, adopted enthusiastically by slave-holding Virginians and despotic French revolutionaries, Burke preferred the actual rights that Englishmen had evolved ad hoc over centuries. In his opposition to building governments on a theory lay the root of the *Reflections*'s attack on the French Revolution and the root of its defence of the British constitution.

But if the constitution that had evolved in Britain was appropriate for Britain, it followed that it might not be appropriate for societies that had evolved differently. In an age that had made General Wolfe a heroic martyr, Burke was sceptical of governments rooted in conquest. He argued that ties between a nation and its colonies could only be rooted in common interests and a shared heritage, never in coercion. His willingness to let colonies go if those ties could not be sustained was, of course, heresy and treason to the handfuls of Protestant Englishmen struggling to maintain and to justify their authority over the Catholics of Ireland, the Hindus of India – and the French population of Canada.

Despite his horror of change based on nothing but abstract theories of man or government, the author of the counter-revolutionary bible had not even been a reliable supporter of the status quo at home. The worshipper of Marie Antoinette might be expected also to have idolized George III. Yet to read Burke on George III is to move from the counter-revolutionary propagandist of the *Reflections* to a vigorous opponent of royal power. In domestic politics, the British tradition that Burke extolled and defended was the Whig tradition of parliamentary supremacy. Whigs looked proudly back to the Glorious Revolution of 1688, when England's Stuart dynasty was deposed and the Dutch Prince William of Orange was made King of England as a constitutional monarch, obliged to seek and follow the advice of Parliament.

The Glorious Revolution fell short of completely or permanently shearing British kings of their independent power. The active, young King George III of the 1760s had often chosen prime ministers for their assent to *his* policies and then struggled to bring Parliament into line. In *Thoughts on the Causes of the Present Discontents*, a long essay he wrote on this subject in 1770, Burke had argued that the king and his cabinet were not truly responsible to Parliament, that they consistently interfered in and circumvented the workings of Parliament. *Thoughts on the Causes* attacked the covert influence the king still maintained and the way royal influence corrupted parliamentarians, who too often served the king's will rather than the interests of the nation. That kind of Parliament, said Burke, became "the best appendage and support of arbitrary power that ever was invented by the wit of man."[13]

The political power of the monarch and his friends was no dead issue in the 1770s. In the midst of the American Revolutionary War, Burke and his parliamentary allies who supported American independence fought a long war against royal influence and royal power. King George had made the refusal of American independence a question of personal dignity, even when it was clear that granting independence was essential to ending the war. In 1779 George declared, "Before I will ever hear of any man's readiness to come into office, I will expect to see it signed under his hand that he is resolved to keep the empire entire." That royal will still shaped national policy.[14]

In 1782, the peace faction in the Commons, strengthened by every defeat in the colonial war, struck back. After the British disaster at Yorktown, the party of which Burke was a key strategist demanded, with the backing of a parliamentary majority, that "the king must not give a veto" to American independence. This blunt demand, rooted in the principle that *any* interference with parliamentary control over national policy was simply unconstitutional, brought George III to the brink of abdication. When the king swallowed his pride and kept his throne by accepting Parliament's decision on the independence of the United States, a crucial step in securing parliamentary sovereignty had been taken. Burke briefly became a cabinet minister in a government committed, with the king's very unwilling consent, to accepting the independence of the former colonies. Since then, no British monarch has successfully withstood the will of the House of Commons on a significant matter of public policy.

It was his advocacy of reducing the monarch from a power in politics to a symbol who reigned but did not rule that made Edmund Burke a congenial figure for Canadian politicians of Edward Whelan's sort. For all his angry radicalism in other areas, Whelan was an orthodox child of Burke in his campaign to promote parliamentary government. Responsible government had brought Whelan into politics in 1846, at the age of twenty-one. He had wrapped himself in the rights of Englishmen and the "defence of the constitution," in language that paraphrased Burke's struggle against George III. Like other reformers from Newfoundland to Upper Canada, he pushed Burke's argument that the elected legislature must control the executive branch. He likened governors and their advisers to arbitrary monarchs, and portrayed fellow reformers as loyal subjects and defenders of the constitution, even in the midst of their agitation for change. Looming inevitably behind them was the parliamentary Burke. The Burke they quoted, however, was not the defender of Marie Antoinette but the crusader against arbitrary royal authority, who nevertheless avoided any tinge of disloyalty by his deference to monarchy as a symbol.

After the achievement of responsible government in 1847, the doctrine that governors must defer to elected representatives was adopted throughout British North America. Paraphrases of Burke rolled out instinctively whenever a governor like Arthur Gordon needed to be educated about colonial political realities – or indeed, whenever colonial politicians bridled against the wishes of the Colonial Office. Charles Tupper used such arguments as confidently as Edward Whelan, and it hardly proved that either of them was a political philosopher. The argument that power must belong to elected parliamentarians was the fundamental assumption of mid-nineteenth-century Canadian politicians. Burke, an impeccably British ancestor, provided much of the rhetorical splendour which the confederation-makers mustered on this issue. In British North America, he was a force for change, not continuity.

The British Parliament whose power Burke himself had fought to expand was a very curious one. The House of Commons Burke defended against royal autocracy was itself wildly unrepresentative of the people of Britain. Britain in Burke's time – and at the time of Canadian confederation as well – was governed by a Parliament for which few Britons could vote. Many MPs held parliamentary seats controlled by a single aristocratic patron. Burke himself held such a seat for most of his parliamentary career, and he unapologetically defended the unreformed House of Commons. In *Thoughts on the Causes*, his attack on the political powers of the king, he associated "the natural strength of the kingdom," which Parliament represented, not with the people, but with "the great peers, the leading landed gentlemen, the opulent merchants and manufacturers, the substantial yeomanry."[15]

That narrow definition of who should elect the House of Commons was barely beginning to change in Britain in the 1860s. When the confederation plan was being debated in Canada, the hot controversy of British politics was a bill intended to increase – slightly – the number of men eligible to vote. Opposition was deep and strong, and the issue made and broke British governments in the 1860s.

Was Britain's unreformed Parliament the model the makers of confederation extolled when they quoted Burke? A surprising number of our historians and political scientists have assumed it was. But the makers of confederation managed to combine reverence for parliamentary rule with a commitment to a broadly based electoral franchise totally unlike Britain's. Edmund Burke had defended the dominance of a handful of property owners in the British Parliament on the grounds that, in truth, they dominated British society. The tightly limited circle of British voters, he had argued, actually modelled and represented real power in British society, just as it should.

In the North American colonies, however, property and the vote had always been very broadly held. There were rich and poor in British North America, but the distinction between them was much smaller than in Britain. Unlike their British counterparts, most families in nineteenth-century Canada could and did acquire property sufficient to give the household head the vote. The same principles that decreed a narrow electoral franchise in Britain supported a broad franchise in British North America.

The issue of voting power in Canada had once been hotly debated in Britain, and Edmund Burke himself had joined the debate. In 1791, when the British government drafted constitutions for the newly created colonies of Lower and Upper Canada, it wanted to prevent them from drifting, like the lost Thirteen Colonies, into hostility and independence. How was that to be done? The Constitutional Act of 1791 was intended to create societies like that of Britain, where long-established patterns of deference would buttress a lasting commitment to Britain, its monarchy, and its Empire. The Canadas would remain loyally British, argued the authors of the Constitutional Act, if they became societies led by a wealthy, secure, respected, and politically privileged local aristocracy, supported by an established church.

As late as the 1840s, John Beverley Robinson, then chief justice of Upper Canada, "bone and sinew of the Family Compact," a beneficiary and a defender of the Constitutional Act of 1791, could still advocate "the control of numerous landlords over a grateful peasantry" as the way British North American society ought to be run. He defended the rule of "the most worthy, intelligent, loyal and opulent inhabitants . . . of high character, of large property, and of superior information" as the proper government for Upper Canada, as for Britain itself. Robinson always said, and believed himself justified in saying, that he was merely defending the constitution the Crown had bestowed on British North America in 1791.[16]

But in this interpretation of the English constitution, the conservative Robinson could not claim the support of the conservative Burke. In 1791, Edmund Burke had argued against the objectives that Robinson came to hold sacred. In the British House of Commons debate on the bill that created Upper Canada, he asserted his view that societies were organic, the product of history and tradition. Government, he always held, should be a reflection of society as it actually existed, not a tool for re-inventing society. "Let the Canadians have a constitution formed on the principles of Canadians and the English upon principles of Englishmen . . . but let there be no wild theories," he declared. It was useless and wrong, in other words, to try to conjure into being a Canadian aristocracy, simply to bind the colony to the mother country. Even at the risk of losing Imperial control over Canada, Burke endorsed a French-Canadian government for French Canada, just as he had endorsed an American government for the American colonists and proposed an Indian government for India.[17]

The 1791 act, with its provisions for encouraging a Canadian landed gentry, was Upper and Lower Canada's constitution from 1791 to 1841. But, as Burke predicted, no Canadian aristocracy took root. The appointed councils that dominated Canadian government between 1791 and the 1840s came to represent, not an independent landholding gentry, but a handful of petty office-holders, dependent on the Crown's patronage. Canadian reformers, presenting themselves as loyal defenders of the rights of Englishmen, argued with all the more force that the constitution of 1791 had to be adapted to local circumstances. The logic of the British constitution, they had been saying since the 1820s, required that, since property was widely held in the Canadian colonies, political power had to be widely held. Political power in British North America, they argued, was the birthright of the elected assemblies, not the appointive councils of the would-be gentry. They dismissed the other view, the ostensibly conservative one advocated by Robinson, as fundamentally unconstitutional.

The reform interpretation triumphed so completely in British North America in the 1840s that, by the 1860s, it was a non-controversial orthodoxy. Old-fashioned "compact tories," hanging on to Robinson's views, had been pushed aside by conservative politicians like Macdonald and Tupper, ready and very much able to secure electoral support for their brand of conservatism. Reformers and conservatives, whatever their other differences, had all become parliamentarians. On the role of parliament, they were all Burkeans, which (despite Burke's counter-revolutionary aura) meant they had all accepted what had been reform arguments and had become orthodoxy after the winning of responsible government in 1847.

What elected representatives had lacked before responsible government was not representativeness; they had always been close to their voters and elected on a remarkably broad franchise for the times. What they had lacked was power. The makers of confederation, as heirs and beneficiaries of the long struggle to secure the authority of elected assemblies over the executive arm of government, quite naturally held an exalted view of representative bodies. Here again, Burke was a crucial exemplar. Once more, he has made the makers of confederation liable to a charge of being conservative reactionaries when they were actually being notably progressive.

The classic statement of the right and duty of parliamentarians to make up their own minds and to vote, not simply as pipelines for their constituents but in accordance with their own convictions, was Edmund Burke's. In 1774, Burke was invited to stand for Parliament in the city of Bristol. To sit for Bristol, then England's second-largest city and its most important west-coast port, would be a promotion from holding a seat through the patronage of a landholding aristocrat. Holding that seat would make Burke a significant figure in Parliament. Yet Burke was frank in telling the voters of Bristol how he expected to act as their member of Parliament. He would not let them tell him how to vote.

> Their wishes ought to have great weight with him; their opinions high respect; their business unremitted attention. . . . But his unbiased opinion, his mature judgement, his enlightened conscience, he ought not to sacrifice to you, to any man, or to any set of men living. . . . Your representative owes you, not his industry only, but his judgement; and he betrays, instead of serving you, if he sacrifices it to your opinion.[18]

Late-twentieth-century opinion often condemned this view of the parliamentarian's role. Burke's declaration was frequently cited as simple élitism, a permission for politicians to dismiss with disdain the ignorant masses who merely elect them. But Burke argued that parliamentary representation was in fact worthless unless parliamentary study and debate could lead representatives to reach informed conclusions, even to change their minds. As for his supposed contempt for voters, it is worth observing what happened to his parliamentary career as Bristol's representative.

Burke did follow his own counsel as Bristol's member of Parliament, and he managed to offend many of the voters there. By 1778 he was clearly in danger of losing his seat. It was a risk he was prepared to run. "He should not blame [his constituents] if they did reject him," he wrote. "The event would afford a very useful example, on the one hand of a senator inflexibly adhering to his opinion against interest and against popularity; and, on the other, of constituents exercising their undoubted right of rejection; not on corrupt [grounds], but from their persuasion that he whom they had chosen had acted against the judgement and interest of those he represented." Soon after, with his defeat certain, Burke withdrew his candidacy on the eve of the election and ceased to be member for Bristol after a single term.[19]

After his defeat in Bristol, Burke was able to stay in the House of Commons only by acquiring once again a seat controlled by an aristocratic patron. He retained the title of member of Parliament, but lost the clout that came from being elected by a key constituency. In modern terms, it was as if a potential party leader had thrown away a House seat for a Senate appointment. Burke took the demotion in stride, for he was more a philosopher in politics than a typically ambitious politician, and relied more on his voice in the House than on raw political power. But few conventional politicians would so willingly have thrown away the Bristol seat. Burke's experience, in fact, proved that elected parliamentarians who were cavalier about their constituents' wishes put their careers in jeopardy. Whatever their theoretical freedom, few conventional politicians were as reckless as Burke was about disagreeing with the voters.

Having fought for a generation to secure the rule of the elected assemblies against appointive governors and councils, Canadian politicians of the mid-1800s held an exalted view of the status of a parliamentary representative. They frequently spoke in Burkean tones of Parliament's independence, and of a legislator's obligation to consider the national good, not simply the local interest. They consistently argued that the elected assembly was the body where legislators should make up their mind and cast their votes according to their convictions.

In 1856, Edward Whelan defended one of his votes in the Prince Edward Island legislature with a paraphrase of Burke. "I have always entertained the notion – and I think I shall never abandon it – that when a member is sent here, he does not appear in the character of a delegate to carry out a certain code of instructions, but rather to act in accordance with the dictates of his own conscience and judgement, and to pursue that policy best calculated to promote the interests, not of his own constituents only, but those of the whole Island at large. It is right that a member should consult with his constituents on public questions, as I frequently take an opportunity of doing, and endeavour to ascertain their opinions and, if possible, reconcile them to his own, should there be any disagreement, but I do not conceive it to be any part of the duty of a member to sacrifice his own conscientious convictions to suit the views of any class of men."[20]

Whelan did not identify Burke, who was far from his favourite philosopher, as the source of his idea or his language, but the similarity is inescapable. Like most Canadian politicians, Whelan both was and was not a Burkean on this point. Canadian politicians endorsed in principle the independence of legislators, but they held no sinecure seats of the kind Burke had waiting for him. They faced broadly based and well-informed electorates, which would not tolerate representatives who did not heed those who elected them. The inescapable fact is that Whelan was much closer to and much more dependent on the voters than Burke had ever been. Whelan believed deeply in the authority of parliamentarians, but he hardly needed Burke's Bristol example to know that disregarding his constituents as flagrantly as Burke had done would simply be political suicide.

The makers of confederation did not much believe in political suicide, and they rarely practised it. Indeed, their relations with voters were much closer than those of later members of Parliament. Nineteenth-century Canadian politics provided many more examples than the late twentieth century of politicians deserting their party out of fear of, or respect for, their constituents.

In that context, the arguments of Edmund Burke, so often echoed by the makers of confederation, achieve a new poignancy in the Canadian context. The struggle of the first half of the nineteenth century in Canada was for responsible government – an executive answerable to the elected parliamentary majority. With responsible government achieved, Parliament had real power and parliamentarians celebrated their independence and authority – all the more so because of the wary eye they had to keep on the voters back home.

During the twentieth century, that situation was reversed. Disciplined and docile legislative caucuses came to understand themselves to be responsible to the party leadership, rather than vice versa. The consequence of this huge accretion of executive power was starkly visible in constitutional politics. At Charlottetown and Quebec in 1864, large, bipartisan parliamentary delegations made constitutions. Leadership was collective. Every delegate was aware he could be held to account by his legislature as well as his constituents. In the late twentieth century, small executive conclaves made the constitutional deals. Leadership was personal. Each government leader, sure of support from his caucus, shouldered the full burden of representing his province. Each took any suggestion of opposition participation, and any likelihood for serious legislative review, as insults to first-ministerial prerogatives.

The great principles of confederation-era parliamentary democracy in Canada – a broad franchise and the constant responsibility of the executive branch to the elected legislators – were clear in theory in the 1830s. They became established in practice after 1847. By the end of the 1850s, with the absorption or marginalization of Clear Grit and *rouge* ideas of direct democracy, they were the undisputed ideology of Canadian political life. That battle had been decided. The philosophy of it was not contested and did not need to be argued.

As a result, the constitution-makers who gathered at Quebec in October 1864 did not need to spell out the overarching political philosophy of the new nation – though they could, when they chose. George Brown, Ned Whelan, D'Arcy McGee, and many others could roll out hours of rotund Victorian rhetoric in praise of constitutional monarchy. But only one lonely resolution of the seventy-two approved at Quebec in October 1864 may be considered "philosophical." The fourth resolution declared that, in Canada government would be administered "according to the well-understood principles of the British constitution." This was later incorporated into the preamble of the British North America Act of 1867 as a government "with a Constitution similar in Principle to that of the United Kingdom." [21]

It sounded simple, but it spoke volumes. There was a tome buried there, and much of it was a gloss on Burke's constitutional ideas. The British and Canadian constitutions would be similar in principle but, given their electoral franchises (determined by their very different social structures), who sat in government would be utterly at variance in the two countries. They were "similar in principle," yet Britain had one House of Parliament devoted to a hereditary aristocracy and an established church, and another whose members were elected on an extremely narrow franchise, in a country where very few householders could vote. In Canada, the upper house would be almost entirely irrelevant, while the lower house, the one that made the government, would be elected by most of the adult male population.

The British and Canadian constitutions might be similar in principle, but they would be operated by societies that were hugely different. The Canadian reading of British constitutionalism gave colonial parliamentarians of the confederation era a tremendous sense of legitimate authority, and they wanted to be free to use it. By proposing a constitution similar "in principle" to that of the United Kingdom, the Canadians actually endorsed a government "formed on the principles of Canadians," as Burke had proposed in 1791.

Edward Whelan certainly believed in using the powers of the state. As a cabinet minister in George Coles's reform government in the 1850s, he had been part of a government that had introduced universal manhood suffrage and given Island children a free, non-denominational public-school system. Other confederation-era politicians had been similarly activist. Leonard Tilley's New Brunswick governments invested in public health and public-works projects, introduced universal manhood suffrage, and adopted the secret ballot. In Nova Scotia, conservative and reform governments both promoted railways and mines and invested in the public-school system.

In Canada East, George-Étienne Cartier and his *bleu* supporters wound up the seigneurial regime inherited from New France and modernized and codified the old civil law. They built spectacular public works like the Victoria Bridge at Montreal. The bridge, which opened to great fanfare in 1860, was only the most visible symbol for state support of railways and other industries. Cartier, the Grand Trunk Railway's legal counsel, was also that railway's most prominent parliamentary advocate when railways were the largest development projects in British North America. In Canada West, reform and conservative leaders introduced new layers of city and county government and expanded public works and public schooling. Scores of mid-nineteenth-century courthouses, city halls, and other public buildings that still stand throughout Ontario and Quebec are testimony to the burst of state activity just before confederation.

In *Colonial Leviathan*, a study of these events, the historians Allan Greer and Ian Radforth speak of "the unprecedented expansion of state institutions and the increasing attempts at government supervision of civic life," once the decades of conflict between appointed executives (which had controlled the institutions of state) and elected assemblies (which had controlled the public revenues) ended after 1847. In all this activity, the politicians were doing more than simply spending money. They were conscious and proud of using the state to mould better citizens.[22]

This was not only the state's role, of course. The temperance movement of the time sprang from the same impulse, seeking to do away with drunken idleness and create a sober, industrious, diligent citizenry. In Quebec, it was the Catholic Church, not the state itself, which expanded schools, hospitals, and other public institutions. Throughout the colonies, charitable societies, churches, and the state worked hand-in-hand to reform and guide the poor, the drunken, the ill-educated, the young, and the female toward the bourgeois standards of conduct judged universally appropriate. To this end, the mid-nineteenth century, seemingly so conservative, saw an expansion of public activity unmatched by any other period until the explosion of Keynesian economic planning and social-welfare programs in the mid-twentieth century.

Virtually all of this public activity, it seems fair to guess, would have been anathema to Edmund Burke. Burke was hostile to most forms of state action. He believed government must reflect the shape of society, not reshape it. Burke did not believe government could do much more than defend the liberty of its citizens. "The state ought to confine itself to what regards the state," he wrote, and his list of what regarded the state was very short. For the poor to expect government to improve their condition, for example, was delusory. The state should not try to relieve their misery even in the midst of a famine, he said. "Patience, labour, sobriety, frugality, and religion should be recommended to them; and all the rest is downright fraud," he declared. "It is not in breaking the laws of commerce, which are the laws of nature, and consequently the laws of God, that we are to place our hope of softening the divine displeasure." [23]

In defence of parliamentary authority, the confederation-era politicians of British North America were wonderfully skilful disciples of Edmund Burke. On the role of the state, however, it is hard to see Burke's influence at all. Conservative or reform, they were determined to put state power firmly under the control of the people's representatives. With that achieved, they delighted in their new freedom, not to restrain the state, as Burke would have advised, but to use state power in pursuit of their goals.

Edward Whelan was certainly no Burkean quietist. The issue that had shaped his political career was the explosive one of land owner-ship. Whelan always advocated a two-plank platform: defending the constitution and smashing the "landocracy." Defending the constitu-tion meant securing responsible government – a bold project in 1846, but one that could be shielded under the mantle of Burke. Smashing the landocracy, however, was both socially and politically radical. It meant breaking up the great estates that owned most of the land of Prince Edward Island, and it meant confronting rival politicians whose fortunes, as well as principles, were threatened. In an era when property was sacred, Whelan wanted Prince Edward Island to attack the property rights of the great landlords who owned most of the Island and kept most of its farmers as insecure tenants.[24]

Though it was flaring up when the confederation delegates met at Charlottetown in 1864, the land issue had dogged Island govern-ments for years. Premier George Coles's government, in which Whelan served, had promised in the 1850s to end the absentee land-lord system and to help Island farmers buy the lands they had worked for generations. It passed legislation to coerce Island land-lords to sell their estates. The land reforms, however, were consis-tently vetoed by the British government. This was hardly surprising: any British cabinet of the 1860s consisted largely of landed propri-etors, men for whom large landed estates were the basis of society and government, to say nothing of their own wealth, standing, and political power. Prime Minister Palmerston, one of whose close rel-atives owned a Prince Edward Island estate, haughtily dismissed any move against the Island landowners as an attack on property that should not be permitted anywhere in the Empire.[25]

Whelan, a cabinet minister in the government that had passed the laws, saw Britain's actions as an attack on responsible govern-ment itself. "It is degrading and humiliating to the colony," fumed

Whelan, "that the proprietors – most of them, or many of them absentees, and quite irresponsible, should exercise so arbitrary an influence at the Colonial Office, as to render nugatory the deliberate action of our legislature. This is a species of despotism." London's intransigence meant Coles's government was unable to deliver on its promises to the tenant farmers who had elected it. It was defeated in 1859. In opposition, Whelan's bitterness grew, and his commitment to constitutional reform wavered. "Talk about the glorious privileges of the British Constitution! We live under a constitution of dispatches dictated according to the caprice of absentee land proprietors," he snarled in 1860.[26]

Whelan then began to speculate about a social contract between the governed and the governing that would have horrified Edmund Burke. "Loyalty with me is not a blind sentiment. The sentiment which springs from a mutual return of advantages is the loyalty which . . . we owe to that sovereign who rules over us. . . . Prince Edward Island has generally exhibited much more loyalty than, under the circumstances of the case, she was perhaps justified in showing." Spoken in a legislature of the British Empire, particularly by a Catholic Irishman, such talk of "a mutual return of advantages" – and the implied right of subjects to abolish the contract when they chose – carried a whiff of revolution.[27]

In 1864, still in opposition, with the landocracy as entrenched as ever, Whelan got an opportunity to endorse the bold measures his words of 1860 suggested. In May 1864, Island farmers founded the Tenant League. They declared they would not pay rent and would resist any sanctions that might ensue, forcibly if necessary. Support for the League spread across the Island. Rents went unpaid. Horn-blowing lookouts surrounded bailiffs who went to enforce payment or to carry out evictions, and, at the sound of the horns, angry crowds gathered to drive the bailiffs back to Charlottetown. The delegates to the Charlottetown conference who went driving through the Island countryside were visiting a landscape in which defiance of lawful authority was almost universal. Within a year, companies of the British army would be needed to aid the civil power in Prince Edward Island.

The Tenant League members were the people for whom Whelan had been fighting the landocracy since the 1840s. They included many of his own voters in the Second Kings riding. And their cause was his: defeat of the landocracy. If Whelan believed the Crown had forfeited its claim to the allegiance of the Islanders, the rise of the Tenant League should have been his moment to declare himself.

Instead, Edward Whelan condemned the Tenant League, and he did so unequivocally. He went back to the other fundamental principle he had declared in 1846: defence of the British constitution. The landlords must be confronted, he wrote in a long newspaper article on the league, but the law had to be respected. "No man has a right to resist the laws for the attainment of any public object . . . until all the resources under the constitution have been exhausted," Whelan wrote.[28]

Whelan's attack on the Tenant League, which bitterly antagonized its members, seems to have had several motives besides his conviction that it was wrong in principle. As a practical matter, Whelan believed defiance of the law would fail, and in failing would set back the legitimate cause. "It may be no difficult matter to bag a bailiff or an agent now and then, but to attempt to bag a company or a regiment of troops would be another affair," he predicted long before troops had been called for. As an Irish Catholic, Whelan probably also guessed that defiance of the law would be more dangerous for the Catholic minority than for Protestant Islanders. League membership cut across Catholic–Protestant divisions, but if religious differences were exploited to divide the tenants, as had often been done before, many League leaders would be protected by their membership in the Protestant ascendancy. Whelan's fellow Catholics would not.[29]

At bottom, however, Whelan was returning to the faith in parliamentary measures that had been wavering in 1860. By the fall of

1864, Whelan thought his faith was about to be vindicated. A new event had given fresh strength to his arguments. Forcible resistance seemed not only wrong and dangerous, but unnecessary. The new event was confederation.

Before the Charlottetown conference, Whelan had dismissed a union of the colonies as meaningless – unless it freed the Island from the interference of the Colonial Office and the landlords. That view was widely shared. When Arthur Gordon of New Brunswick floated the idea of uniting the three Maritime provinces, Leonard Tilley and Charles Tupper made sure the proposal included a plan for buying out the Island's landlords. During the conference itself, George Coles pushed for that commitment. The Canadian visitors, particularly George-Étienne Cartier, who had assisted the buying out of the seigneurial landlords of Canada East, were encouraging. The conference passed no resolutions on the Island lands, but Coles said that they had accepted the principle of breaking up the estates. John Gray of New Brunswick, well known to Islanders for his role in a commission that had attempted to settle the land question in 1861, said as much at one of the Charlottetown banquets. Denouncing tenancy as the greatest drawback to the Island, he publicly confirmed that "the removal of this grievance would certainly follow as the result of colonial union."[30]

Between the Charlottetown and Quebec meetings, Edward Whelan exulted. Confederation would drive landlordism "to the wall," he wrote in the *Examiner*. Once confederation was achieved, he saw at once, the new federal government would stand between the Island and the Colonial Office. Island legislation to assist the tenants would no longer be vetoed by the landlords' powerful friends in London. And, most wonderful, confederation would end the problem that had always vexed Island reformers: how to finance the end of tenancy. The much larger treasury of the federated colonies could readily provide money for a fund that would assist poor farmers to buy their land.[31]

Whelan became a sudden and permanent convert to confederation about the time of the Charlottetown conference, and with good reason. He had found the promise of an end to the Island's most intractable social and political problem – and also a solution to the issue that was estranging him from his restless Tenant League constituents. Even a rival newspaper, hostile to confederation, admitted that, if the new confederation could buy out the landlords, "the islanders almost to a man will hold up both hands for the union." If confederation could end landlordism peacefully and profitably, Whelan would have a victory for parliamentary principles – and fine prospects for re-election and a return to power. No wonder the confederation proposal had restored his faith in constitutional measures.[32]

Whelan came from a generation that had done well by the British constitution. In the aftermath of the disastrous and counter-productive 1837 rebellions in Upper and Lower Canada, reformers like him had re-dedicated themselves to change through constitutional means, and they had won. Proclaiming their absolute loyalty to the constitution, they had successfully turned the system of government inside out. The rule of appointed governors and their appointive councils had given way to the rule of legislatures elected on a broad public franchise and sympathetic to vigorous state initiatives.

In defeat and opposition in the early 1860s, Whelan's constitutional faith had wavered. The Tenant League's adoption of extra-legal means, however, drew Whelan back to his fundamental faith that constitutional means were, both tactically and as matters of principle, the right ones. In September 1864, confederation looked to Whelan a fresh step in constitutional reform. It promised not only a glorious transcontinental destiny but also an end to landlordism, the last vestige of the bad old days that still lingered in Prince Edward Island. As the *Queen Victoria* ploughed through the Gulf of St. Lawrence, the next great reform triumph must have seemed to lie just over the horizon.

Quebec delivered a shattering disappointment to those hopes. In the Island delegation, Coles and Whelan, espousing liberal principles, sat with landowners like Edward Palmer and Heath Haviland, who were deeply suspicious of any change that might threaten their standing. Even though they fought bitterly amongst themselves, both groups asserted the rights of Islanders against central authority. The Island delegates quickly became the most obstreperous critics of the plan the Canadian delegates were putting forward. Demanding provincial equality in the Senate and more seats in the House, the Islanders challenged the rep-by-pop deal by which the Canadians had agreed on a federal union.

The Canadians began to denounce Island arguments as the complaints of greedy malcontents. And suddenly the proposal to buy out the Island's landlords vanished from the confederation agenda. Possibly the Islanders' demands had irritated the Canadians into closing the purse strings. Perhaps a dawning recognition that the Canadians were not going to live up to the land commitment made at Charlottetown helped ignite the hostility of the Islanders. Whatever the case, the Canadians would not budge on the land question. Support for confederation evaporated in the Island delegation. A land purchase, said Andrew Macdonald, was the only advantage he could see in confederation, but the motion that he and Coles put was not even included in the minutes of the meeting. The Islanders voted, often alone, against one resolution after another, and Whelan seems to have voted with the Island majority.

By the time the delegations returned to Prince Edward Island, George Coles, the leader of Whelan's party, had changed course dramatically. Since Charlottetown, he had favoured confederation as the way to end landlordism. When confederation failed to deliver, he made common cause against it with Edward Palmer, who had always resisted both it and any challenge to landlords' rights. In rejecting confederation, Coles had made an astute political calculation. With the tempting prospect of an end to landlordism snatched away, the tough take-it-or-leave-it offer of confederation seemed mostly an affront to Island pride and self-sufficiency. Mass meetings across the Island condemned the idea of confederation. By an overwhelming majority, the legislature in Charlottetown instructed the government to have nothing to do with colonial union of any kind. In a couple of years, Coles would ride the anti-confederate crusade back to the premier's office.

Edward Whelan would come back into office with Coles, but Whelan had not repudiated confederation. Although he had voted against many of the resolutions at Quebec, he told the Island legislature, "we got what I think should be accepted as a compromise." At Quebec he had been fascinated by glimpses of the complex, diverse political world that confederation would create. He had caught the national vision, and he began to make disparaging jokes about "this patch of sandbank in the St. Lawrence." He also seems to have calculated that federal union and the removal of Colonial Office interference would quickly make landlordism extinct, whether the money was provided or not. All through 1865, 1866, and 1867, he stood among the tiny, unpopular minority of Island confederates.[33]

Whelan, of course, held no sinecure post. He had to win his seat in every election, and, in 1867, the unpopularity of his views caught up with him. Anti-confederates resented his support for union. Tenant League supporters resented his refusal to support them. The bishop of Charlottetown and the local priest resented his blunt declarations that clerics ought to stay out of politics. The Irish community, Whelan's core constituency, shared all three resentments. Whelan lost a by-election in the spring of 1867 and was out of politics when confederation went ahead on July 1 without Prince Edward Island. He was dead before the end of the year, not yet forty-four.

Even serious historians have been tempted into suggesting that Whelan died of a broken heart, a kind of martyr for the confederation cause. Surely this is nonsense. Whelan was a seasoned political pro. He would hardly have pined away over a by-election, and his confidence that Prince Edward Island would soon embrace confederation had not wavered. "He was a fast liver," said one of his reporters in an obituary, and photographs of Whelan suggest the beefy, thick-necked look of a man who worked too hard, ate too much, and drank too often. Almost certainly he died of these enthusiasms, and not from heartbreak.*

Whelan's legacy seemed small. Edward Palmer once accused him of saying little during the Quebec conference because he was too busy making notes of the proceedings. Whelan admitted as much, but if he intended to make his fortune with a book about confederation, he never got the chance. All he produced was a small compilation of speeches from the conference banquets, "a very humble and unpretending affair," in his own words. It cost him £150 to print, "and I haven't received a shilling for it yet," he told a friend. The larger book, if there was one, never appeared. Whatever notes he kept at Quebec were probably lost with all his papers in a house fire a few years after his death. His only surviving child drowned in 1875.[34]

Even his political predictions mostly went awry. He thought confederation would end landlordism, while Tenant League actions threatened only disaster and defeat. Instead, the tenants broke the landlords themselves. Whelan expected the landlords would invoke the law to smash the illegal resistance with armed force. But in face of the rent strike, it was the landlords who wavered. Leading landlords soon declared themselves ready to sell out to the tenants, and a wave of purchases eroded the great estates. Once they themselves became landowners, Island farmers shed their radicalism – but it had been the threat of forcible resistance, not Whelan's parliamentary tactics, that had won their fight.

---

* Circumspect accounts of unexpected deaths in Victorian times invite speculation about either alcoholism or syphilis, but Whelan's decline seems too rapid to suggest either. George Coles became insane within a year of regaining office in 1867, and died insane in 1875, aged sixty-five. That Coles, by all reports a solid, respectable, bourgeois paterfamilias, may have been one of the classic gentlemanly victims of Victorian syphilis seems impossible to confirm but cannot be ruled out.

Whelan also predicted that Prince Edward Island would soon beg to be allowed into confederation. Reckless investments in railways did force the Island to seek terms, but by 1873 Canada was at least as eager as the Islanders to complete the union. Prince Edward Island persuaded Ottawa to guarantee six Commons seats, two hundred miles of railways, permanent communications with the mainland, and generous financial terms. There was a large grant to complete the buying out of the landlords, and in 1874 Prince Edward Island began the expropriations of large estates that Whelan had advocated twenty-five years before. Terms less generous than these would have secured the support of the Island's delegation, and perhaps the Islanders as well, in 1864. Governor General Lord Dufferin, officially visiting the new province in 1873, wrote Prime Minister Macdonald that Islanders were "quite under the impression that it is the dominion that has been annexed to Prince Edward Island, and in alluding to the subject I have adopted the same tone."[35]

Did Edward Whelan's support of an unpopular confederation and his condemnation of the radical Tenant League prove he had betrayed the humbler classes and gone conservative? Had he begun to endorse the authority of a parliamentary élite over the wishes of the people? Hardly. Just after the Quebec conference, he declared he would defer "reverently" to public opinion, since the issue of confederation had to be put to the public. Confederation could only be ratified, he said, in "the several local legislatures, the constituencies of each province in public meetings assembled, and at the hustings." When the Island legislature declared in 1866 that it would never accept confederation on any terms, Whelan offered a lonely dissent: it would be up to the people to accept or reject confederation, and if they eventually accepted it, no legislative veto should stop them.[36]

Whelan's commitment to both democracy *and* confederation, his insistence that confederation was both right for his province and the right way for "the humbler classes of society" to fight the landocracy, suggests the underlying radicalism that still attended the idea of responsible government. Responsible government and parliamentary democracy had been reform causes in British North America; it was only by yielding to them that conservative politicians had surged back to power in the 1850s and 1860s. But Whelan still expected parliamentary democracy and confederation to change the world, not to conserve it. That enduring activist strain confirms what a flexible instrument the British constitution still seemed in the 1860s. The other confederation-makers, whatever their goals, were more like him than not in their eagerness to use parliamentary government to do things, not to prevent them.

During one of the Sunday breaks of the Quebec conference, Edward Whelan found a few moments to visit the monuments and battlefields of the city. He told his readers he was still "nearly a stranger to the historic places in this old city," but he hoped to have a chance to remedy that before leaving Quebec. Edmund Burke, also a lover of history and tradition, might have shared Whelan's eagerness to explore the ramparts and ancient landmarks of Quebec. We can imagine the two of them haunting the sites of the Quebec conference like quarrelsome ghosts, deeply in harmony over the value of parliamentary government, deeply divided on the uses of the state.[37]

Burke's warnings against all kinds of state activism were largely unheeded in Whelan's day. Burke, who thought the governments of his day had no business either feeding the poor or funding the colonization of Nova Scotia, would have been appalled by Whelan's enthusiasm for using the Canadian state to expropriate private property in Prince Edward Island and to build railways across the continent. In the late twentieth century, however, echoes of these ideas of Burke's once more reverberated loudly. Few modern "neo-conservatives" were quite so explicit about the necessity of letting the poor starve, but Burke's insistence that the state must not try to change the society it served was alive and walking the corridors of power in the 1990s.

Parliamentary government, however, the idea on which Burke and Whelan were in harmony, commanded very little reverence in late-twentieth-century Canada. In the 1990s, not even parliamentarians gave more than lip service to the notion that a parliamentary seat was, or should be, a significant and important office. Sadly, it was where Burke and Whelan were most compatible – in believing that parliamentary government was a legitimate and effective way to resist arbitrary authority and to articulate the will of the nation – that the legacy of both had become most wraithlike and insubstantial.

CHAPTER FOUR

Under the Confederation Windows

~

THE HOSTS OF the Quebec conference hoped the old city and its spectacular site would welcome the visitors with a Laurentian fall to match the Island summer that Charlottetown had provided so lavishly in September. But before the delegates arrived, Quebec City's blazing autumn colours were whirled away in an early snowstorm. Mercy Ann Coles, who came from Prince Edward Island with her father, the ex-premier, would grumble to her diary about watching endless rain pound down on the roof outside her hotel window. Nevertheless, Quebec City could glitter even in the rain. With its viceregal court and its military garrison, in an era when the court and the officer corps were the acme of society, Quebec offered unparalleled conditions for dignified celebration.[1]

The liveliest descriptions of the Quebec conference's ceremonial side come from women. Frances Monck, the governor general's niece, who had left her baby in Ireland to visit Quebec, met many of those who had come "to arrange about a united kingdom of Canada." In the diary she kept, she generally approved of what she saw of the conference, looking with amused toleration even upon the Catholic

95

clergy's edict against intimate dancing. Charles Tupper she found forward in his courtesies. George-Étienne Cartier struck her as "the funniest of little men," always lively and amusing, and apt to break into song after dinner. She thought George Brown handsome and D'Arcy McGee remarkably ugly. During one conference dinner, Edward Chandler of New Brunswick told her "a great deal about the happiness of slaves, and how miserable they are when emancipated."[2]

Frances Monck assessed the ceremonial side of the conference with the detachment of one long used to the elegant entertainments of the British aristocracy. Mercy Coles, one of many delegates' wives and daughters who came along to Quebec, was better placed to express a colonial view of the conference. She had grown up in the small town of Charlottetown, in the home of a successful middle-class brewer who also happened to be premier. Neither Mercy nor her father would have got in the door of English society of the kind Frances Monck knew, but George Brown had been much taken with the Coles women when he met them in Charlottetown. As soon as the Coles family settled at the Hotel St. Louis ("a very nice hotel and every comfort one can wish for"), Mercy was surrounded by ministerial admirers from Charlottetown – not only Mr. Brown, but also Cartier, Macdonald, and McGee. "Major Bernard tells me we are to have grand times," she wrote the night she arrived. "The first word almost he said was 'I hope you brought the irresistible blue silk.'" She had.

In her diary Mercy Coles seemed oblivious to the conference itself, which she could not attend and about which her father seems to have told her little. Constrained by mid-Victorian ideas about a woman's role, she shopped with a daughter of Upper Canadian delegate William McDougall and gossiped about the daughters of New Brunswickers Steeves and Fisher ("The Misses Steeves seem to be possessors of the parlour downstairs. I think they never leave it. There is a Mr Carver who seems to be the great attraction. He is a beau of Miss Fisher's but they monopolize him"). She saw the sights around Quebec in a party led by Premier Gray, whose invalid wife was home in Charlottetown with barely a month to live. She even put up with bad behaviour from D'Arcy McGee ("Before dinner was half over he got so drunk he was obliged to leave the table. I took no notice of him. Mr Gray said I acted admirably").

At the end of the first week of the conference, Mercy Coles fell ill; indeed, she may have had diphtheria. After Colonel Gray's homeopathic remedies failed, her parents called in Dr. Tupper, and Tupper attended to her before and after conference sessions for ten days ("Dr Tupper came in and found me out of bed standing in my bare feet. Get into bed this minute, he said, you want to catch your death of cold. I tumbled in pretty quickly, he felt my pulse and looked into my mouth and said you are a good deal better"). In her sickbed, Mercy Coles missed most of the great balls and dinners of the Quebec conference and had to content herself with collecting the photographic visiting cards of the delegates ("Mr Tilley gave me such a nice card of himself. All the gentlemen have been having their likenesses taken. Papa's is only tolerable"). When she was able to dine in company again, she was delighted by the kind inquiries of John A. "The conundrum!" she wrote as Macdonald, trying to draw George Coles away from his deepening disaffection from the Quebec plan, courted his family.

Edward Whelan was another admiring observer of the social whirl attending the Quebec conference. "If the delegates will survive the lavish hospitality of this great country, they will have good constitutions – perhaps better than the one they are manufacturing for the confederation," he wrote home. Whelan had argued against secrecy in the conference, but felt bound by the rules. In the reports he sent his newspaper in Charlottetown, he was circumspect about the decisions being made.[3] Instead he described every dinner and ball. Whelan even hinted that the intercourse of Maritimers and Canadians was not restricted to dancing and dining. In an after-dinner speech at the end of the conference, he paid tribute to the way the Maritime delegates had been "caressed" by their hosts. "This was not intended to apply to the fair ladies of Canada," he said to appreciative laughter. "For the delegates all being married men were, of course, like Caesar's wife – above suspicion." Perhaps Whelan had special targets among his fellow delegates as he went on, "If not so circumstanced, they would be as dead as Julius Caesar long ago!" Whelan had left his own wife at home.[4]

After another ball, which lasted until three in the morning, Whelan wrote, "I think it would be advisable to be somewhat reticent hereafter regarding the social parties in which the delegates engage in this stupendously hospitable city, lest it be supposed they do nothing but frolic." In fact, the social whirl of Quebec, though more sustained and more glitteringly adorned, was actually less significant than Charlottetown's. At Charlottetown the entertainment had helped build the trust that convinced the delegates to proceed to Quebec. At Quebec, however, the work of drafting a constitution had to be faced.[5]

The hours the delegates spent in conference at Quebec suggest the gravity with which they faced the task. They gathered on sixteen different days between October 10 and October 27. They failed to meet only on the two Sundays, and they averaged over six hours a day in formal session. At first they sat from 11 a.m. until 4 p.m., but, as they warmed to the work and its difficulties, they revised that schedule into a 10:00 a.m. to 2:00 p.m. session, followed by a second session from 7:30 p.m. until midnight. The afternoon break was not for leisurely teas, but for additional lobbying, caucusing, committee work, and the drafting of resolutions. Throughout the Quebec conference, the delegates permitted themselves only a fifteen-minute lunch break, during which they grabbed lunches in the next room – this in an era when civil servants with a six-and-a-half-hour workday always took a two-hour lunch.[6]

Whelan marvelled that "the cabinet ministers – the leading ones especially – are the most inveterate dancers I have ever seen," and Mercy Coles described her father coming home from a ball "with every stitch of clothes wringing wet with perspiration. He never had such a time." But mostly the delegates joined the dancers after midnight, and mostly they went back to work early the next morning. Reporters who were turned away from the doors of the working sessions described the conference much as Mercy Coles did, by its glittering hospitality and its rivers of champagne. For the delegates, however, Quebec meant mostly a conference room heaped with papers and hot with debate, and the drumbeat of rain at the windows.

Painting "The Fathers of Confederation" on a Canadian government commission in 1884, Robert Harris lent splendour to the room where they met by endowing it with spectacular arched windows. Through a large central window flanked by smaller ones in the same style, Harris presented a panorama of the St. Lawrence, the river of Canada. The richly symbolic view was accurate enough, but the windows – which would give the name "confederation window" to a style – were the painter's own invention. The real windows were identical in size, and were framed in sturdy wooden casements, rather than the delicate leading of Harris's imagination.[7]

The working sessions of the Quebec conference took place in a makeshift reading room in what was supposed to be a post office. In 1864, the Quebec City legislative building was an unprepossessing structure, though it occupied the magnificent cliff-edge site once adorned by the eighteenth-century palace of the bishops of New France. After the episcopal palace burned in 1854, the new building on the site was pressed into service as a legislature when Quebec temporarily became capital of the Province of Canada in 1860. (After the capital moved to Ottawa in 1865, the post-office-turned-legislature, where the makers of confederation met, burned down in its turn in 1883. This fire took place while Harris was working on his painting, which itself was lost in Ottawa's Parliament Hill fire of 1916. Since the Second Empire-style Assemblée Nationale on the heights beyond the city walls was already under construction, its predecessor seems to have gone largely unremembered and unlamented.)

The weather may have been disappointing, the meeting room undistinguished, and the grind of work relentless, but the conference at Quebec in October 1864 was a remarkable event, the longest, largest, most inclusive, most productive, and most successful constitutional conference in the long history of Canadian constitutional palaver. The long-vanished reading room on the cliff-edge at Quebec is where confederation was made. In sixteen working days, the thirty-three delegates of more than a dozen political factions from six provinces negotiated, drafted, debated, and passed seventy-two resolutions that set out the essentials of the constitution that has governed Canada ever since. Since the deal they made at the conference table at Quebec is substantially the Canadian constitution of the late-twentieth century, the agreements hammered out in mid-October 1864 are the ones that really matter.

Charlottetown's one crucial resolution – in favour of federation "if the terms of union could be made satisfactory" – had given Quebec its agenda. Back in 1859, faced with an early flurry of union talk, Britain's colonial secretary had advised governors in the colonies not to put too much stock in early enthusiasm. "The success of such a measure must depend much on details," he wrote then, "and unless all interests are provided for, fresh sources of discontent will arise." This proved nicely prescient of the task that would keep the Quebec delegates at the table. If there was a constitutional deal to be made, the delegates would sit around the table under the not-quite-confederation windows and hammer at the details until a deal was made.[8]

The delegations at Quebec formed a larger body than those at Charlottetown. Only Nova Scotia's delegation was unchanged from Charlottetown, and there were ten new faces around the table. Prince Edward Island and New Brunswick had both recruited additional advocates of union into their delegations. The Canadian delegation, on its home turf, had swelled from eight to twelve – the whole Canadian cabinet. And a new delegation was present: Newfoundland's. Informed too late to attend at Charlottetown, Newfoundland's legislature sent two observers to Quebec. As if to prove how widely the value of bipartisanship in constitution-making was understood, the Newfoundlanders had sent conservative Frederick Carter of Protestant, mercantile St. John's and Catholic reformer Ambrose Shea of the outports.

The Quebec sessions began on Monday, October 10, with the election of Sir Étienne Taché as chairman. A veteran politician, first elected as one of LaFontaine's francophone reformers in 1841, Taché had been made nominal premier of the united Canadas by the three-way coalition whose real (and rival) powers were Brown, Macdonald, and Cartier. Leaders of the other provinces were elected honorary secretaries to the conference, and Hewitt Bernard, Macdonald's civil-service deputy and future brother-in-law, was appointed to keep the actual minutes. As at Charlottetown, the conference rejected the pleas of journalists, who argued that regular reports to the press would be a valuable corrective to rumours, even if the statements of individual delegates had to be kept secret to permit frank discussion.

Early in the deliberations at Quebec, George Brown burst out in a moment of frustration: "I appeal to the other provinces!" The conference had agreed that voting would be by province; each province would cast a single vote, except the united Canadas, which would have two. Talk was free: Brown, losing a dispute in his own delegation, was hoping he could sway the other delegations to his personal view. If there seemed sometimes to be as many viewpoints as delegates, however, there was also strong pressure for consensus. Brown's plea went unheeded here and, after all the talk, many resolutions passed by concurrence – unanimously, without even a pause for provincial caucusing before the vote.

After setting out some general principles, the conference devoted most of its time to an exploration of federalism: how to constitute the national and provincial governments and how to divide authority among them. Loud and long, influential confederation-makers had proclaimed their preference for a strong central government. From large provinces and small came wistful declarations that, if possible, the best union would be a legislative union, in which the national Parliament would be the only legislature and there would be no provinces. A legislative union was the properly British model; no states or provinces rivalled the sway of Parliament in London. A federal union, dividing power between a national and state governments, was suspiciously American. It was indeed, said delegates frequently, the flaw that had led the United States to civil war.

Macdonald and Tupper and Galt and others could sing the praises of legislative union, however, only because they knew it was an absolute non-starter, never for one moment to be taken seriously at Charlottetown or at Quebec. The enduring existence of provinces with their own governments and powers was a first principle of confederation in the 1860s. A federal union that would provide a substantial measure of autonomy to both Canada West and Canada East – that was the bargain that had brought Brown and Cartier into the coalition government of the united Canadas. Brown had established that Canada West would not remain in the existing union without rep-by-pop, and Cartier had insisted Canada East would not remain with it. Federalism, by separating the two regions, was the mechanism that might satisfy both. Brown and Cartier's shared understanding of that ruled out all serious consideration of legislative union even before the conferences began.

The Maritimers, unwilling to sink their local autonomy in Maritime union, were just as unfavourable to a legislative union, in which they would be overwhelmed by either of the Canadas, let alone both of them. Any union with the Canadas was going to be looked at sceptically there, but one that annihilated all local governments had no chance of being accepted. Whatever lip-service might be given to clear, simple legislative union, federalism was the only feasible proposal. Tupper at one point spoke of diminishing local governments as much as possible, but he instantly admitted the conference could not "shock too largely the prejudices of the people in that respect." In the Maritime provinces, the degree to which the

Quebec resolutions respected local autonomy would be a fundamental issue on which confederation would be judged.

Any delegate could talk about the simplicity and cheapness of a
single legislature for the whole country and how appropriately
British that would be, but not a single delegation supported a complete legislative union. Later, battling with provincial governments,
Prime Minister John A. Macdonald would speak wistfully of New
Zealand, where the national government had the power to abolish
local authorities, and did so. But at Quebec, when another delegate
cited the New Zealand constitution, it was Macdonald who dismissed the analogy. New Zealand's experience was irrelevant, he
said. That was a legislative union.

Only federalism, in fact, made a written constitution essential.
On the British model, with undivided sovereignty reposing in a
single parliament, Canada would hardly have needed a written
constitution any more than Britain did in the 1860s (or the 1990s).
Federalism and the division of powers between governments was
what required the weeks spent drafting the resolutions at Quebec.

Reading the debates at Quebec, however, one looks in vain for
ringing declarations of provincial rights. Provincial rights had been
at issue from the first glimmerings of confederation, but the principle was hardly explicit in the agreement. The French Canadians,
having struck their deal within the cabinet of the united Canadas,
had remarkably little to say on that issue. George Brown, entranced
by all the seats Canada West would have in the new federal Parliament, hoped that local governments would be small and economical. As late as August 1864 and again soon after the Quebec
conference, the *Globe* endorsed the independent authority of the
provinces, but during the conference itself Brown spoke of the
provinces becoming mere municipal institutions, as if his quasi-sep-
aratism of 1859 had never existed. Charles Tupper, who by personality as well as circumstance was a leader among the Maritimers at the
conference, cheerfully advocated diminishing the powers of local

governments. Guarantees of provincial authority, in fact, have to be found in the texts of the resolutions they passed, rather than in the speeches they made to each other. Even in the resolutions, they are deeply buried.

The delegates got into meaty issues of power and its allocations on the fourth day, Thursday, October 13, when John A. Macdonald introduced a resolution, drafted by the Canadian cabinet, on what would become the Senate. His resolution ignited a week of fierce wrangling, first over the composition of the Senate, then over how senators would acquire their offices.*

The argument over the Senate was the longest of the conference and the one which brought it closest to breakdown. But the time the delegates spent fighting about the Senate was hardly an index of how important the upper house was. Rather, the shape of the Senate, as the first substantial question on the agenda, became the issue on which the delegates began to test each other for soft spots and stone walls. The Maritimers, who fuelled the debate, wanted more influence in the Senate, but implicitly they were demanding more influence in the conference, too, where it was mostly the Canadians who presented the resolutions and the others who reacted to them.

"For the first few days, the leading delegates of the lower provinces exhibited caution and vigilance upon every question affecting the interests of these provinces," said Prince Edward Island's Edward Palmer approvingly. What their vigilance would expose, however, was how very little the Canadians were willing to bend. After the Senate confrontation, leading Maritime delegates displayed their willingness to make substantial compromise for the sake of confederation – much to Palmer's dismay.[9]

The Canadian delegation's Senate proposal offered sectional equality. The three "sections" – Ontario, Quebec, and the Maritimes –

---

* At Quebec, the delegates spoke of a "legislative council," not a Senate. Throughout, I use the name that was adopted later.

would each have the same number of seats in the upper house of the new federal Parliament. The Canadians were acting as if Maritime union had gone ahead, and the Maritimes were to be treated as one province. A negotiator of long experience, Macdonald presented this as a concession to the Maritimers, noting they were receiving "equality" in the Senate, although their collective population was smaller than either of the Canadas.

The Maritimers saw it differently. Leonard Tilley, then Charles Tupper, and then Charles Fisher, one of the newly appointed New Brunswick delegates, tried in succession to expand the Senate representation of the Maritimes. They may have been testing the Canadians, for they offered no clear principle in place of sectional equality. Their amendments simply attempted to secure a few additional seats for their region. The argument ground on through Thursday and Friday to Saturday, October 15, but all the Maritimers received was a lesson in the intransigence of the Canadians.

George Brown apparently suggested that, if the Maritimes could have extra senators, so should Upper Canada. That, said Hector Langevin at once, was anathema to Lower Canada. The hint that they might be endangering the *bleu*-Grit alliance at the heart of the Canadian coalition seems to have trumped the Maritimers' claims. But the arguments were heated. "Matters do not certainly look very promising," wrote Edward Whelan on Friday night, just before the first great ball. Saturday's sessions were no better.[10]

After the Sunday break at the end of the first week, the Prince Edward Islanders launched an even more serious challenge. In August, George Coles had thought that confederation should be based on equal provincial representation in the House of Commons. Charlottetown squashed that idea; the Canadians had established that rep-by-pop was indispensable. Now Coles's fellow reformer, Andrew Macdonald, observed plausibly that, if rep-by-pop had to prevail in the Commons, "the upper house should be more representative of the smaller provinces, as it was to be the guardian of their rights and privileges." Each province (not merely each section) ought to have equal representation in the federal upper house, said Macdonald, as American states did in the Senate of the United States.[11]

Perhaps some deal-making had been going on during the Sunday break. Or the Canadians may have feared that, if the deadlock continued, Andrew Macdonald's idea might win over Maritime moderates whose less-far-reaching Senate proposals had already been rebuffed. In any case, the Canadians held a private caucus after Andrew Macdonald's Monday-morning proposal and changed their tactics. They revived a motion Charles Tupper had put forward at the start of the debate. The three Maritime provinces together would start on an equal footing with Ontario and Quebec in the Senate, but there would be additional Senate seats for the Atlantic region if Newfoundland joined confederation. Tupper's suddenly resurrected motion was quickly passed.

The Canadians had moved, but not far. They preserved most of their principle of sectional equality – Newfoundland's Senate seats, they suggested, would be balanced by future seats for the North-West when it joined confederation. The Maritimers had gotten the satisfaction of extracting a concession from the Canadians, but they had won only a handful of extra seats to distribute. Andrew Macdonald's proposal for a different kind of Senate was, as he acknowledged in his own notes, "not entertained."

His fellow Islanders, who still liked the idea of their small province having as many senators as any other, seem to have endorsed his threat that, if the Canadians "made no allowance," the Island might prefer to remain out of confederation. In response, the Canadians implied that they hardly cared whether Prince Edward Island came in or stayed out. In the vote on the distribution of Senate seats, Prince Edward Island cast the first of several lonely dissents to conference resolutions.

The other Maritime delegations had turned a deaf ear to Andrew Macdonald's plausible contention that the Senate could not be the guardian of provincial interests unless all provinces were equally represented in it. No Maritime delegate gave an unequivocal explanation of why they accepted a mere handful of extra seats in the Senate as a substitute for provincial equality there. But a hint at an answer emerged from the next big issue of the conference: how senators were to be selected.

The delegates took up the method of selecting senators as soon as the division of seats had been settled. Should senators be elected or appointed? If appointed, should they be appointed by federal or provincial governments? Should members of the existing upper houses have priority in appointment and, if so, should opposition as well as government parties be represented? These questions took up another couple of days of the conference's fast-dwindling time. Motions and amendments were debated and withdrawn or defeated at a bewildering rate.

Finally, on a motion by Nova Scotian reformer Jonathan McCully, the delegations voted by concurrence – unanimously – that senators would be appointed for life by the federal government (although the first Senate would be a bipartisan one, appointed from all parties in proportion to their existing strength in the upper house of each province). The decision for "sectional" (that is, regional) rather than provincial equality had already established that the Senate was unlikely to become an effective guardian of provinces' interests. The decision to let the federal cabinet appoint the senators killed any possibility of that.

The appointive principle was ridiculed, even at the time. In the Canadian legislature, Christopher Dunkin would call the appointive Senate "just the worst body that could be contrived – ridiculously the worst." The best defence of it, he joked savagely, was that its appointees would be old men, upon whom death would provide a strange kind of constitutional check when nothing else did. Others condemned the Senate plan as reactionary, a return to the bad old days before responsible government, when appointive councils wielded autocratic power on behalf of a narrow élite of the wealthy and well-connected.[12]

In the decision to go back to appointed senators, the 1960s historians saw proof of the conservatism of the makers of confederation, of their doubts about democracy and their search for ways to hem in the unreliable will of the people. They defended the Senate decision by defending the delegates' conservatism, emphasizing the confederation-makers' dislike of American precedents and their concern that untrammelled democracy would undermine the dignified, British character of colonial society.

Yet it was not the conservative delegates who most vigorously supported the appointive principle. Jonathan McCully, who moved the crucial motion, was a reformer, and George Brown supported him vigorously. As reformers, they believed in government being made, and kept, responsible to the voters. A wide (male) franchise, representation by population, strict control of government by the legislature: these had been touchstones of reform politics for a generation. Yet Brown and McCully spoke for many reformers in their vehement opposition to elective upper houses, and the reason was not some vestigial reactionary tinge.

The main body of reformers did not want the Senate elected quite simply because an elected Senate would be a legitimate and powerful body. Reformers understood that an upper house's function was always conservative. An upper house existed to place a check upon the democratic excesses of the widely elected lower house, and it tended to become the preserve of wealthy men, relatively insulated from constituent pressure. "We must protect the rights of minorities, and the rich are always fewer than the poor," John A. Macdonald put it genially during the conference's discussions of the Senate.[13] Brown believed in the rights of property, but he did not want a conservative upper house that felt itself entitled to challenge the House of Commons. Election was the one sure way to give senators that sense of entitlement, so election of senators was anathema to reformers like Brown.

All schemes for a powerful upper house were modelled on the United States Senate. The American Senate was much smaller than the House of Representatives, and both the scarcity of seats and the significant property qualification required of senators favoured wealthy candidates. In short, the United States Senate had been conceived by the American founders as a conservative check on the democratic House of Representatives. As such, it had been very successful. Indeed, when the triumph of responsible government suddenly made the once-tame legislatures of British North America into such powerful institutions, it was conservatives who looked to the American Senate for inspiration. In the 1850s, in the first decade of responsible government in British North America, conservative politicians began to push for an elective upper house (then called the Legislative Council), because they wanted a rival to the newly powerful lower house. They wanted an élite counterweight to the too-representative assemblies and too-powerful cabinets empowered by responsible government. The united Canadas got an elective upper house in 1856, by the votes of an odd alliance of conservatives and Brown's Clear Grit rivals (who believed all public institutions should be elective). Brown was among those who opposed the change. Eight years later, when elected councillors were slowly replacing the life-tenure appointed councillors in the united Canadas, he still thought it had been the wrong decision, and he was no longer in the minority.[14]

George Brown had always looked balefully upon the growing influence and confidence of the elected upper house. Reformers – and many moderate conservatives who had accepted and thrived under responsible government – did not want a powerful, conservative Senate confronting and confounding the Commons. And that was the point around which the consensus formed at the conference. Most of the delegates, and all the influential ones, were the children of responsible government. Leonard Tilley and his New Brunswick reformers had cut their political teeth in that struggle, as had Coles and Whelan from the Island and Shea from Newfoundland. Nova Scotians McCully and Archibald were Joseph Howe's heirs and allies. Just as much as them, conservative politicians like Nova Scotia's

Tupper, Macdonald of Canada West, and Cartier of Canada East had thrived under responsible government. Conservatives or reformers, they all believed in the shiny new-model parliamentary government that the colonies had been enjoying for less than twenty years. They had cut their ties not only to the ultra-democratic Clear Grits but also to ultra-tories who yearned for a gentlemanly upper chamber with real power to block the Commons.

The makers of confederation understood a powerful upper house to be a threat to parliamentary power. The constitutional text of their day was John Stuart Mill's 1861 book *Representative Government*. In it, Mill had succinctly explained why the British House of Lords no longer posed a very significant challenge to the authority of the British House of Commons. "An assembly which does not rest on the basis of some great power in the country is ineffectual against one that does," wrote Mill. Once the House of Lords had rested on a great power, the landed aristocracy. But the influence and authority of great landowners had waned in Britain, and so had the power of the Lords. In 1861, Mill savoured the paradox: the strength of the House of Lords lay in its weakness. Its members could enjoy their dignified perquisites, wield back-corridor influence, and even function as a chamber of sober second thought – but only so long as they posed no direct challenge to the Commons, which claimed to rest on the power of the people of Britain.[15]

Ultimately, Mill's view was the view of the delegates at Quebec. Their commitment to responsible government was such that no competing interest could induce them to create a rival power to the lower house. They could accept a chamber of sober second thought. They could welcome a source of legislative ideas and suggestions. They could anticipate a place in which to reward and honour their friends. But if they permitted the upper house to acquire independent and credible authority, they would fatally undermine their deepest commitment: parliamentary democracy rooted in the responsible government achieved in the 1840s and 1850s.

Brown would explain the reasons for the appointive Senate at a public gathering a week after the conference closed. He had always opposed elective upper houses, Brown told a cheering crowd that had gathered to welcome the delegates to Toronto on their post-conference tour of the Canadas, "not because I was at all afraid of popular influence, but because I felt that while the lower house controlled the government of the day and the government of the day appointed the members of the upper house, the people had full and efficient control over the public affairs. The question, I think, fairly presents itself whether two elective chambers, both representing the people and both claiming to have control over the public finances, would act together with the harmony necessary to the right working of parliamentary government."

Brown went on: "And there is still another objection to elective councillors. The electoral divisions [in the upper house] are necessarily of enormous extent. . . . The difficulty of obtaining personal access to the electors, and the expense of election is so great as to banish from the house all who are not able to pay very large sums for the possession of a seat."[16]

Even elected councillors could share this opinion. During the debate on confederation in the Canadian upper house, Walter McCrea would declare that "but for the elective principle having been applied to this house, I should never have had the honour of a seat within its walls," yet he went on to rank himself "among those of the reform party who think that making the members of this house elective was a step in the wrong direction," because it undermined the more directly representative Commons.[17]

This was orthodox doctrine to more than the reformers. By the 1860s, responsible government ideas were the broad middle ground of colonial politics. Clear Grits still held out, at least in principle, for elective offices at all levels – from dogcatcher to governor general. (Indeed, the old Clear Grit William McDougall later claimed that during the conference he had urged an elective Senate. If he did, the minutes failed to note it.) Some diehard ultra-tories also hoped to resist the too-democratic Commons from an upper house which would be both reliably conservative and powerful. But Brown, Tilley, McCully, Whelan and other reform delegates agreed with conservatives like John A. Macdonald, Cartier, and Tupper: parliamentary democracy was fundamental. The power of the Commons guaranteed it. An elective Senate was a threat to it.

The confederation-makers, despite all the days they spent wrangling over details of the Senate, agreed on one thing about it: it must be weak. The Senate they designed was attacked from the start as unrepresentative, unable to defend provincial interests, a retirement home for party hacks. But no one has ever successfully shown the Senate to be strong, or to pose a credible challenge to the authority of the House of Commons. That was the essential requirement of the men who designed it.*

Faith in responsible government, rather than a yen for élitist autocracy, best explains why the delegates settled on an appointive Senate. It also suggests why Charles Tupper, Leonard Tilley, and other delegates from the small provinces had not pushed harder for provincial equality in the Senate or for provincial appointment of senators. Even if its members were unelected, a Senate representing the provinces (and appointed by them) could claim to represent a "great power" – not the voters, but the provinces themselves. A Senate authorized to speak for the provinces, like an elected Senate, could have claimed the moral authority to challenge the legislative supremacy of the Commons. Maritimers like Tupper and Tilley believed in parliamentary democracy that put real political power in the lower house, more than they believed in a Senate that would

---

* Only in the 1980s did the appointive Senate begin to challenge the authority of the Commons by rejecting important measures that were thought to lack popular support. It was able to justify its actions only because the Commons was widely held to have forfeited its own traditional role as an independent check on arbitrary government.

be a voice for the regions. The provinces would have to be protected elsewhere.

The argument on the Senate changed relatively little at Quebec, but it confirmed how much the Canadians were running the conference. The Canadian cabinet had done most of the detailed planning for the conference. Key resolutions had been drafted, debated, and redrafted by the coalition partners in the Canadian cabinet before the meeting. When the Canadians introduced a resolution, the Maritimers usually began with spontaneous questions and random opinions, and the Canadians could respond with apparently author- itative replies based on their prior discussions. They set the agenda.

By the end of the Senate debates, it was becoming clear that the delegations from Nova Scotia and New Brunswick were willing to accept that agenda. Prince Edward Island increasingly was not. Prince Edward Island's disgruntled isolation, exposed in the Senate argu- ments, was confirmed in the brief argument about the Commons that followed. On the evening of Wednesday, October 19, *le tout Québec* was preparing for the ball being offered that night by the speaker of the Canadian Legislative Council. But until ten that evening, the delegates themselves were in the conference room, debating George Brown's resolution that, in the new House of Commons, "the basis of representation would be population."

Brown's resolution marked the triumph of his ten-year crusade for rep-by-pop, but its approval by the delegations should have been automatic. The Canadian coalition and the Charlottetown consen- sus had both been rooted in agreement upon rep-by-pop; there could be no confederation on any other principle. Indeed, most of the dis- cussion that evening turned on technical details. But when the vote was taken, Prince Edward Island stood opposed. After the vote, and again on Thursday morning when Brown demanded an explana- tion, Heath Haviland, Edward Palmer, and Andrew Macdonald all denounced rep-by-pop. They wanted more seats in Parliament than the mere five to which the Island's population would entitle it.

Edward Whelan, staunch confederate though he was, had voted with them to swing the Island delegation against the motion.

The Island's delegation was split. Premier Gray and Provincial Secretary Pope, both warm supporters of confederation, were embarrassed by the repudiation of the Charlottetown consensus by their cabinet colleague, Attorney-General Palmer. But Palmer had always been cool to confederation, and he was willing to rally the Island against it if it meant no power in the Senate and only five seats in the Commons. Andrew Macdonald, who perhaps still smarted from the dismissive rejection of his Senate proposal, voted with Palmer. Haviland and Whelan, who had not been in the Charlottetown sessions, were enthusiasts for confederation, but seem to have felt obliged to make a stand on rep-by-pop after the Island's inability to gain anything on the Senate question.

"Prince Edward Island would rather be out of the confederation than consent to this motion," said Heath Haviland bluntly, but the Islanders were abused more than cajoled. Canada East's Alexander Galt lamented that "it would be a matter of reproach to us that the smallest colony should leave us," but to avoid that unfortunate situation, he urged the Islanders, not the other delegates, to reconsider. And when Galt presented the financial terms of confederation in the last days of the conference, it became clear that the Canadians had reneged on the commitment that the Islanders thought they had won at Charlottetown, namely, that the new nation would provide a fund for buying out the Island's landlords and establishing freehold tenure. For Island delegates who had seen political salvation in confederation's promise to end landlordism, this was a disaster. It clinched George Coles's opposition to confederation and ruined Edward Whelan's hope of persuading Islanders to support it.[18]

With the Islanders virtually written out of confederation, the conference proceeded to the workings of the federal and provincial legislatures. On Thursday and Friday, October 20 and 21, John A. Macdonald moved a series of resolutions. Several were routine, but the status of the provincial lieutenant-governors provoked a revealing exchange. Would they be appointed by the Imperial government, as was the governor general? Or would the federal government appoint them? Macdonald got what he wanted, a statement that the provinces would be subordinate in this to the national government.

That great issue, the independence or subordination of the provinces, came up again on Monday, October 24, in resolutions that set out the division of powers between the provinces and the federal government. These resolutions brought in a new player, who had not been at Charlottetown and thus far had said little at Quebec. This was Oliver Mowat, an Ontario reformer who had come into the coalition government with George Brown.

Like John A. Macdonald, Mowat was a Kingston Scot of unpretentious background and large ambitions, and, like Macdonald, he had chosen law as his path upward. He had been a law student in Macdonald's own Kingston office and might have been his partner. Instead, as Macdonald launched his political career, Mowat moved to Toronto and prospered in the arcane field of chancery litigation. "I do not see where it all came from," he said disingenuously as he tallied up the income a decade of practice had brought him.* [19]

Despite his family's conservative connections and his own utter lack of radical passion, Mowat went into politics as a reformer. John A. Macdonald resented this betrayal by his former protégé, but Mowat seemed no great threat. Knowledgeable and useful in administrative work, he seemed too "desky" for real political success. He peered at the world through small, round glasses set on a small, round face. He was pious, a non-drinker, a dull speaker, and he lived a life of bourgeois propriety, proud to call himself a "Christian statesman." In the rough and tumble of Canadian politics, he hardly seemed a match for the likes of John A.

---

* One of his fellow practitioners was more explicit. "That's the business I like," said Skeffington Connor about chancery law, "the pace dignified and slow, the pay handsome, and a gentlemanly understanding among practitioners to make it handsomer."

Mowat, however, would one day be a political giant, the first great provincial premier of confederation. As premier of Ontario from 1872 to 1896, Mowat would virtually set the mould for provincial premiers, and he would do it by declaring loudly that the provinces mattered. Far from being minor branches with no more than municipal duties, said Mowat, the provinces were sovereign powers within confederation. "The provinces are not in any accurate sense subordinate to the Parliament of Canada," was the way he put it. "Each body is independent and supreme within the limits of its own jurisdiction." [20]

Defending the rights of provincial governments proved to be brilliant politics in Oliver Mowat's Ontario. Premier Mowat would become (to the extent it was possible) even duller and deskier as he aged in office, but the voters of Ontario supported him every time he got into a jurisdictional fight with Ottawa. Mowat had rooted himself in the great Upper Canadian political heritage. By resisting autocratic Ottawa, he made himself the heir to the Baldwin reformers who had resisted autocratic British governors and the Brown reformers who had resisted "French domination" of Ontario under the union. Mowat never lost an Ontario election. He was premier until he went to Ottawa in 1896, age seventy-six, to be Wilfrid Laurier's minister of justice.

Mowat's success on the platform of provincial rights infuriated John A. Macdonald, who was Ottawa for most of the time that Mowat was Ontario. Macdonald as prime minister insisted on the supremacy of Ottawa over the provinces. He insisted that the Quebec conference had authorized the central government to dominate the provinces — and that Ottawa's pre-eminence was crucial to the survival of the new Canadian nation. Mowat, said Macdonald furiously, "with his little soul rattling like a dried pea in a too large pod — what does he care if he wrecks confederation?" [21]

Donald Creighton shared Macdonald's opinion of Oliver Mowat as a dangerous wrecker. Creighton, who was born in 1903, came to maturity in a surge of postwar nationalism in the English Canada of the 1920s. His views solidified in the 1930s, when English-Canadian constitutional scholars agreed that only a strong national government could wield the powers needed to fight the Great Depression. Impatient with provincial sensibilities or provincial rights, Creighton agreed absolutely with Macdonald that strong central government was vital to Canada – and that centralized authority had been the aim and consensus of the Quebec conference. In Creighton's story of confederation, anti-confederates were merely misguided. Oliver Mowat was a villain.

Mowat, said Creighton, was "a remarkable combination of determination, effrontery, and legal cunning," who knew well that his provincial-rights views "differed from – and, in fact, completely contradicted – the original conception of confederation." Mowat may have called himself a Christian statesman, said Creighton icily, but "attacking principles which he had previously endorsed and attacking a constitution which was partly his own handiwork apparently did not cause him a moment's concern." Creighton even accused Mowat of attempting to falsify the memory of what happened at the Quebec conference.[22]

To clinch their case that the delegates at Quebec had guaranteed Ottawa's supremacy, Donald Creighton and John A. Macdonald could cite a string of resolutions on federal and provincial powers which were debated and passed between October 20 and 25. Had not the delegates established a clear hierarchy when they agreed that lieutenant-governors would be appointed by Ottawa, while Ottawa's governors general would be appointed by the Queen? Had they not given Ottawa the power to make laws "for the peace, welfare, and good government of the federated provinces," as well as authority to legislate "respecting all matters of a general character" in the new nation? Had they not given to Ottawa all the great powers: trade and commerce, finance, foreign affairs, and indeed all powers not specifically listed as belonging to the provinces? Had they not, in the financial resolutions debated on Saturday, October 22, and again on October 26, given Ottawa most of the nation's revenues and made the provinces dependent upon federal allowances (unless they were ready to move into the then-explosive matter of direct levies on property)? Above all, had they not specifically given the government in Ottawa the power to disallow any law passed in any province, for any reason or for no reason at all?[23]

They had. These were apparently overwhelming powers. For Donald Creighton and English-Canadian constitutional scholars of the 1960s who defined the history of the confederation process, they confirmed that the founders had decreed a national government with all the powers needed to harness and direct "the expanding energies and requirements of a potentially great nation," as Creighton put it. He quoted John A. Macdonald's conference speech of Monday, October 24, when Macdonald denounced proposals for stronger provinces as American in inspiration. Macdonald declared, "We should concentrate the power in the federal government and not adopt the decentralization of the United States," and the motion he was supporting passed without opposition.[24]

The records of the Quebec conference contain many statements echoing Macdonald's. The confederation-makers did want a strong central government to fulfil their nation-building ambitions. They put much stock in the British example of undivided sovereignty in a single Parliament. If they doubted, the civil war in the United States provided strong lessons about the dangers of schism in a loose federation, while the republic's very size (and the size of its armies) suggested that only a strong, united Canada could hope to stand up against its threats and pressures.

The delegates' commitment to strong central government was demonstrated in their reaction to the states-rights argument of New Brunswick's Edward Chandler on October 24. Chandler, Frances Monck's expert on the happiness of slaves, objected to giving the federal government all powers not specified as provincial. It should be the other way around, he declared, with federal powers strictly listed and the provinces acquiring all the many powers that had gone unspecified. "I am rather inclined to agree with Mr. Chandler," said Robert Dickey of Nova Scotia. A few other delegates expressed equally qualified sympathy.[25]

But the attack against his proposal was overwhelming. Henry from Nova Scotia, Haviland from the Island, Chandler's fellow New Brunswickers Johnson and Gray, and Brown from Ontario all tried to show Chandler his error. The most powerful assault came from Charles Tupper, who called federal primacy "a fundamental principle ... and the basis of our deliberations," and from John A. Macdonald. Macdonald connected Chandler's proposal to its origins in the United States, where, he said, the principle that "every man sticks to his individual state" had led to civil war. "It would be introducing a source of radical weakness," cried Macdonald, winding up a long speech. "It would ruin us in the eyes of the civilized world." Chandler was routed, left vainly protesting that his plan was "not precisely the same" as in the United States.[26]

Oliver Mowat said not a word in support of Chandler's lonely fight for provincial rights. In fact, the resolution Chandler was attacking was Mowat's own. It was Oliver Mowat himself who had introduced the essential resolutions on federal and provincial powers, and he had certainly helped draft them. At least since Creighton wrote his confederation histories, the case that Oliver Mowat accepted a dominant federal government at Quebec, only to renege on this fundamental principle of confederation when he became premier of Ontario, has seemed damning.

Yet Mowat, in his own defence, might wish to emphasize elements of his Quebec resolutions that the historians of the 1960s minimized. First among these was the list of powers granted to the provinces. By its terms, provincial governments won exclusive authority over education, hospitals, and charities. They would control the public lands and the income from them, and govern all matters of property and civil rights. They could levy direct taxation, which in the context of the 1860s essentially meant putting taxes on property. They would have full authority to create and supervise municipal institutions. They would run the prisons, the police forces, and the administration of justice. They would have authority over the whole sphere of what Mowat initially called "private and local" matters and which in the final draft became "generally all matters of a private or local nature."

These were broad and substantial powers. From Canada West to the Maritimes, in fact, there was a significant caucus committed to preserving substantial provincial authority – even as it acknowledged the need for strong central authority. Leonard Tilley would later argue that eleven of every twelve laws he had seen passed in New Brunswick before confederation were in fields that would remain within its powers after confederation. What Ottawa had acquired, he implied, were Imperial powers transferred from London, rather than local powers removed from the provinces. George-Étienne Cartier hardly needed to say that French Quebec could never join a nation dominated by Protestant anglophones unless its local government had the powers to protect the vital institutions of francophone society. And Brown's reformers had long wanted to get Upper Canada free of the union to run more of its own affairs through a legislature "beyond the control of the central power, set apart from it, untouchable by it" (as Brown's *Globe* had put it just as the Charlottetown conference opened). Even John A. Macdonald concurred. When it was suggested the federal government might "sweep away" the provinces, he told the conference, "This is just what we do not want. Lower Canada and the lower provinces would not have such a thing." [27]

There were, nevertheless, those crushing federal powers of reservation and disallowance in Mowat's own resolutions, which transferred London's Imperial authority to Ottawa and expressed the yearning of many delegates for a single, clear focus of constitutional authority in the new nation. They allowed Ottawa to delay or simply to nullify any piece of provincial legislation whenever it chose. Reservation and disallowance seemed to give the federal government a sledgehammer against the provinces.

Mowat did not confront disallowance and reservation directly at the conference. He may, however, have schemed to undermine them in the drafting of them. John A. Macdonald said of his own constitutional drafting at Quebec, "I must do it all alone, as there is not one person connected with the government who has the slightest idea of the nature of the work." But Mowat was an expert in administrative law, abundantly qualified for legal drafting, and a friend described him as the delegate chiefly responsible for putting the Quebec decisions "into constitutional and legal shape." At least part of what Macdonald had to do himself, perhaps, was wield a restraining hand upon Mowat's drafts.[28]

With Macdonald looking over his shoulder, if not actually holding the pen, the final draft of Mowat's resolution on the division of powers was something he described late in his life "only as the best practicable in view of the different interests and sentiments of the members of the conference and those they represented." His first version, he claimed, had been much more explicit about the equality of the federal and provincial governments. But changing some words did not necessarily mean yielding on the principle. For Creighton was right: Mowat was cunning. He was a skilled and very successful lawyer, who almost certainly considered himself a better lawyer than John A. Macdonald. If the conference was reluctant to oppose directly the idea of a supreme national government, Mowat could try to build in restraining principles that he drew from his legal specialty, the law of chancery.[29]

The jurisdiction of the common-law courts and the jurisdiction of the chancery court were separate territories of English and Canadian law until they were merged late in the nineteenth century. (As premier and attorney-general of Ontario, Oliver Mowat supervised their merger in his province.) Common-law judgments were bound by the letter of the law and by strict judicial precedent. The chancery court, on the other hand, left scope to consider natural justice and to apply "equitable principles," if strict application of the black-letter law would lead to an injustice. It was the subtle challenges of working out and applying these equitable principles that made chancery procedures so slow, so intellectually satisfying, and so lucrative for practitioners like Mowat. When he was a judge, one of Mowat's critics called him an "equity fanatic," always ready to overthrow a common-law rule or a legislative statute on some principle of natural justice. Today, he might be called a judicial activist.[30]

From his successes in chancery, Mowat understood how principles of natural justice could modify the constitution the delegates were drafting. He was well placed to calculate that, in passing their resolutions, the Quebec delegates were embedding in them equitable principles strong enough to challenge the rule of disallowance. The black letter of the disallowance clause, he could have calculated, might one day be exploded by the deeper principles of responsible government.

During the Quebec conference's discussions of provincial powers, Nova Scotian reformer Jonathan McCully declared that the provinces must be "miniature responsible governments." Seizing on this phrase, Donald Creighton emphasized the word "miniature," as if McCully had wanted to underline the minor and dependent status of the provinces. But the part of McCully's phrase that must have echoed around the conference table was "responsible government." In the political context of the 1860s, responsible government – rule by a government that answered to a popularly elected legislature – was the fundamental shield of the rights of British North Americans. It was a sacred thing.[31]

Creighton was ill-placed to ponder what "responsible government" meant to the delegates. The defining moment of his historical career had come when he grew bored with the colony-to-nation history of Canada that limped from Robert "Responsible-Government" Baldwin through a tedious series of constitutional abstractions towards the national independence of Canada. Creighton brilliantly shifted the emphasis away from reform-minded advocates of colonial self-determination. He directed attention to the tory entrepreneurs and politicians who transformed the commercial empire of the St. Lawrence into the continent-spanning Dominion of Canada. Reform obsessions had been sidelined in the 1860s, Creighton argued. In confederation, he saw the strategic calculation and nation-building vision of John A. Macdonald. Creighton had no more patience for reform soliloquies on responsible government than for reform arguments that the reason to appoint senators was not to make them dignified and aristocratic (as conservatives suggested), but to make sure the Senate was toothless.

But even the tory nation-builders stood squarely on reform foundations. By the 1860s, the political culture of the colonies made it almost impossible to justify outside interference with a responsible government. In law, the Colonial Office's authority over British North America was absolute. The achievement of responsible government in the 1840s and 1850s, however, had made it unacceptable for London to interfere arbitrarily with the internal affairs of the colonies in any but rare and extreme cases. When the British cabinet overruled Prince Edward Island's attempt to legislate an end to land-lordism, Edward Whelan had called London's interference "degrading and humiliating" and "a species of despotism that strikes at the root of one of our most valued privileges – that of self-government." Such things would never happen in Canada, Nova Scotia, or New Brunswick, Whelan said bitterly.[32]

Indeed, governments throughout British North America had largely defanged London's ability to control local politics. In the debate on confederation, one veteran politician said London had not disallowed a Canadian law in twenty-five years. When a colleague cited one lone example, he retorted, "in that case we got our own way in effect directly afterwards." Reformer or tory, no British North American politicians were willing to have their legislatures dictated to by London on local matters where local voters insisted *they* must be heard. It was being answerable to their own electorates that enabled confederation-era politicians to delegitimize interference from London, even as they proclaimed themselves loyal subjects of the Queen.[33]

If there was a Machiavellian brilliance in Oliver Mowat's work at Quebec, it lay in perceiving that what had reduced London's Imperial power to ceremonial trappings (of the sort so bitterly resented by New Brunswick's Arthur Gordon) would just as effectively undermine the powers Ottawa might one day claim to find in the Quebec resolutions. If the provinces were responsible governments answerable to their own electorates, Ottawa would find itself unable to interfere with them in their allocated spheres, just as London already had.

The power of disallowance was plainly there in the Quebec resolutions. But if Ottawa tried to disallow what a provincial government had enacted, it would be interfering in the action of a government responsible to its own local electorate. By attempting to negate the will of the voters, Ottawa would instantly become the old Family Compact, the autocratic appointed governor, the interfering Colonial Office of the bad old days. It would be wrong in politics, and it would be contrary to natural justice.

It may have been Mowat's guess, as he and Macdonald drafted division-of-powers resolutions for the conference, that the crucial item in the deliberations, then, was the unequivocal agreement that the provinces, miniature or not, were responsible governments. Though George Brown, who should have been a reliable supporter of Ontario's determination to control its own affairs, had said in his newspaper that "a responsible ministry in each province would certainly not be the cheapest system which could be adopted," the provinces' status as responsible governments was clearly understood at Quebec. In fact, the principle was confirmed in the resolutions that John A. Macdonald had himself introduced.[34]

In the battle of the draftsmen in the Canadian delegation at Quebec, John A. Macdonald put his faith in disallowance and other federal powers he had had written into the resolutions. He believed that, armed with them, "the central power must win in the long run.

My own opinion is that the general government or parliament should pay no more regard to the status or position of the local governments" than they would to municipal corporations. Mowat may have reasoned, however, that responsible governments were sacred in mid-nineteenth-century Canada, and that the principles of natural justice to which he had devoted his legal career would secure the rights of the provinces' responsible governments against Macdonald's black-letter rules of disallowance.[35]

By the late stages of the Quebec conference, Macdonald may have been growing aware of Mowat as a threat, for he paid him the compliment of getting rid of him. One of Canada West's three chancery judges died in Toronto on the very day that Mowat was introducing at Quebec his crucial resolutions on the respective powers of the federal and provincial governments. Macdonald was the attorney-general for Canada West and, to the chagrin of several conservative allies who were angling for the appointment, he offered it to his Grit rival Mowat.

This rare offer – there were only three seats on the chancery bench in Canada West, all life appointments – was irresistible to a dedicated counsel like Mowat, particularly considering the minor role politics seemed to offer him. He accepted the judicial appointment. As a judge, he could not participate in the debates that followed the conference, and for years he offered no views about the terms of confederation. As a result, the reform-based, provincial-rights interpretation he would have been uniquely able to present was almost entirely unspoken in English Canada. As the confederation battles were fought, as the Dominion of Canada came into being, and as John A. Macdonald and his view of confederation came to dominate national politics, Mowat would spend eight quiet years as a judge in Toronto.

In October 1872, Mowat would leave the bench in spectacular fashion, shedding his chancery robes to assume the premiership of Ontario. Prime Minister Macdonald was by then making frequent and enthusiastic use of the disallowance powers granted to the federal government in the British North America Act. Mowat almost at once confronted him. The conflict that had been buried in the backrooms of the Quebec conference became one of the great constitutional struggles of Canadian history.

The judicial war Mowat and Macdonald would fight between 1878 and the 1890s involved a long series of cases about provincial authority and the right of Ottawa to override provincial law. In 1880, John Wellington Gwynne of the new Supreme Court of Canada gave Macdonald just the verdict the prime minister wanted. "The Dominion of Canada is constituted a quasi-Imperial power," he ruled ". . . while the provincial governments are, as it were, carved out of, and subordinated to, the Dominion. . . . Nothing can be plainer . . . than that the several provinces are subordinate to the Dominion government."[36]

Mowat would have none of this. "I claim for the provinces the largest power which they can be given," he told the Ontario legislature in 1882. "It is the spirit of the B.N.A. Act and it is the spirit under which confederation was agreed to. If there was one point which all parties agreed upon, it was that all local powers should be left to the provinces and that all powers previously possessed by the local legislatures should be continued unless expressly repealed by the B.N.A. act. . . . The provinces are not in any accurate sense subordinate to the Parliament of Canada; each body is independent and supreme within the limits of its own jurisdiction."[37]

Defending Ontario against Ottawa's interference made good politics in the late nineteenth century. Indeed, it revived the crusading fervour of the old Ontario reform tradition. The lawyer and journalist David Mills, who would one day succeed Mowat as federal minister of justice under Wilfrid Laurier, denounced Macdonald's use of the power of disallowance as "war upon responsible government." Macdonald's cabinet was a "Star Chamber," he wrote, and it was attempting to impose an autocratic and tyrannical power upon the free people of Ontario. Macdonald himself was a new King James II – significantly, James was the monarch deposed in the

Glorious Revolution of 1688, when the triumph of Parliament over autocratic monarchy was confirmed in England.[38]

John A. Macdonald's attempts to use federal power simply strengthened Mowat's hold on Ontario. Since every quarrel with Ottawa increased his popularity at home, Mowat did not flinch from rhetoric as inflamed as Mills's. "Confederation was well worth maintaining if the constitution was faithfully administered," he told the Ontario legislature in 1882. "But if [the provinces'] power of passing laws within their own legitimate sphere was to be subject to the whim of a minister or ministers at Ottawa, . . . then it was not worth maintaining."[39]

Mowat did not need to pursue this separatist threat seriously. He had one more constitutional court to which he could appeal. In the 1880s (until 1950, in fact), Supreme Court of Canada judgments could be appealed to an Imperial tribunal, the Judicial Committee of the Privy Council (which sometimes included judges from Canada and other Commonwealth nations, but which sat in London). At the Privy Council, Mowat won a string of resounding victories that killed the federal power of disallowance and permanently established the provinces as powerful partners in confederation. "The object of the [British North America] act was neither to weld the provinces into one, nor to subordinate provincial governments to a central authority," said the Privy Council in 1892. At last, Mowat had someone reading the provincial-powers clauses of the British North America Act the way he thought he had drafted them in 1864. "In so far as regards those matters which by section 92 are specially reserved for provincial legislation, the legislation of each province continues to be free from the control of the Dominion, and as supreme as it was before the passing of the act."[40]

The privy councillors had decreed that, whatever the British North America Act said about disallowance, interference with the workings of a responsible government in its own sphere was fundamentally unjust. The words remained unchanged, but Ottawa lost the power of disallowance, much as the Colonial Office had lost it with the coming of responsible government. The equitable principles of interpretation upon which Mowat had built his legal career had triumphed over the black-letter rules in which Macdonald had put his trust.

At the end of the Quebec conference, with his baggage gone and the train waiting, George Brown scribbled a note to his wife. "You will say our constitution is dreadfully tory – and it is – but we have the power in our hands (if it passes) to change it as we like. Hurrah!" This has always seemed a poignantly sad prediction. Brown's party would be out of power in Ottawa for most of the rest of the century, and the constitution drafted at Quebec largely resisted formal amendment for more than a hundred years. But perhaps at some point during the conference, Brown had had Mowat at his elbow, Mowat with his enigmatic smile and his equity-lawyer mind, hinting that Canada West would find the federal government's big guns as easy to discredit as the autocratic rule of the bad old days before responsible government.[41]

The Mowat resolutions on the division of powers and Alexander Galt's financial resolution were the last large issues of the Quebec conference. Galt's financial proposals were another demonstration of the Canadians' control of the Quebec agenda. Mowat's resolutions had confirmed that the provinces would receive the revenues of their Crown lands and would be entitled to levy direct taxes. But direct taxes were almost unknown and much feared in the 1860s. (George Brown, who took his free-trade principles seriously, was rare in his eagerness to see direct taxation of property replace customs tariffs as a main source of public revenue). On the whole, the financial terms gave blunt evidence of Canadian primacy. Although the Maritime provinces had substantial net assets and the Canadas substantial liabilities, Galt's resolution transferred to the federal government most of the assets and liabilities of the old provinces. The federal government would also acquire control of customs duties and tariffs, though the sea-trading Maritimes needed low tariffs much more than the revenue-hungry Canadas did.

Had these fiscal proposals been introduced at the start of the conference, they might have launched intense, even fatal, disagreement. Even in the last days, with confederation almost a *fait accompli*, the financial terms provoked hard bargaining. Soon after Galt introduced them on Saturday, October 22, they were handed over to a committee for further work. When the committee members – Galt and Brown for Canada, Tilley, Tupper, Pope, and Shea for the four Atlantic delegations – returned on Wednesday, they proposed new details but no fundamental change. Tilley, who had an eye for a balance sheet, had secured for New Brunswick a special grant of $63,000 a year for ten years. Tupper, less preoccupied with monetary details, got nothing similar for Nova Scotia. As part of the bargaining, the delegates had also agreed on a railway from Quebec to Halifax – considered a boon to the Maritimes and particularly to Halifax, but long viewed sceptically by Upper Canadians. Prince Edward Island, perhaps to teach it a lesson about the perils of resisting the Canadians on so many issues, got nothing for its land problem.

The conference wound up at Quebec on Thursday, October 27. A ceremonial tour of the Canadas followed. Some delegates left for Montreal on the afternoon train, but the key ones spent most of the day in a desperate scramble to get the resolutions into coherent form and caught the night train at 9:00 p.m.

What they had produced in their sixteen days of arguing and voting was a strikingly utilitarian document. There is no poetry in the Quebec resolutions. The colonists had addressed the philosophical questions of government in the responsible-government struggles two decades earlier. They treated their constitution as a machine for running governments, and their resolutions were almost entirely about governmental mechanics. Explosive issues of language, religion, ethnicity, and national identity were not ignored, but they were left almost entirely unstated in the text.

"Since they had entered the province of Canada," reflected Nova Scotia delegate Robert Dickey about the experiences of the Quebec delegates, "the managers of railways had contributed in a very great degree to their pleasure, comfort, and accommodation." The railwaymen, who understood exactly what the new nation could mean for railway development, had been keeping in touch at the St. Louis Hotel throughout the conference.[42] When it ended, they were happy to lay on special trains to take the delegates wherever they chose to go. After Charlottetown, the delegates had gone on to Halifax, Saint John, and Fredericton, giving speeches and promoting their new proposal everywhere. Now the railways would speed the Quebec delegations through the Canadas. In their last official session, held at the St. Lawrence Hotel in Montreal on Saturday, October 29, the delegates formally adjourned the Quebec conference, and the Charlottetown conference too, at least until Maritime union returned to the political agenda. Then it was more speeches, more dinners, more champagne.

The weather at Montreal was as bad as at Quebec, and a military review and fireworks display in honour of the delegates was cancelled, but there was another lavish ball. At a six-hour luncheon the next day, the delegates described their agreement to a large and enthusiastic crowd. Then they and their families went by Ottawa River steamer to Ottawa. They dined in the spectacular new parliament buildings, still under construction. Then, in a few whirlwind days on the railways, they visited Prescott, Kingston, Belleville, Cobourg, Toronto, Hamilton, and even Niagara Falls. Conference secretary Hewitt Bernard refused to give in to the agonies of gout, but John A. Macdonald succumbed to drink at Ottawa. Mercy Coles, having the time of her life, was much more forgiving of him than she had been of D'Arcy McGee two weeks earlier. At each town, there were tours and civic receptions, and even George Coles and Edward Palmer were persuaded to say kind things about confederation – which they were later to regret.

The very brief stop at Cobourg was made mainly to gratify the local delegate, James Cockburn, a loyal supporter of Macdonald, who, so far as the record shows, had said not a single word throughout the conference. But the tour was acutely political, too, for the decisions of Quebec still had to be ratified. The men of the confederation conferences were merely delegates, with no power to bind their respective provinces. The Quebec resolutions were merely their proposals, and would lack all official standing until given legislative approval. "I should see no objection to any consultation on the subject amongst the leading members of the governments concerned," the colonial secretary had instructed the colonies in 1862, "but whatever the result of such consultation might be, the most satisfactory mode of testing the opinion of the people of British North America would probably be by means of resolution or address proposed in the legislature of each province by its own government." Only the legislatures could grant legitimacy to the Quebec resolutions.[43]

The delegations at Quebec represented the cabinets of all five provinces, as well as three of the four political parties of the united Canadas and both leading parties in each of the Atlantic provinces. From the perspective of the late twentieth century, when the functions of Canadian legislatures had become largely ceremonial, it was difficult to imagine that legislative approval of the Quebec resolutions would have been more than a formality. In the 1860s, however, no legislature could be taken for granted. To get their plan through, the delegates had to begin to seek public approval as part of the campaign to win legislative approval.

So the grand tour of the Quebec delegations coincided with a flood of press coverage in newspapers controlled by the delegates – and in the hostile press as well. The resolutions, and commentary on them, were soon published throughout British North America. So were the speeches the delegates made to public meetings at all the stops on their tour. Their opponents were soon organizing counter-demonstrations, but for a time the confederation delegates had a clear advantage. The largest of their post-Quebec public meetings was in Toronto, late at night on Thursday, November 3. With Mercy Coles watching from her window at the Queen's Hotel on Front Street, Tupper, Tilley, and Toronto's own hero of the hour,

George Brown, stood on a gallery just beneath her and spoke to five thousand cheering citizens.

That was almost the end. The festive excursion to Niagara Falls was the last gathering of the personnel of the great confederation conference. When her family parted from the others after a visit to the falls ("I can't, it is quite impossible to describe them. They far exceeded anything I ever expected to see"), Mercy Coles was grief-stricken.[44] It was time for the delegates to face the reactions back home.

CHAPTER FIVE

If Brother André Went to Parliament Hill

~

SHORTLY BEFORE confederation, twenty-year-old Alfred Bessette left Quebec's rural d'Iberville County and the relatives who had raised him and went seeking work in the United States. In the 1860s, emigration was carrying a flood of young people like him from the crowded farms of rural Quebec to the factory towns of New England. Unlike most of them, young Bessette did not stay in the States. Small and sickly, he proved as ill-suited to the American factories as to the farms where he had grown up. Shortly after confederation, the young man returned home, to bleak prospects.

Soon, however, Alfred Bessette found a vocation. He had always been given to prayer, penance, and meditation, and his local curé encouraged him to approach the Congrégation de Sainte-Croix, a clerical order that had recently opened a college nearby. For an illiterate son of the rural peasantry, the priesthood was beyond reach, but the Congrégation included lay brothers who devoted themselves to manual labour in imitation of St. Joseph the carpenter, and Bessette joined these. At the order's college in Montreal, Alfred Bessette gave up his name and became Brother André. In time, he

133

was assigned to be the college doorman – in effect, to be a house-hold servant to the teaching order and its students. It seemed an appropriately humble vocation for one of the weakest and most vul-nerable children of rural French Canada. Yet, during his decades of service as doorman and servant, Brother André would become one of the pre-eminent men of early-twentieth-century Quebec.[1]

Brother André began to visit the poor and sick of the neigh-bourhood around the college. He also began to work cures. During his charitable visits, Brother André would offer to rub sores or dis-abled limbs with oil that he collected from the lamps at the statue of St. Joseph in the college chapel. Many professed themselves cured, often instantly. Admiration for the humble brother's healing skills and his holiness began to spread. Devout Montrealers seeking relief from illness or injury made their way to the doorman's cell. Brother André attributed all his feats to his patron saint and insisted he was only St. Joseph's "little dog."

To have a miracle-working cult arising in Montreal initially dis-mayed sophisticated Catholics and some of the Catholic hierarchy. But Brother André's simple piety disarmed his critics, and his pop-ularity among working-class Montrealers became immense. He won tolerance and support, and then he won permission to build a shrine to his saint on the slopes of Mont-Royal near his college. St. Joseph's shrine became a place of pilgrimage, a minor North American Lourdes, with Brother André as its guardian and guiding spirit. Pilgrims left alms, and in 1915 the small shrine was removed to make way for a vast church, the Oratoire Saint-Joseph.

For the rest of his life, Brother André devoted himself to caring for the pilgrims and completing his shrine. As devotees flocked to the Oratoire, and stories of cures multiplied, Brother André humbly but ceaselessly solicited the millions of dollars his shrine required. He would talk to anyone, pray with anyone, take an offering from anyone. By the 1920s, frail and elderly, he travelled widely every year to raise funds, but he was particularly cherished by the poor Montrealers to whom he preached quiet Christian acceptance of life's hardships, even as he sought to heal their pain. Montreal shops displayed collection boxes for Brother André, in much the way they might now support cancer research or environmental protection. Brother André became a talismanic figure for French Canada, but particularly for francophone Montreal. The simple, devout, barely literate son of the rural peasantry had become to Montreal what the parish curé was supposed to be for rural farm families of Quebec: a familiar friend and counsellor, the benefactor of a village society secure in the embrace of traditional ways.

Except, of course, Montreal was not a rural village. It was a big city, growing and industrializing since before confederation and reaching a million in population before Brother André's death in 1937. Hundreds of thousands of francophone Montrealers lived in walk-up apartments, worked in factories, and worried about the rent and crime and unemployment. They lived lives not very dissimilar from those of urban workers elsewhere in North America. One of the miracles of Brother André, simple pastor to a great metropolis, was to help his people retain something of their comforting traditional way of life in the modern, anonymous, secular world of the city.

In Brother André's lifetime, religion and agriculture were said over and over to define the essence of French Canada, to be the shields that guarded French civilization on an English continent. From the 1850s to the 1960s, many of Quebec's leaders believed its security lay in being at heart rural and agricultural. Only as a nation of devout Catholic farm families was Quebec safe from the urban, secular, materialist values of English Canada and the Americans. They sometimes said (in a metaphor now mercifully extinct) that English Canada might be the husband, authoritative and worldly, but French Canada would be the wife, perhaps deferential but the nurturer of culture and faith. To be true to itself, Quebec would remain a Catholic society and a traditional one.

Despite its cities and industries, the development of Quebec – and particularly francophone Quebec – did lag behind that of Ontario and the adjoining American states. Far into the twentieth century, francophone Quebec preserved more of the characteristics of traditional, pre-industrial society than its anglophone neighbours: a high birth (and death) rate, limited opportunities for mass education, and a strong dependence on traditional industries and traditional leadership.

But the difference was only relative. Commerce, capitalism, industry, and city life made their inroads in Quebec slightly more slowly than in neighbouring regions, but by the early twentieth century a substantial bloc of Quebeckers had long since left behind traditional rural society. But what endured for them, almost as much as for their rural cousins, was the conviction that the devout, traditional farming community was the truest part of French Quebec. From the 1840s into the 1960s, Quebec's leaders often believed their task was like Brother André's: to celebrate and safeguard traditional values in the midst of a world that was too English and too secular.

Quebec's political leaders had the harder task in this regard. If Brother André went to Parliament Hill, he went secure in his faith, seeking only to bring a blessing and take away a few alms. Secular political leaders had to bridge two worlds. French Canada's minority position in the Anglo-Protestant modern world meant its representatives had to deal as skilfully with English Canada as with their own francophone community. In the 1860s, the statesman charged with that double responsibility was George-Étienne Cartier, Quebec's pre-eminent representative in the making of confederation.

By 1864, George-Étienne Cartier had been the dominant politician of Canada East for a decade. A political rival conceded that "by his energy" and "his intimate acquaintance with the strong and the weak points of his fellow countrymen," Cartier had made himself "chief of the French-Canadian nationality," and the only person who could have imposed confederation upon it. Cartier did not disagree. Criticized by another rival for failing to consult widely, Cartier said cheerfully, "That is quite correct. I do not consult anybody in making up my mind." His irritating self-sufficiency regularly provoked his foes. "The honourable member never sees a difficulty in anything," said Christopher Dunkin in the legislature when Cartier dismissed a particular difficulty arising from the Quebec resolutions. "And I have been generally pretty correct in that," responded Cartier.[2]

Cartier was fifty in 1864, a small, wiry man with a large head and a shock of white hair. On the surface, he seemed a genial, uncomplicated companion, fun-loving, and not much daunted by his less-than-perfect command of English. A furious worker, he preferred noisy parties over quiet solitude for relaxation, and he could be counted on to pound the piano and lead the singing in every quiet moment of the confederation process. As the leader of the conservative *bleu* caucus and long-time ally of John A. Macdonald, Cartier had built his political success on the principle that traditional French-Canadian society could survive and prosper by accepting the union of the Canadas. To his English-speaking colleagues, he was at once a hard-headed lawyer, perfectly comfortable in a mostly English business milieu, and a proud, sentimental defender of his French heritage.

Only his closest associates knew how intimately Cartier lived with the complexities of that dual allegiance. He proclaimed himself a proud son of the people, and he often represented rural Verchères in Parliament – but he had made a fortune as a big-city railway lawyer. Cartier exalted Catholicism and worked hard at cultivating alliances with the clerical hierarchy – but his private life was irreligious, and he spent much of his adult life in an adulterous relationship with his wife's cousin. An apostle of traditional family life, he was both neglectful and controlling with his daughters, who grew up despising him.

Above all, Cartier was the defender of French Canada's traditional ways, composing sentimental anthems in praise of his people, urging his voters to hold fast to the land and work it with love. But he was also a fervent admirer of the British Empire, a monarchist who wore English-tailored clothes, talked of retiring to London, and named one of his daughters "Reine-Victoria." He once declared that a French Canadian was an Englishman who spoke French.[3]

Cartier's family had lived with these complexities a long time. In the agricultural Richelieu valley, the Cartiers had been merchants and landholders rather than plain farmers. Cartier's grandfather had been a member of Lower Canada's assembly in 1809. George-Étienne, born in 1814, was christened "George," rather than "Georges," in honour of George III. His parents ran through much of the family wealth, but George-Étienne received a solid education and became a lawyer in 1835.

Like most politically active young French Canadians, Cartier was quickly drawn into Louis-Joseph Papineau's Patriot movement. Quebec's elected assembly, dominated by Papineau and his English and French supporters, had in the 1830s become stifled by conflict with the governor's appointed councils. Representative government on the British model had become a sham. The Patriots increasingly favoured radical action and the recourse to arms if necessary.

For Cartier, as for many of his generation and class, the Rebellion of 1837 was a defining moment. When the Patriot leaders had been agitating for constitutional reform and the rights of elected politicians against the appointed councils of the Crown, scores of young men like him had been active in petition drives, protests, and rallies. But when the confrontation flared into violence late in 1837, peasant farmers provided the manpower for armed resistance to the British troops and the loyal militias who advanced on Patriot strongholds in the countryside. The peasants were less attracted by constitutional slogans than by the prospect of fundamental change.

The farmers who died behind the stone walls of Saint-Denis and inside the shattered church at Saint-Eustache when the British army wiped out the rebellion had seen themselves as oppressed by more than a theory of government. Burdened with poverty on overcrowded lands with exhausted soils, they were as likely to blame their miseries on seigneurs and their rents, priests and their tithes, and usurious merchants, as on Queen Victoria and her distant governor at Quebec. Once the farmers decided the goal of the uprising was to end taxes, tithes, and dues, the Patriot agitation threatened to become a peasant-driven revolution against the existing social order in French Canada. Peasant anger put muscle behind Patriot resistance, but it threatened and alarmed Patriot supporters from the landowning and mercantile class – Cartier's own friends and allies.[4]

Cartier did not abandon the Patriot cause when fighting flared. He had been among the leaders at Saint-Denis, faced the British cannon, and went into hiding with a charge of treason on his head. For the rest of his life, he spoke proudly of having fought for the rights of his people. But after facing both the horrors of a defeated rebellion and the spectre of a peasant uprising, Cartier made a swift and permanent conversion to parliamentary process. In his bid for a pardon, he swore that he had resisted oppression but never forfeited his allegiance to the Crown. When he emerged in politics soon after, it was as a follower of Louis-Hippolyte LaFontaine, an ex-Patriot who had rejected violent means in favour of parliamentary tactics.

When he joined LaFontaine, Cartier was returning to a political tradition with deep roots in French Canada and in his own family. As soon as Britain had called an elected assembly in Lower Canada in 1792, French-Canadian leaders had begun to master – and to appreciate – the intricacies of English parliamentary processes. Cartier's own grandfather had been one of them. Another, the lawyer and journalist Pierre Bédard, was among the first in British North America to work out the principles of colonial self-government and legislative control that are summed up as "responsible government." Republican and radical theories drawn from France and the United States always competed with parliamentary models in French Canada, but after the disastrous rebellions, LaFontaine's advocacy of parliamentary methods triumphed. Even in the face of a union between Canada East and Canada West intended by Britain to punish and assimilate French Canada, LaFontaine argued that French Canada would be able turn the union to its advantage.

French Canada could thrive within the British Empire, LaFontaine and his followers argued. They became apostles of British liberties, British parliamentary processes, and the British monarchy. Treated with respect, they argued, French Canadians would be the Crown's most loyal subjects. In 1846, the doctor-politician Étienne Taché, who in 1864 would chair the Quebec conference, made the ringing declaration that, if Britain respected the rights of French Canada, "the last cannon which is shot on this continent in defence of Great Britain will be fired by the hand of a French Canadian."[5]

The achievement of responsible government in 1848 put the elected assembly in control of political life in the united Canadas. The French-Canadian voters who elected a crucial bloc of members to that assembly suddenly had power. It was Cartier, first elected in 1848 and securely established as LaFontaine's successor by 1854, who built an enduring political base upon that fact. He welded his bloc of parliamentary supporters, the *bleus*, into a cohesive party solidly behind his leadership. With their support he could achieve LaFontaine's ambition: a partnership between French and English politicians in which French Canada's interests would never be neglected.

Anglo-French partnership proved good for Cartier personally. No longer confined to the legal work of the small French-Canadian middle class, Cartier grew wealthy as the lawyer to the Grand Trunk Railway and other businesses of English Montreal. For political success, his *bleus* had to show that, whereas Patriot resistance had brought only blood and defeat to Quebec, they could deliver benefits. Cartier delivered. French Canada began to receive the benefits of modernization, without opening the door to outside influences that might threaten the control of the church and of middle-class political leaders like himself.

In the 1850s, Cartier and the *bleus* helped end the regime of seigneurial landlords – not by seizing the land, as the peasants of 1837 might have wished, but by assisting them to pay the seigneurs generously for it. In place of the ancient legal system inherited from New France, they drafted a revised code, much better adapted to the needs of the Montreal business community, French and English. They used the revenues of the state to help the Catholic bishops spread education out to the countryside. For the first time, substantial numbers of young French Canadians began to learn to read and write. (Alfred Bessette, born in 1845, did not, but it was a newly opened rural college that put him in touch with the religious order he joined.) Even traditional farm life began to change, as an expanding market and agricultural reform campaigns helped wean farm families from traditional crops towards more commercially viable dairying and market gardening.

Cartier took care that such changes did not threaten the entrenched powers of French-Canadian society. In turning Quebec away from a dead-end confrontation between peasants and landlords, the *bleus* encouraged commerce, education, and an expanding middle class. But it was all done under conservative auspices, in ways that did not threaten the church hierarchy or the Montreal bourgeoisie (whether French or English). Quebec could still aspire to be rural, agricultural, and Catholic. Cartier, a city man, rhapsodized about the sacred bond between his people and their land as frequently as he blessed the British Empire.

From 1854 to 1864, Cartier and the *bleus* made the union of the Canadas work for Canada East. The *bleus*' effective control of the largest bloc of French Canada's legislative seats made them the controlling bloc in Parliament. Cartier became the linchpin of the Anglo–French partnership, without whose support no policy and no party was likely to succeed. That position enabled him both to deliver the benefits of union to Quebec – and to protect the traditions of his people from alien influences. Throughout the decade that George Brown campaigned for rep-by-pop and against "French domination," Cartier and the *bleus* insisted that the union was inviolable. It could not be changed, they said. Merely to question it was to insult and threaten French Canada, and for years the *bleus* had demonized Brown as a dangerous bigot.

So when Cartier led the *bleus* into a coalition with Brown based on confederation and rep-by-pop, he was making an enormous political conversion, and taking an enormous risk. He was abandoning the positions on which he had built his career. After twenty years of insisting that the union was essential to the survival of his people, he was suddenly agreeing to consign it to the dustheap – in partnership with the man he had always denounced as an enemy to French Canada. The survival of his people, not merely of Cartier's political career, was the measure by which confederation would be judged in Quebec. For Quebec's political master, confederation was a gamble with nightmarishly high stakes.

Nevertheless, Cartier had compelling reasons to come over to confederation. He liked some key elements of the idea. He was, after all, a growth-oriented bourgeois railway lawyer, a proud partner in the expanding British Empire. Partnership with English Canada had brought him both personal wealth and political success, and he believed it had been good for his people as well as for his business clients. Cartier was no more immune to state-building, continent-spanning ambition than Tupper or Brown. "Shall we be content to maintain a mere provincial existence, when, by combining together, we could become a great nation," he told the Parliament of the united Canada in 1865, and no one doubted he was sincere.[6]

Cartier could also calculate that the union of the Canadas, attractive as it had been for almost a quarter-century, might not long endure. Canada West, with 300,000 more people than Canada East, was expanding the population gap more every day. Its unwillingness to tolerate the sectional equality that gave Cartier's *bleus* such influence could only grow stronger. The *bleus* had to calculate that rep-by-pop campaigners might come to control Upper Canada so totally that only a handful of allies in Lower Canada would enable them to turn the tables and make Cartier's *bleus* a perpetual minority. Failing that, the Upper Canadians might convince the ultimate arbiter, the British government, simply to repeal the increasingly unbalanced union. Cartier feared that, once out of the union, Quebec would be ripe for annexation to the United States and rapid assimilation. Cartier's phobia about American republicanism and the tyranny of the majority was one of the wellsprings of his fervent devotion to the British monarchy. In the United States, he argued, Quebec would be consigned to the fate of Louisiana, where the French language and the Catholic faith were already considered as good as lost. When they considered the dark possibilities of seeing the union abolished, the *bleus'* resistance to changing it began to waver.

Accepting Upper Canada's demand for rep-by-pop, Quebec would lose the precious half-share in the national Parliament that had become its bulwark against hostile or assimilationist policies. But in a *federal* union, Quebec might see the union preserved, and still shelter its vital interests. Back in 1859, when the Upper Canadian reformers had proposed a federal union, they had suggested all significant powers would go to the provinces. That concept had changed by 1864, but the confederation bargaining of 1864 still presumed that "local matters" would be consigned to the provinces. That was Brown's peace offering to Cartier, and Cartier recognized it.

Brown's cry of joy when the Quebec resolutions were complete – "French Canadianism entirely extinguished" – has often been taken as an assimilationist chant, but Brown always used "French Canadianism" as an ugly shorthand for French-Canadian interference in Canada West's affairs, and securing an end to that necessarily meant hands off French Canada's affairs. Even Edward Whelan, visiting from far-off Charlottetown, grasped in a couple of weeks at Quebec that "the French desire most ardently to be left to the undisturbed enjoyment of their ancient privileges – their French language, civil law, literature, and language. It is utterly impossible to anglicize them."[7]

In the spring of 1864, when Brown was floating the idea of federation in the union Parliament, Cartier's government partner, John A. Macdonald, had condemned federalism as a foolish, dangerous notion. "We should have a legislative union, in fact, in principle, and in practice." Brown leapt in. Was that the policy of the Macdonald–Cartier government? "That is not my policy," said Cartier grimly. The House laughed to see a wedge put so neatly between the unshakeable partners, but Cartier's answer was the decisive one. Quebec could not accept rep-by-pop *and* legislative union, since in a single legislature its representatives would always be in a minority. If rep-by-pop had to come, federation must come too.[8]

Cartier quickly calculated that the trade was worth making. In a federal state, the province would protect the powers then thought necessary to the survival and prospering of rural, Catholic, and agricultural French Canada – its legal code, the administration of property, and education, charities, and health. With those secure, language and culture would take care of themselves. At the same time, Quebec could preserve the economic benefits of a larger union. Cartier seems never to have doubted that French Canada's needs would be protected in a federal state, both by the powers of its new provincial government and by the continuing clout of Quebec's members in the national government. Taché, his nominal leader, declared that confederation was "tantamount to a separation of the provinces, and Lower Canada would thereby preserve its autonomy together with all the institutions it held so dear." Had he been a maker of slogans, Cartier might have called the plan sovereignty-association.[9]

Cartier was not a maker of slogans or a parliamentary speech-maker. He set his terms for confederation in the back rooms of the *bleu* caucus and in the coalition cabinet before leaving for Charlottetown. He spoke little in the conferences, though he did weigh in heavily when any of his fundamental requirements seemed threatened. Even in the public speeches he made, after the conferences and in the parliamentary debate on the Quebec resolutions, he chose blandness over detail. Instead of minutely analysing confederation's benefits, he preferred mostly to celebrate the agreement and to sneer at its critics. It was his job to know what was good for Quebec, he seemed to be saying, and he had decided on confederation. Do you think you can do everything? challenged an opposition member. Cartier replied disdainfully that he was sure he was capable of forming a government for the new nation. "Well," said the critic, "it will take more than a bold assertion and capacity for a hearty laugh." Cartier did not bother to reply.[10]

Confederation had critics in Quebec. The *bleus* were the largest but not the only political party in Quebec. Ranged against them were the *rouges*, proud heirs of Papineau's Patriot cause. (In the parliamentary debate on confederation, Cartier's dismissive reference to Papineau would provoke them to a furious defence of the man "every true French Canadian holds in veneration."[11]) In the 1860s, the *rouges* offered French Canada a political vision almost the reverse of Cartier's. They were liberals and sometimes radicals, heirs of the French and American revolutions. Where *bleus* defended traditional society and an alliance with English Canada, *rouges* proposed both a secular society and a French one, a Quebec independent of both clerical and British influence.

Federalism in itself was not necessarily anathema to the *rouges*. In other circumstances, they might have been natural federalists. In 1858, when Antoine-Aimé Dorion had been George Brown's unfortunate fellow victim of the double shuffle, they had been struggling to shape a common policy that would give each section of the Canadas greater autonomy to run its own affairs. Dorion still led the *rouges*. Far from being an embittered old rebel, he was liberal more than radical. Four years younger than Cartier, he too was a middle-class Montreal lawyer with commercial interests, and he was perfectly fluent in English. Unlike previous *rouge* leaders, he was a practising Catholic. Under his influence, the *rouges* were mellowing, in a society where clerical influence was on the rise. If Cartier could talk with Brown, why should not Dorion?

But *rouges* and reformers had drifted apart. Cartier, whose credentials as a defender of tradition were secure, could consider the leap to accepting rep-by-pop. The *rouges* no longer could. In the conservative Quebec of the 1860s, it was radical enough for *rouges* to question clerical authority by defending freethinking intellectuals and secular education. For them also to waver from the defence of sectional equality seemed suicidal. When Brown and Cartier began talking about federalism in the spring of 1864, Brown hoped to bring *rouge* leaders into the coalition. Instead, the *rouges* took up the traditional *bleu* repudiation of rep-by-pop, proposing that the sectional equality of Canada East and Canada West should be entrenched forever. The *rouges* stayed out of the coalition of 1864 and declared themselves opposed to its federal policy.

Cartier, the only provincial leader willing to bear the risk of making confederation alone rather than have to share credit for it, seems to have been glad to find the *rouges* so hostile to the coalition. It was said that, when Brown and Cartier met to form their new partnership, Cartier only embraced Brown after making sure no *rouge* leaders were following the western reformer into the room. Instead, the *rouges* would attack the *bleus* for making a unprincipled surrender to George Brown. They accused Cartier of endangering French Canada simply to preserve his hold on power. *Bleus* retorted that the *rouges* had turned away from federalism "not by patriotism or national spirit, but simply by party spirit."[12]

The isolation of the *rouges* left them out of the constitutional process. Quebec became the only province where the main opposition party did not have delegates at the confederation conferences. Had Dorion and one or two of his *rouge* colleagues joined the negotiations at Quebec, they could have strengthened the reform-minded, provincial-rights caucus there. Their readiness to challenge Cartier would have forced clarification of issues he was willing to blur, and their participation should have improved both the resolutions and the debates about them which followed. If dissatisfied, the *rouges* could still have repudiated the outcome of the conference, as several members of the Maritime delegations soon did. Instead, Quebec was the only province where one party presumed to negotiate for a divided population. The *rouges*, having had no part in making the new constitution, were certain to oppose it.

In February 1865, the legislators of the united Canadas gathered again in the building where the confederation terms had been negotiated in October. The vital order of business was a resolution requesting the Imperial government to enact a new constitution for British North America based on the Quebec resolutions. The *rouges* launched their attack on it with their usual parliamentary skill. Governor General Monck, in his Throne Speech, had looked forward to the rise of "a new nationality" under confederation. Dorion swiftly moved that, as French Canadians and loyal subjects of the Queen, they wanted no new nationality. Confederation's supporters found themselves obliged to vote down this apparently unimpeachable statement of loyalty, as if confederation's aim was to assimilate the French and break up the Empire.

In the debate on the resolutions themselves, Dorion, his followers, and anglophone allies Luther Holton and Lucius Huntington launched withering attacks on the agreement. How could confederation protect British North America against the United States when it simply created a longer border to defend? Why promote a customs union between colonies which had no trade ties? What good were bold promises that union would bring intercolonial railways if confederation was, as Dorion put it, only "another haul at the public purse for the Grand Trunk," which would bankrupt all the colonies together?[13]

What about this crazy idea of letting the government appoint members of an unelected upper house? *Rouges* condemned it as reactionary and autocratic, a tory plot to reimpose the rule of unelected councils sure to be hostile to French Canada. The federal union was at once too centralized and too dependent on the will of the Maritime provinces, they said. Dorion urged the union to solve its own problems rather than "going on its knees and begging the little island of Prince Edward to come into this union." Henri Joly, *rouge* member for Lotbinière, concluded a string of criticisms by proposing the rainbow as confederation's symbol. "By its slender and elongated form, the rainbow would afford a perfect representation of the geographical configuration of the confederation. By its lack of consistence – an image without substance – the rainbow would represent aptly the solidity of our confederation."[14]

Mostly, however, the secular, freethinking *rouges* took up the natural grounds of the conservative *bleus*: confederation as a threat to the institutions, religion, language, and way of life of French Canada. The *rouges* stressed the danger of ethnic conflict, tried to show the Catholic Church was opposed to the union, and denounced confederation's originators as the implacable English enemy, the heirs of Lord Durham. "The union having failed to produce assimilation," said a *rouge* newspaper, "they have turned to a more powerful, more terrible instrument: federation."[15]

In his fiery contribution to the legislative debate, Joseph Perrault, *rouge* member for Richelieu, made much of this theme. Perrault was no nostalgic Patriot. Just twenty-seven, he was an agronomist, trained at English universities, who urged modernization for Quebec's farms. But facing the confederation plan, he made embattled tradition the theme of a long speech, packed with historical references. He argued that it had been the ambition of the English since long before the conquest "to destroy the influence and the liberties of the French race" in Canada. Confederation was the work of George Brown, the "imported fanatic," "the man most hostile to Lower Canadian interests." It would be "a fatal blow to our influence as French Canadians" and "decreed our national downfall." French Canadians would find it would be "disastrous to their institutions, their language, and their laws" and "threaten their existence as a race." Perrault acknowledged he was in favour of "the creation of a great political organization spread over an immense territory" – but not "at the price of our absorption."[16]

Other *rouges* made similar declarations. It was the terms of confederation, not federal union itself, that inspired their wrath. "The confederation I advocated," said Antoine-Aimé Dorion, "was a *real* confederation, giving the largest powers to the local governments and merely a delegated authority to the general government – in that respect differing in toto from the one now proposed." He declared that the Quebec conference had proposed a legislative union in disguise, with "local governments whose powers will be almost nothing, which will only burden the people with useless expenses."[17]

This was the crucial point. The *rouges* and their allies pointed to the unequal division of powers, to the federal authority to disallow, to federal appointment of the lieutenant-governors and judges. They highlighted every clause that emphasized central power and every statement delegates had made extolling strong national authority. They seized on all the elements designed to create a strong central government – and found them too strong. The English-Canadian majority had gained rep-by-pop, they charged, while French Canada would receive a provincial government whose powers were only illusory.

Why had French Canada's representatives at Quebec allowed this to happen? It was treason, said several of the *rouges*, and Cartier was the traitor. He had undertaken a cynical betrayal of French Canada. Maurice Laframboise, *rouge* member for Bagot, accused Cartier of assisting the disappearance of the French-Canadian race for the promise of a baronetcy. Henri Joly compared him to a banker who had been entrusted with the fortune of the French Canadians – their nationality – and sacrificed it without a scruple, for private gain.

If political opinion in Quebec endorsed the *rouge* charge that the *bleus* had failed to safeguard its interests in so fundamental a matter, Cartier and his party would be finished. On November 8, 1864, a *bleu* journalist wrote ominously to one of Cartier's cabinet colleagues, "I won't hide from you that there is a certain malaise among our warmest, most devoted friends. It will need much prudence and zeal – both at the same time – to keep them all beneath our banner. Don't trust too much in Cartier. He is surrounded by flatterers who don't express the feelings of most people."[18]

The recipient of that letter was Hector Langevin, *bleu* politician, solicitor-general of Canada East, and a delegate at Charlottetown and Quebec. Like Cartier, with whom he had articled, Langevin was the lawyer son of a mercantile family, though his home and power base was Quebec City, not Montreal. At thirty-eight, he stood second to Cartier among Quebec's confederation-makers. One of Langevin's brothers was an aide to a bishop, another about to become a bishop himself.

Langevin had decided early he was too ambitious to be a priest; he seems to have aspired all his life to be a *"grand fonctionnaire."* Even at thirty-eight, he was a stout, formal figure with a fussy little goatee. In later years, he grew fatter as he grew more powerful, and he joked contentedly that "a minister should be a man of gravity, if he wants to weigh in the balance." Langevin's personal life was much more conventional than Cartier's. He was always lonely when politics separated him from his wife and children. Never very sociable, he stood a little apart from the dinners and balls of the confederation process. Personal style, ambition, and the traditional Quebec–Montreal rivalry all kept him slightly removed from his leader. By the London conference of 1867, he would come to think Cartier spent too much time fighting for confederation in the salons of the great and powerful, leaving Langevin alone at the conference table to struggle with all the vital details of the legislation. (The other *bleu* delegate at the Quebec conference, a remarkably self-effacing politician named Jean-Charles Chapais, from Kamouraska, said barely a word in the conference or the legislative debate. He was dropped from the London delegation.)[19]

Still, Langevin understood that "my political future depends entirely on the success of the measure." He had to stand with Cartier. On February 21, 1865, well after the senior ministers had made their speeches, Langevin rose in the Parliament of the united Canadas to defend both his leader and confederation. In a long and powerful speech, Langevin appealed to ambition, saluting confederation because "we have become sufficiently great" for it. He quoted reams of financial statistics. He argued tangled issues of national defence and arcane matters of church-state relations. He even defended the appointive Senate.[20]

But the issues Hector Langevin kept coming back to were the national interests of Quebec. French Canadians were "a separate people," he declared. They could never accept a position of inferiority, and he denied they would have to. "The central or federal parliament will have the control of all measures of a general character . . . but all matters of local interest, all that relates to the affairs and rights of the different sections of the confederacy will be reserved for the control of the local parliaments." This talk of a new nationality that had alarmed the *rouges* meant the creation of a great country and a powerful nation, he said, but not at all the dismantling of "our different customs, manners, and laws."[21]

Unlike Cartier, Langevin was willing to confront the most explosive issue of confederation in Quebec: the threat to local autonomy pointed to by its critics. Lieutenant-governors would be appointed by the federal government, he agreed, but that would give them no more authority for "arbitrary acts" against the local government than the existing constitution gave to the governors appointed from Britain. The power to disallow local legislation had indeed been shifted from "a second or third class clerk" in the Colonial Office to a responsible government in Ottawa. But under responsible government, Imperial London had rarely used that power, and Langevin denied that a cabinet in Ottawa would have broader grounds for using disallowance against the provinces. In any case, should Ottawa try, members from every province would oppose it, "lest they should one day experience the same treatment."

Oliver Mowat, gone to the chancery bench, was not in the Canadian legislature to argue the case he would make as premier of Ontario, that responsible government made provincial sovereignty inevitable. (Christopher Dunkin, who became so incisive a critic of the Quebec resolutions, had told Mowat when he left for the bench that his participation had been the best guarantee something good would come of the conference.) Langevin, however, was rooting his case in the same set of ideas Mowat would defend as premier of

Ontario. In the late twentieth century, praise for responsible government would sound like the merest cliché of platform oratory. But to the politicians of the 1860s, conscious heirs of the achievement of that principle, it mattered vitally. Responsible government was the sovereignty of the 1860s.

Antoine-Aimé Dorion had charged that the Quebec delegates had plotted to produce "the most illiberal constitution ever heard of in any country," because confederation would obliterate responsible government. "There will be no such thing as responsible government attached to the local legislatures." The appointive Senate, the powers confided to Ottawa, federal disallowance, lieutenant-governors dominating the provinces – all these proved confederation was a tory plot against the people, Dorion said. Confederation was not only an misallocation of powers between local and central governments. It was an attempt to restore arbitrary power against the influence of the people.[22]

Langevin confronted the *rouge* leader directly. "Now we enjoy responsible government," he cried. "This great constitutional guarantee we take with us into the confederation." Étienne Taché, titular head of the Canadian coalition and a living link to the campaign for responsible government, had declared earlier in the debate that the war of races in Canada had been extinguished "on the day the British government granted Canada responsible government." Langevin argued on the same grounds that a self-governing people could not be oppressed. Within confederation, Quebec was and would remain distinct. Since responsible government had been preserved in the confederation settlement, he insisted, "our position then is excellent, and all those who frankly give expression to their opinions must admit that the representatives of Lower Canada at the Quebec conference have carefully guarded her interests."[23]

Langevin gave his long speech to a noisy House. He was frequently interrupted and frequently flung out charges of his own. But his most impassioned moment came in response to Henri Joly's image of Cartier as a corrupt banker who had squandered the treasures entrusted to him. Langevin gave a long survey of Cartier's achievements and turned Joly's image inside out. "The country," he said of Cartier – and by "country," he meant French Canada – "confided to him all its interests, all its rights, all its institutions, its nationality, its religion . . . and he restored them guaranteed, protected, and surrounded by every safeguard in the confederation of the British North American provinces." Langevin concluded with one final insistence that confederation "will afford the best possible guarantee for our institutions, our language, and all that we hold dearest," and sat down amidst cheers.[24]

Despite speeches of great length, detail, and sometimes even power, the Canadian Parliament's debate on the Quebec resolutions was weakened by a hint of inconsequence. The members had been told at the start that they could not change the resolutions, no matter how long they debated. "These resolutions were in the nature of a treaty," John A. Macdonald said several times as he launched the debate. They were the result of long negotiation and many compromises among several provinces. If each legislature began to revise the terms of the treaty, "we could not expect to get it passed this century."[25]

Macdonald's cheerful refusal to countenance any change to the agreement made at Quebec troubled even some of his supporters. It infuriated his opponents. They denounced it as more evidence of the anti-parliamentary arrogance of the confederation planners. But Macdonald could refuse to be troubled with the inconvenience of amendments only because he and his partners were sensing that the House was behind them. No nineteenth-century ministry could count on passive, complaisant support from its backbenchers the way twentieth-century party leaders could. Had enough of the Canadian backbenchers seen trouble for themselves in the confederation resolutions, Macdonald would not have been so high-handed. Both Charles Tupper and Leonard Tilley had returned from the Quebec conference to discover they could not get the Quebec resolutions through their legislatures, despite the large majorities their parties enjoyed. They each backed down. In Prince Edward Island and Newfoundland, the legislatures made sure the Quebec terms were not even brought up for debate, while Tupper and Tilley eventually sought approval for resolutions that held out hope of "better terms." Macdonald and Cartier would have done the same if their seats in government depended on it. They persevered only because they calculated they had the votes to do so.

Indeed, the Canadian caucuses did not waver. Among the Upper Canadians, Sandfield Macdonald of Cornwall, ex-premier of the union and its staunchest defender, voted against the Quebec resolutions. So did Malcolm Crooks Cameron, a prominent Toronto lawyer and a deep-died tory, Joseph Rymal, a homespun Clear Grit farmer from Hamilton, and a few others. From early in the debate, however, it was clear they and a handful of others would not shake the Upper Canadian consensus in favour of confederation. George Brown had forged it through years of effort, and Macdonald's adhesion made it unbreakable.

In Lower Canada, caucus solidarity was equally firm. Had the *rouges*' charges – that confederation put the survival of French Canada at risk – stuck, Cartier and Langevin could not have prevented wholesale defections of *bleu* backbenchers to Dorion's side. Instead, confederation gained supporters as the debate went on. Louis Archambault of L'Assomption came to the session intending to oppose confederation, he said. During the debate, he changed his mind. He would support confederation on the Quebec terms. Edouard Rémillard of Bellechasse, formerly a supporter of Dorion's, told the House that, when it came to protecting the rights and institutions of French Canada, he had more confidence in Cartier than in his former leaders.

When an opposition member challenged him to put confederation to the people, George Brown predicted that, if the House failed to support confederation, the government would sweep every seat in Upper Canada in a snap election. In Lower Canada, Cartier and Langevin faced more doubters and more opposition. But, as the debate continued, they too seem to have grown more confident. Dr. Beaubien of Montmagny expressed a belief that was growing rather than wavering among the *bleu* backbenchers when he declared that he had found opinion leaders "in every parish" were coming to support confederation.

Beaubien was exaggerating. Particularly in *rouge* strongholds around Montreal and on the south shore, protest meetings and petitions denounced confederation. But initial suspicion of the Quebec plan had failed to develop into general hostility. The church hierarchy got over its shock at what one influential cleric called "the union of this fanatic [George Brown] with our states-men."[26] Vigorously lobbied by Cartier and Langevin, and by Langevin's clerical brothers, the bishops dismissed the *rouges*' cry of alarm and came to support confederation very strongly. Even Henri Joly had to concede that Cartier had lulled the all-pervasive feeling of uneasiness the confederation plan had first provoked in Quebec into "a sleep of profound security." The success of the *bleus*' public-relations offensive reassured their supporters, and few of their elected members defected.

On March 10, 1865, the legislators of the united Canadas sat long into the night. After more than a month of debate (it would fill 1,032 pages in the transcript published soon afterwards), the Quebec resolutions came to a vote not long before dawn. Peter Waite found a sardonic report of the proceedings in the anti-confederate Stratford *Beacon*.

The House was in an unmistakeably seedy condition, having, as it was positively declared, eaten the saloon keeper clean out, drunk him entirely dry, and got all the fitful naps of sleep that the benches along the passage could be made to yield. . . . Men

with the strongest constitutions for parliamentary twaddle
were sick of the debate, and the great bulk of the members
were scattered about the building, with an up-all-night, get-
tight-in-the-morning air, impatient for the sound of the division bell. It rang at last, at quarter past four, and the jaded
representatives of the people swarmed in to the discharge of
the most important duty of all their lives.[27]

The members may have been jaded, tired, and hung-over, but by
the time backbencher Thomas Ferguson of Simcoe County uttered
the last words of the debate, they knew what they wanted to do. "I
take upon myself," said Ferguson, "though with great reluctance, the
responsibility of voting for this measure." It was hardly a clarion call
but, reluctant or exultant, most of the others had made the same
choice. They voted ninety-one to thirty-three in favour of a confederation on the terms agreed at Quebec. Despite the united opposition of the *rouge* members, confederation had received majority
support from among francophone members.

After the vote, the alliance of the church and the *bleus* grew even
stronger. Bishop Bourget, the powerful, ambitious bishop of Montreal,
who had often clashed with Cartier on other issues, remained cool
to the *bleus*' coalition with George Brown and to confederation itself.
As it moved toward ratification, however, clerical support for confederation would become nearly unanimous. Once the British
Parliament passed the British North America Act early in 1867, the
Quebec bishops issued a declaration that confederation, now the
law of the land, must be accepted, respected, and made to work.
Submission to lawful authority was orthodox church teaching, of
course, but many clerics used the declaration as a fresh weapon in
their old war with the *rouges*, even threatening to deny the sacraments
to anyone who would vote for an anti-confederation candidate.
The *rouges*' attempt to position themselves as defenders of traditional, Catholic French Canada against the confederation threat

had completely failed, and the clerical offensive helped ensure that the *rouges* were badly beaten in the general election of 1867.*

In fact, *rouge* opposition to confederation had begun to flag after the legislature approved the Quebec resolutions. There began to be hints that *rouge* hostility was less intense than *rouge* rhetoric. Even before confederation was completed, *Le Pays*, the leading *rouge* newspaper, began to argue that liberals should be seeking "to give more elasticity to the federal structure and to push back the centralizing elements . . . so as to make a veritable confederation."[28] By then, George Brown was busily wooing old *rouge* allies, seeking to build a liberal coalition that could challenge Macdonald and Cartier in the new confederation.

The reform of confederation, not its abolition, became the future course of most of the *rouge* opposition. Antoine-Aimé Dorion, Luther Holton, and other leading anti-confederates gradually conceded that confederation was not a plot against responsible government and became provincial-rights federationists. After confederation, in effect, they defended what had been Langevin's reading of the Quebec resolutions against John A. Macdonald's centralizing inclinations. In alliance with advocates of provincial autonomy like Ontario's Oliver Mowat and reconciled anti-confederates of Atlantic Canada, they helped bring the Liberal Party to power in Ottawa in 1873.

Maurice Laframboise and young Joseph Perrault lost their seats in 1867, and Perrault left politics. But Henri Joly soon became a supporter of confederation who served as both premier of Quebec and

---

* A recent book, Marcel Bellavance's *Le Québec et la confédération: un choix libre?* (Québec: Septentrion, 1992), argues that clerical interference on the side of confederation supporters should have invalidated the elections, but, given that all sides agreed that defending the influence of the church was one of Quebec's vital requirements in confederation, it seems unreasonable to expect that the church should not have used that influence. New election laws a decade after confederation, however, prohibited the kind of direct political intervention the bishops made in 1867.

lieutenant-governor of British Columbia. Antoine-Aimé Dorion became a founder of the Liberal Party and an Ottawa cabinet minister under Prime Minister Alexander Mackenzie. The man who had argued that federal appointment of judges would be a threat to French Canada's legal system ended his days as Sir Antoine-Aimé Dorion, Chief Justice of Quebec.

One of Dorion's anti-confederate protégés was Wilfrid Laurier, a young *rouge* lawyer who launched his long public career in the fight against the Quebec resolutions. Laurier wrote in March 1867 that in confederation the union that had been intended to destroy French Canada had at last achieved its aim. But Laurier too came to accept that confederation did not threaten the survival of French Canada and its institutions. In 1894, when he was poised to become prime minister of Canada, his adviser Joseph-Israël Tarte foresaw a glorious union for "Quebec and the Mowat party," a union that would respect "all races and all the agreements which were the basis of confederation."[29]

Laurier's 1896 victory would remove Hector Langevin permanently from power. After 1867, Langevin and Cartier had both preferred federal over provincial politics. Despite his annoyance that Macdonald received a knighthood and became sole prime minister, Cartier at first played a role in Ottawa similar to that he had known in the union. He acquired the territorial interests of the Hudson's Bay Company for Canada, negotiated British Columbia's entry into confederation, and helped launch the national railway. But Cartier's power in Montreal was already wobbling. New alignments arose to challenge his political networks, and he lost his seat in 1872. Then, brought down by kidney disease, he went off to his beloved London, with both his wife and his mistress in tow, and he died there in 1873. The Pacific Scandal was breaking in Ottawa, exposing the huge donations that railroad barons had made to Conservative leaders in exchange for the Pacific railway contract. Cartier's old patrons in the Grand Trunk Railway had been squeezed out of the contract, but when he died his executors still thought it prudent to burn all his papers.

Hector Langevin succeeded Cartier as leader of the Quebec wing of the Conservative Party. He spent twenty more years wielding the high authority to which he had always aspired. In 1866, taking a new cabinet post with important patronage possibilities, Langevin had said it was a position where he could be useful to his friends while rendering service to his country. When Macdonald gave him a growing share of responsibility for party patronage on a national scale, his career, perhaps inevitably, was tarnished by spectacular corruption scandals. He had to resign from cabinet in 1891, and Laurier's accession to power left him no avenue by which to return. Even before then, however, the power of Langevin and the *bleu* machine in Quebec had been broken.

In the post-confederation years, Langevin had become an Ottawa man, forced by his place in cabinet to acquiesce in Macdonald's attacks on provincial power. His inability to prevent the cabinet from letting Louis Riel's death sentence be carried out in 1885 helped destroy the Conservative Party in Quebec. The rights-of-the-provinces argument he had made so powerfully in 1865 became the property of Liberals, many of them his old *rouge* adversaries. In the wake of the hanging of Riel, Honoré Mercier built a nationalist coalition based on the vigorous assertion of provincial rights, traditional values, and clerical power. Mercier denounced Langevin for attempting to sit in Ottawa and control Quebec at the same time, and, in 1887, he swept to power as premier of Quebec. He and Oliver Mowat soon organized the first meeting of provincial premiers. Chaired by Mowat but held at Quebec, it proposed that the British North America Act be amended – to increase provincial powers, naturally. It was Mercier who first gave political sanction to the rising theory that confederation was a compact made between sovereign provinces and changeable by them.

For a century after 1860, Quebec got roughly the split which Cartier seems to have foreseen and Langevin defended. From the 1860s to the 1960s, French Canadians could participate in building a national state and a national economy if they chose to co-operate with the dominating English majority. Within Quebec itself, French Canada's traditional leaders continued to direct a society in which French language, religion, and traditional culture held sway. For all who believed it was the destiny of Quebec to be rural, agricultural, traditional, and Catholic – and in 1865 that was almost everyone in Quebec's public life – confederation confirmed Cartier's and Langevin's predictions much more than those of their critics and opponents in Quebec.

No one foresees the emergence of a saint. But Cartier and Langevin, both hard-headed, secular political managers, had helped create the environment in which Brother André thrived. As they intended, confederation helped Montreal consolidate its status as the financial and industrial capital of Canada, confirmed by the new national railroad as the gateway to the west. Industry thrived in the growing city, and resource industries blossomed throughout the province, often under English auspices. At the same time, the distinctly French-Canadian leadership of provincial society was preserved.

When Quebec controls its own land, several *bleu* members had declared in the confederation debates, it would be able to put an end to the migration to the United States that was bleeding the population of rural Quebec. After 1867, the province did launch "colonization" projects, guiding Quebeckers to the frontiers of Quebec rather than toward assimilation in New England. It was a priest, Father Antoine Labelle, who became the "apostle of colonization"; eventually he became Quebec's deputy minister of colonization.

Clerical leadership of a public campaign such as land development was typical of the new Province of Quebec. The province had no department of education for a century; the province assisted the church to defend its authority in that field. The schools, colleges, technical institutes, and universities of French Canada were nearly all religiously run. It was the same with hospitals and charities. As industry grew, the church took a leading role in workers' organizations and labour unions. Clerics became increasingly influential in cultural and intellectual life. The expanding responsibilities of the church symbolized how Quebec was simultaneously a modernizing society and a traditional one, a society with both the wealth to build Brother André's shrine and the inclination to do so.

The miracle worker of Mont-Royal died at the age of ninety-one in 1937, and his death was soon followed by the initiation of efforts to see him canonized a saint. His mighty shrine to St. Joseph, already looming over the northern slopes of the city to which he ministered, was completed in 1957, twenty years after his death.

Considered from the end of the twentieth century, Brother André, in career and personality so different from George-Étienne Cartier, seems like the patron saint of the Quebec that Cartier sought to defend. Each represented a Quebec that wanted agriculture and the church to be the soul of Quebec – and yet provided no obstacle to economic development dominated mostly by English Canadians. By the time Brother André's shrine was finished, however, those very policies had assisted in making French Quebec urban and modern and industrial. By then, it took a Maurice Duplessis to rule Quebec as if it were still the traditional society it had been in 1860. In his youth a student at the college where Brother André kept the door, Duplessis was a brutal, amoral, and sometimes hard-drinking politician. He was, however, *le chef,* the master of traditional French Canada as surely as Cartier in his prime had been.

After Duplessis's death in 1959 came the "Quiet Revolution," the explosive emergence of secular, modern, fashionable, relentlessly democratic Quebec. The Quiet Revolution seemed sudden and total because it was the abandonment of an illusion as much as a real social change. The demographics of Quebec had never been completely different from the rest of North America, and by the 1960s most Quebeckers, like other Canadians, were already leading urban ways of life. Quebec had moved beyond traditional faith and traditional agriculture, even when those things still defined it for the outside world and for itself. In the Quiet Revolution, Quebec abruptly abandoned the traditional image to seek new ways of defining and expressing itself in the modern world. Quebeckers began to reject clerical domination with the same determination that had gotten George Brown labelled as an anti-French bigot a century earlier.

If being rural farm families and devout, traditional Catholics no longer defined the French civilization in North America, what did? For many in Quebec, the answer was nationalism and the state. The Quiet Revolution dramatically changed the relationship between Quebeckers and what Cartier and Langevin had called "our religion, our institutions, and our laws." Abruptly, the bargain on which they had brought Quebec into confederation looked obsolete. A new division of powers began to seem urgently necessary.

A new constitutional deadlock, much longer than the one that preceded the breakthrough of 1864, began to dominate Canadian politics in the late twentieth century. In Quebec, the dominant figure in that deadlock was Robert Bourassa. Much like Cartier and Langevin, he went almost alone into the constitutional conferences, the leader of a single party attempting to define the constitutional needs that would ensure the survival of a people. His task was even more difficult than theirs. In the 1860s, French Canada was a cohesive society, generally respectful and deferential to its political and clerical leaders. Cartier and Langevin were able to strike a deal which a broad cross-section of French-Canadian society could accept. Even though the *bleus* and the *rouges* fell into partisan division on confederation, Cartier's *bleus* were powerful enough and popular enough to escape the consequences.

Robert Bourassa, a single party leader trying to incarnate both sides of a society absolutely divided as to whether federalism or separation was the choice best suited to the survival and flourishing of Quebec, was never so fortunate. Often distrusted by both federalists and separatists, accused by English Canadians of demanding too much, and by French Quebeckers of yielding too much, he was never able to see a new constitution ratified. Perhaps there exists a new constitutional settlement that will define Quebec's distinct requirements for the twenty-first century as successfully as confed-eration did in the 1860s. But it hardly seems likely that any single leader or single party will be able to find it, or see it accepted in the new Quebec.

CHAPTER SIX

Leonard Tilley and the Voters

~

I N 1987, after eleven first ministers had spent a couple of days
negotiating the Meech Lake accord, Premier Richard Hatfield of
New Brunswick returned home and called a general election before
the accord had been ratified by his provincial legislature. Hatfield
and his party suffered a disastrous defeat, and the Meech Lake accord
never recovered.

In 1864, after thirty-three bipartisan delegates had spent almost
three weeks negotiating the Quebec resolutions, Premier Leonard
Tilley of New Brunswick returned home and called a general election before the resolutions had been ratified by his provincial legislature. Tilley and his party suffered a disastrous defeat, and . . .

The script changes here. Despite the defeat of Tilley's government, confederation survived to be ratified in New Brunswick a year
later. Tilley returned triumphantly to power in a second election,
and the constitutional process of the 1860s culminated in the
passage and gradual acceptance of the British North America Act.
Tilley had made himself the only Canadian politician who has ever

faced the voters twice on constitutional issues and survived. Since "everyone knows" that the nineteenth-century makers of confederation excluded the public from Canada's constitution, Tilley's experience opens a window on the relations between politicians and voters in the confederation process.

Leonard Tilley has dropped almost completely off the radar screen of Canadian history. The only substantial study of his career is twenty-five years old, an unpublished and almost unavailable academic thesis.[1] Standard texts in Canadian history refer to him routinely as "Samuel Leonard Tilley," though he never used his first name. Even more completely than the other key makers of confederation, Tilley has become almost entirely faceless.

Tilley was hard to make interesting. He had a genial style, but was not witty, drunken, or flirtatious. A widower, he was the devoted single father of seven children, a steady, churchgoing, evangelical Christian, who taught Sunday school and had made his living running a drugstore. As a politician, he was more an administrator than a leader or a crowd-pleaser. He never became prime minister. Even his enthusiasms were muted. Early in his career, Tilley was best known as a crusader against alcohol, but even as Most Worthy Patriarch of the North American Sons of Temperance, he was unfanatical. He went through all the confederation dinners without touching the champagne, but he never complained about its presence either.

At the end of his life, when he was Lieutenant-Governor Sir Leonard Tilley, with fifty years of political success behind him, eulogists would emphasize his United Empire Loyalist origins. But Tilley was never one of the gentlemanly office-holders from the old colonial élite who kept the loyalist flame in New Brunswick. He rarely mentioned his antecedents, who had been part of the anonymous rank and file of the American refugee migration into New Brunswick. The son of small shopkeepers in the Saint John River valley community of Gagetown, Tilley at thirteen moved to Saint John as a pharmacist's apprentice. At twenty he was a partner in a successful retail drugstore there, and he soon moved into local politics.*

His politics reflected his origins. Tilley was another of the heirs of responsible government. He helped achieve the rule of Parliament in New Brunswick in 1854, and it helped him to rise from nowhere to domination of the province. Tilley was for reform: a secret ballot and an expanded voters' list, more public education, businesslike administration of government, economic development. As a key cabinet minister in the government of Charles Fisher, Tilley delivered on much of that agenda. Tilley was also for temperance when it was a great and highly controversial issue. In fact, his attempt to legislate prohibition in New Brunswick brought down the Fisher government in the infamous "Rummies" and "Smashers" campaign of 1856. Tilley learned a lasting lesson about electoral politics. "Our legislature was at that time in advance of public sentiment," he said later. When the reformers returned to power, Tilley became more cautious about legislating his own enthusiasms.[2]

Responsible government had vastly expanded the powers of cabinet government, and Tilley rose on his ability to shoulder the burden. He mastered the details and understood the finances, and he dominated cabinet sessions. He also kept his elbows up. In the schism-prone party politics of mid-century New Brunswick, he made enemies in his own caucus as often as beyond it, but he was rarely outmanoeuvred. In 1861, when Premier Fisher became tangled in a scandal, Tilley ruthlessly organized his removal from cabinet and took over himself. Soon after, the voters gave the reformers a

---

* The most famous statement of loyalist pathos – "I climbed to the top of Chipman's Hill and watched the sails disappearing in the distance, and such a feeling of loneliness came over me that, although I had not shed a tear through all the war, I sat down on the damp moss with my baby in my lap and cried" – was attributed to Leonard Tilley's great-grandmother by loyalist historian W. O. Raymond. Tilley never mentioned it, or her, to his authorized biographer.

comfortable majority, which was still supporting Premier Tilley in 1864, when he led New Brunswick's delegations into the discussions of Maritime union and then of confederation. (Fisher, who had remained in politics, was one of the delegates with him at Quebec.)

In all the provinces, legislatures normally met for a month or two early in each calendar year. The plan at Quebec had been to have the Quebec resolutions approved at Quebec, Fredericton, Halifax, Charlottetown, and St. John's, Newfoundland, early in 1865. The Imperial Parliament would then receive what it wanted: simultaneous requests from the provinces to have British North America united on terms negotiated by colonists and approved by their legislatures. On that timetable, the new nation might have come into being late in 1865 or early in 1866. Leonard Tilley's New Brunswick election determined it would not happen so fast.

Tilley knew as soon as he came home from Quebec that confederation would be a hard sell in New Brunswick. He personally had put aside his own earlier suspicion that, in a British North American union, "we of the lower provinces would be placed in a less favourable position than we now occupy." But many of his compatriots still held precisely that view. As soon as the Quebec plan was published, opposition erupted. "The storm that burst upon the delegates from New Brunswick was like the hurricane of the tropics," wrote Tilley's fellow delegate John Gray. Tilley soon saw that the New Brunswick assembly, which had been elected in 1861 and would have to face the voters in 1865, was unlikely to approve the Quebec resolutions.[3]

From the perspective of the 1990s, Leonard Tilley's inability to have confederation approved in the New Brunswick legislature requires some explanation. Tilley was the undisputed leader of a government with a solid majority, and on the Quebec resolutions he had the support of leading opposition members. In those circumstances, modern premiers and party leaders would simply instruct their backbenchers, and the thing would be done. By late-twentieth-century standards, only remarkable carelessness – or an equally remarkable scrupulousness about consulting the people – would cause an incumbent premier to call an election with such crucial business unfinished. We need not attribute either carelessness or scruples to Tilley, however. He did not choose to have an election. His hand was forced.

In Halifax, Charles Tupper was aghast at the election talk in New Brunswick. "I hope you will assist me in pressing Tilley to push it through without going first to the people," he had just written to John A. Macdonald. Macdonald seemed to share Tupper's opinion. "It shakes one's opinion of Tilley's statesmanship," he wrote when he heard the election commitment had been made.[4]

It is easy to assume that Macdonald was angry because he had been counting on Tilley to ram confederation through the legislature against the will of the population, leaving the frustrated opposition impotent to stop it. In that circumstance, so familiar from late-twentieth-century Canadian politics, one would assume that the government's rivals would be delighted to see Tilley playing into their hands by calling an election. Oddly enough, however, the New Brunswick opposition shared Macdonald's view of Tilley's action.

At the end of 1864, Albert Smith led the opposition to Tilley in the New Brunswick legislature. Smith was a long-time reform champion, more radical than Tilley on most issues, and particularly set against taxpayer subsidies to railway corporations. He had been Tilley's attorney-general until 1862, but he had objected to Tilley's generosity to railway promoters and had left the cabinet. Confederation confirmed their rivalry. Smith, who abominated Maritime union, had refused to be a delegate to the Charlottetown conference, and he proved equally hostile to the larger union negotiated at Quebec. Since the leading conservative politicians had joined the confederation movement, Smith became the effective leader of opposition to the Quebec resolutions in New Brunswick. He weighed in against them with all his characteristic fervour – but he did not want a snap election.

Since it was generally agreed that opposition to confederation was widespread and growing, an Albert Smith with the instincts of the 1990s would have been invoking the rights of the people and demanding the election that could put him in power. Smith did not see it that way. Instead of pressing for the election, he called Tilley's decision to call one "an act of tyranny."[5]

The explanation for the actions of both Tilley and Smith lies in the way Canadian politics worked under responsible government in the nineteenth century. John A. Macdonald had not, in fact, assumed that Tilley could ram confederation through a tame legislature. When he urged Tilley to meet the legislature, Macdonald knew the outcome would be uncertain. "Tilley should have called his parliament together and, in accordance with the agreement of the conference at Quebec, submitted the scheme," he wrote after Tilley had gone down to defeat. "Whatever might have been the result in the legislature, the subject would have been fairly discussed and its merits understood, and if he had been defeated, he then had an appeal to the people. As it was, the scheme was submitted without its being understood or appreciated, and the inevitable consequences followed."[6]

Macdonald was making the argument (the amazing argument, by late-twentieth-century standards) that legislative debate mattered. Albert Smith, from the opposite side of the confederation issue, believed the same thing. Both denounced the snap election, because it pre-empted the legislative debate. Both asserted that an important public issue should be debated in Parliament, no matter what the outcome. Macdonald did not urge Tilley to use his control of a compliant legislative majority to impose his policy on an unwilling province. He argued instead that the legislature was the best place from which to *convince* the population. Albert Smith denounced the election call for the same reason, because he calculated the opposition forces could win over the legislature by force of argument – and increase their electability by doing so.

Tilley's decision to dissolve the legislature depended less on his own calculation, however, than on the reaction of his cabinet and caucus. In the 1860s, as today, government policy required the support of a legislative majority. In the 1860s, however, party policy was subject to the approval of the party caucus. Tilley quickly found neither his ministers nor his backbenchers ready to give confederation the automatic and docile support a modern party leader expects. He had a hard fight with his cabinet over confederation, and one of his ministers, George Hatheway, resigned to join Albert Smith. It was worse in caucus. Many of the reform members who had kept Tilley in power since 1861 refused to endorse the Quebec resolutions.

John Gray, the one-time "weathercock" who had become the strongest supporter of confederation among the conservatives, was also running into dissent in his caucus. Even his fellow delegate Edward Chandler had reservations about the Quebec terms. With revolt brewing in both the government and the opposition caucuses, confederation's supporters simply lacked the votes to carry it through the legislature. Tilley could either fight and lose in the legislature and be forced to call an election, or he could dissolve the legislature immediately and debate the issue on the hustings instead, where the outcome was less predictable. With his caucus support dissolving, he preferred an election to humiliation in the House, and he agreed to postpone all action on the Quebec resolutions until after the election. By mid-November, Tilley and Smith were busy meeting the people.*

More precisely, they were meeting those people who had a vote. Something close to universal male suffrage prevailed in New Brunswick in 1864, and it was little different in most of the other

---

* Tilley later claimed Lieutenant-Governor Gordon forced the election on him, and that interpretation has often been repeated. Carl Wallace, however, in "Sir Leonard Tilley," authoritatively discounts Gordon's influence and explains why Tilley made the claim.

British North American provinces, despite the widely held notion that there was no little or no democracy in the mid-nineteenth-century colonies. As early as 1810, Sir James Craig, a governor of Lower Canada whose usual inclination was to throw critics of his policies into jail, had complained bitterly that "scarcely one farmer in a thousand" was without a vote in that colony, while in 1832 the assembly he had fought with celebrated the fact that the right of voting remained "nearly universal."[7]

When the first legislative assemblies were called in the British North American colonies, a radical choice had been required: either let almost all men vote or let almost none. The choice hinged on the amount of property that a voter would be required to own. Most colonial families owned property, but most were frontier farmers, whose properties had infinitesimal cash value. Setting any significant level of property ownership as a requirement for voting would disenfranchise almost everyone. Instead, a low requirement – "the forty-shilling freehold" – gave a vote to almost every household. Even the tenant farmers on the seigneuries of Quebec and the estates of Prince Edward Island got the vote. By the 1830s, with formal discrimination against Catholic, Jewish, and Quaker voters abolished, male property owners nearly all had the vote.

By the 1850s, the achievement of responsible government meant legislatures with genuine authority over the internal affairs of British North America were elected by an electorate as wide as any in the world. Britain still had a very limited franchise, and few European countries were democracies. The United States had adopted the principle of universal manhood suffrage in 1845, but many groups, most notably the slaves, remained disenfranchised, and significant limits to voter power remained. At confederation, United States senators were appointed by state governments, not elected. As late as 1877, Congress installed a president who had been soundly defeated in the popular vote.

Most British North American colonies still required voters to own a token amount of property, and thereby excluded transients, hired men, and adult sons living at home (though policing of the polls to prevent them from voting was very haphazard). In practice, the right of voting for members of the assembly was not far short of universal for males in most of British North America. In Canada East, where poverty and dislocation of the kind Brother André experienced in his youth had disenfranchised a growing number of men, the proportion had fallen as low as 70 per cent by the 1860s, and opponents of Nova Scotia's decision to restore a property requirement in that decade claimed that as many as a quarter of voters there might lose their vote. Even those colonies, however, still allowed more men to vote than most countries, and the other British North American colonies were even closer to universal male suffrage.

Oddly enough, it was reformers, the advocates of responsible government and a broad franchise, who were most reluctant to remove the last vestiges of a property requirement. The vote was nearly sacred to reformers; they resisted giving it to those who, they felt, neither earned it nor cared how they exercised it. In 1855, Tilley's reform colleague Charles Fisher had argued, even as he widened the franchise, that allowing every man to vote would give too much power "to money and multitude."[8] It would enable the rich to cancel out middle-class votes, he said, by buying the votes of desperate poor people.

For the same reason, the great reform crusader Joseph Howe had brought back a property requirement in Nova Scotia after a conservative government had eliminated it. If a county with 5,000 voters had 2,400 men on each side of an issue, said Howe, the balance would be tipped by two hundred impoverished and apolitical voters, who only wished elections were more common so they could sell their vote more often. It was the reformers' faith in the vote that impelled them to keep access to it from being too easy. George Brown defended token limits to exclude the unconcerned and uncommitted, but he was not far wrong when he declared that everyone in Canada West who seriously wanted a vote could have one, and it was much the same in New Brunswick and Prince Edward Island.

Everyone male, that is. Women could not vote. The property requirement eliminated most of them, and when it was noticed in the 1830s that some women who had property were voting, the colonies enacted laws to disenfranchise all women. Men and women were considered different by nature and destined for different realms: women for the domestic sphere, men for public life. In the reign of Queen Victoria, middle-class men increasingly expected to support their wives and dependents at home, while they monopolized "public" life. The doctrine of "separate spheres," which disenfranchised women, was getting stronger in the 1860s.

In some ways, the conviction that men and women occupied separate spheres could empower women. Nurturing the young was women's role, and so women could claim substantial influence over education and charitable work. As public schools expanded, women came to dominate the teaching profession throughout British North America. (Leonard Tilley had met his wife when they were Sunday-school teachers together.) Defending and raising society's moral standards was also women's domain. Since the boundary between moral suasion and public campaigning was hard to define, women's moral role sometimes enabled them to enter directly into political activity.

Temperance, a moral issue that became a political crusade, had drawn thousands of New Brunswick women into politics in the 1850s. As a temperance campaigner, Leonard Tilley had long worked closely with women who organized meetings, spoke, marched, and gathered petition signatures in tens of thousands. George Hatheway, the politician who quit Tilley's cabinet in opposition to confederation, said it was crucial for a politician to have "the good opinion of the fair portion of the community." He claimed he "would rather have one lady canvasser than a dozen men."[9]

Women were also beginning to crack open some of the formal prohibitions on their participation in public life. A few were already going to university and pushing for access to medical schools and professional careers. Emily Stowe, a Canadian trained in the United States, opened a medical practice in Toronto in the year of confederation.

A decade later Dr. Stowe would help organize the first Canadian campaigns for woman suffrage. Though women would be denied the vote until the end of the First World War, women's-rights campaigners would force the generation of politicians empowered by confederation to debate (and vote down) woman suffrage regularly.

Suffragists demanded the vote as a right rooted in the equality of men and women. Men frequently justified male suffrage as providing a "household franchise," exercised by the (male) head of the household. They argued that wives and daughters deserved the vote no more than hired men or sons who deferred to the authority of the master of the house. There was no justice in giving women the vote, they argued, if that simply gave their husbands or fathers control of extra votes. Women might argue about confederation – and what roles they may have played in influencing the choices their husbands and fathers made remains largely unstudied. But they could not vote.

One reason to deny women the vote was what George Brown celebrated as "the manly British system of open voting." Until the 1870s, nearly all British North Americans had to vote in public. Brown's adjective "manly" was carefully chosen, for the tumult and violence that often accompanied "open" voting helped justify the exclusion of women. Even more important was the belief that it was manliness which required a public statement of one's political convictions. Voting and manliness went together, and advocates of open voting argued that no man who demanded a share of civic responsibility should refuse to declare his allegiance publicly. Only cowardly men would hide in a ballot booth. Advocates of the secret ballot argued that open voting encouraged vote-buying, but their rivals retorted that the secret ballot sacrificed "moral control" of voting; it actually encouraged corrupt behaviour by those who would say one thing and do another.

Open voting prevailed in most of British North America until a decade after confederation, but not in New Brunswick. Leonard Tilley had been in the government that had introduced voting by ballot there in the 1850s. In New Brunswick's confederation elections, voters wrote the name of their chosen candidate on a slip of paper and delivered it to the electoral officer. The full secret-ballot system, with printed ballots, screened voting booths, and other controls, was introduced to the world by South Australia in 1856, but New Brunswick had already accepted the essence of the process.*

Campaigning in mid-nineteenth-century British North America was direct and personal. Given the independent authority of individual members, voters had reason to assess the man as closely as the party with which he was associated. With only a thousand voters in many constituencies, an experienced local member would know most of his supporters personally, and most of his opposition, too. Long, careful cultivation of personal and communal loyalties was vital. If that did not seem to be succeeding, then persuasion, coercion, and intimidation came into play. The task of a constituency team was to get supporters to the polls, and also to keep opponents away. Early Canadian electoral folklore is filled with doctored voters' lists, reports of "treating" the voters, intimidation, and discussions of the price of a vote. It was a rough-and-ready process.

Honest elections depended on each individual's will or ability to reject coercion and stand by his principles. (That is, George Brown might have said, elections depended on the "manliness" of each voter.) It was because individual votes were crucially important that corruption lurked around every polling station. In the late twentieth century, skewing the vote had become almost entirely a wholesale process, where media buys, spin campaigns, and the well-timed release of tailored surveys were the best ways to influence national campaigns. In the 1860s, voting was personal, and the economics of political corruption were still retail. If the parties were equally

---

* Despite its sacred status in the twentieth century, the secret ballot became largely theoretical once the buying of individual votes became uneconomic. Today, survey researchers and canvassers expect to predict consumer and voter preferences within three percentage points, ninety-nine times out of a hundred.

corrupt and equally funded, corruption might cancel itself out, but it was never eliminated.

In New Brunswick's 1865 election, "confederation or no confederation" was the overwhelming issue. Tilley, Gray, and other confederation supporters held several big meetings in Saint John in November. Soon Tilley was out on a "stumping expedition through the central counties," and arranging meetings across the province. Unfortunately for Tilley, the "strong current running against federation" that he had observed in November grew stronger as the campaign progressed. Tilley was popular and persuasive enough that anti-confederate leaders refused to debate him, and he had all the machinery and funds of government with which to tempt the voters. In mid-campaign, he believed he was "making good headway against the suspicions and fears of our opponents." In fact, confederation was making very little headway at all.[10]

Confederation was not an urgent necessity in New Brunswick. None of the Maritime provinces faced the political crisis that drove the Canadians to seek a new arrangement, and the Quebec resolutions were a very "Canadian" proposal – from the "oily brains of Canadian politicians," said Albert Smith.[11] Maritimers had experienced years of frustrated bickering with the Canadians on many issues, and felt no incentive to solve Canadian problems. Confederation, with its promise to reorganize all the familiar political identities and commercial ties of each of the colonies, had come up suddenly in the Maritimes, offering little but the sheer ambition of the thing as an incentive.

Confederation's weakness was compounded by a host of local irritants. Tilley's government, in office a long time, had lost supporters on a series of controversies even before confederation emerged. Tilley, an evangelical Protestant who had never cultivated Catholic votes effectively, had recruited no Catholics to the Charlottetown and Quebec delegations, and the Acadian and Irish-Catholic minorities of the province regarded both him and confederation warily. Saint

John merchants and shippers, normally allies of Tilley, feared new tariffs and fiercer competition (with good reason), and argued that maintaining both federal and provincial governments would require increased taxation. Smith and his allies campaigned against both the details and the consequences of the Quebec resolutions. "Do you wish Canada oats, beef, pork, butter, etc., to come into this country at one half the price you are now receiving? Do you wish the whole revenue of this country to be handed over to . . . the dishonest statesmen of Canada?" Every issue seemed to go against Tilley and confederation.[12]

When the results of the New Brunswick election were complete, early in March 1865, only eleven declared supporters of the Quebec resolutions survived in a house of forty-one members, and Albert Smith took over as premier. "We have been pounded, really pounded," wrote John Gray as the results came in. "I could not believe that the constituency which I have represented for fifteen years could have embraced so many fools or could have been so thoroughly blind to its own interest."[13]

Gray had grounds to be bitter, perhaps; he had lost his seat. So had Tilley, but Tilley was remarkably unperturbed. In late-twentieth-century terms, the election should have given Albert Smith an unshakeable "mandate" for four or five years, but in the 1860s parliamentary democracy never put a legislature in such a straitjacket. Tilley had already calculated that Smith's collection of reformers and conservatives would be hard-pressed to find an alternative to confederation – or to agree on anything else. Already, he was guessing that putting Smith into office might turn out to be the best way to expose his weaknesses and wean away his backbench supporters. "All our friends are plucky, sanguine of early success, and intend fighting earnestly for a reversal," said Tilley within weeks of his electoral defeat. He calmly foresaw that "the day is not far distant when a majority of the electors of this province will declare in favour of a federal union."[14]

In the Canadian legislature, then in the midst of its confederation debate, the *rouges* and other opponents of confederation used the New Brunswick results to argue that confederation should simply be abandoned, since it was now dead in the Maritimes (the Prince Edward Island and Newfoundland legislatures had already refused to proceed with the Quebec resolutions). Instead, Macdonald moved to force an immediate vote on the Quebec resolutions. Canadian backbenchers were as free as those in New Brunswick to abandon the government if they judged it wise to do so, but the coalition leaders were confident that their members still supported them and the confederation plan. Indeed, the Canadian legislature seemed undaunted by the New Brunswick results. Its members closed the debate and approved the Quebec resolutions with a nearly three-to-one majority.

There was no such confidence in Nova Scotia. Charles Tupper had returned from Quebec full of his usual confident bluster. He had always declared that the legislature was the appropriate place for the Quebec resolutions to be ratified or rejected. Since the legislature included a large majority of his supporters, and since the opposition leaders were also with him, he foresaw no elections. He seems to have expected to have the Quebec resolutions quickly ratified.

Instead, Tupper encountered the same surging resistance as Tilley. Nova Scotia felt no more urgent spur towards constitutional change than New Brunswick, and many of its commercial and political leaders were horrified by the terms Tupper had accepted at Quebec. Albert Gilpin Jones, who had organized Tupper's electoral triumph eighteen months earlier, denounced him and called the financial terms a disaster for the province. Thomas Coffin of Shelburne, Thomas Killam of Yarmouth, and Archibald McLelan of Minas – all sailors and shipbuilders, and all members of the legislature – spoke out for the province's powerful shipping and trading interests. "Nova Scotia had more ships in the port of Calcutta in any day of the year than . . . in all the ports of Canada," McLelan said scornfully, but Canadian tariffs would force Nova Scotia to abandon its free-ranging, low-tariff sea trades.[15] Halifax merchant banker William Stairs predicted high taxes and high tariffs to subsidize costly Canadian experiments with railways, industrial development, and westward expansion.

Hearing such arguments, Jonathan McCully fumed about the conservatism of the rich. He accused those who had "money made" of blocking the ambitions of those who were seeking new opportunities. But that kind of counter-attack only seemed to confirm that confederation would force radical economic change upon the province. In fact, Tupper, who had gone to Quebec with four lawyers and no businessmen, had accepted financial arrangements that would make it difficult for Nova Scotia to avoid rapid bankruptcy if it joined the union. Confederation's critics savaged these terms, and even would-be unionists declared them impossible to swallow.

Not all objections came from the pocketbook. A potent mix of quasi-national pride and Imperial loyalty led many Nova Scotians to fear that confederation would make their province a very junior partner in a new and unwelcome nationality. The old, established province, once the richest of the British North American colonies, still saw itself as the senior colony, the most cultured and best endowed with higher learning. In its newspapers and meeting places, the public men of the province launched a searching critique of the Quebec resolutions, and, by the end of 1864, a consensus against confederation seemed to have formed. Joseph Howe thrilled with pride. "People were told that opposition would be vain," he wrote. "They had to study the measure, to look for leaders, to cast off the trammels of party, to form new combinations and to defend their institutions from this sudden surprise as they best could. Nothing illustrates more finely the high spirit and intellectual resources of Nova Scotia than the rapidity with which all this was done."[16]

Howe had come late to Nova Scotia's confederation debate. The ex-premier and elder statesman had been busy with his duties on the Imperial fisheries inquiry, and at first Nova Scotian opposition to confederation blossomed without him. But he was only sixty, as assertive as ever, and sure that he understood Nova Scotia and its needs more deeply than anyone. He had often looked forward to uniting the British colonies of North America, but the Quebec resolutions and their strongly "Canadian" emphasis appalled him. From the beginning of 1865, Howe strengthened the anti-confederate cause with his prestige and his phrase-making.

Howe made confederation a question of the rights of Nova Scotians. Responsible government had been his great achievement, and he reminded Nova Scotians of "the great battle by which the appointment of our own officers, the control of our own revenues, the management of our own affairs, was secured to Nova Scotians." Howe denounced the Quebec resolutions as a scheme to transfer those precious rights to a government answerable to Upper and Lower Canadians, not Nova Scotians. "This crazy confederacy" was not merely misguided, he said, it was illegitimate. It was unconstitutional.[17]

As resistance to the Quebec plan swept the province, Tupper's comfortable legislative majority crumbled. One of his cabinet ministers, John McKinnon of Antigonish, resigned rather than endorse the Quebec resolutions. Even Robert Dickey, government leader in the upper house and a delegate to both Charlottetown and Quebec, declared his lack of enthusiasm for the terms. Opposition leaders Archibald and McCully never wavered in their support for the Quebec agreement – they "stood by me like trumps," said Tupper rather possessively – but most of the reform caucus renounced them. They dumped Archibald from his position as party leader and leader of the opposition and chose William Annand in his place.[18]

Annand was Howe's most devoted admirer, nicknamed "Boots" for his devotion, and the editor of Howe's collected works. A journalist by profession, he had made fellow reformer Jonathan McCully editor of his influential newspaper, the *Morning Chronicle*. Since Charlottetown, McCully had made the *Chronicle* a strong voice for confederation. But McCully was only the editor. Annand owned the paper. As soon as Annand committed himself to the anti-confederate cause, he fired McCully, and the *Chronicle* began to publish

Howe's rush of anti-confederate fury, the "Botheration Letters." McCully scrambled to start a new newspaper, the *Unionist*.

In the first days of 1865, Tupper still claimed to believe the Nova Scotia legislature might endorse the Quebec resolutions when it met in February. "I hope we will carry the day," he wrote to John A. Macdonald. But when Tilley called the election in New Brunswick and went plunging toward defeat, he took the prospects for ratification in Nova Scotia down with him. "Had he waited," Tupper complained to Macdonald, "by great sacrifices and exertions, we could, I think, have secured a bare majority." After the collapse of confederation in New Brunswick, however, the Nova Scotia members would not annoy their constituents in a pointless gesture. "A number here who might have been disposed to sacrifice their own position to achieve an important object would not be willing to do so without any practical result to be attained," Tupper told Lieutenant-Governor Richard MacDonell mournfully.[19]

Thwarted in the New Brunswick assembly, Tilley had faced a general election. Thwarted in the Nova Scotia assembly, Tupper preferred the strategy of delay. Since Nova Scotia's assembly could not be persuaded to vote in favour of the Quebec plan, Tupper encouraged it not to vote on it at all. Annand and Howe were endorsing the old dream of rebuilding greater Nova Scotia through Maritime union, so Tupper indulged them. Declaring blandly that "immediate" action on the larger Quebec plan had become "impracticable," he persuaded the legislature to renew negotiations for a union with New Brunswick and Prince Edward Island. When, as he fully expected, Prince Edward Island dismissed the idea as flatly as it had at Charlottetown, the anti-confederates' claim to have a feasible alternative to confederation was neatly skewered. Almost the entire debate on his "Maritime union" resolution had focused on confederation, but Tupper had avoided a negative vote on it.[20]

For the rest of 1865, Tupper avoided asking the legislature or the electorate to decide on confederation. Tupper insisted it was all up to the legislature. "If the people's representatives are satisfied that the country is opposed to this union, they can reject it, or they can obtain a dissolution by asking for it," he said, promising that the government would "leave its decision to the independent action of the legislature." But the opponents and doubters also shrank from forcing the issue. Even when by-elections swelled the anti-confederate ranks, they allowed Tupper to pursue his policy of delay. The Quebec resolutions lay on the table, neither endorsed nor rejected, and Tupper remained in power. His optimism revived. "Twelve months will, I believe, find a decided majority in the present parliament in favour of confederation," he declared in April 1865, and he was prepared to wait.[21]

At first, delay seemed most likely to compound Tupper's problems. With confederation blocked, perhaps permanently, in the Maritimes, some Upper Canadian reformers began to urge the achievement of their goal, rep-by-pop, by federating Upper and Lower Canada alone. The coalition held to its commitment to the larger plan, but Upper Canada was unlikely to wait forever for rep-by-pop, when three Maritime provinces were on record against the union proposed at Quebec. Then Leonard Tilley's prediction began to come true.

During 1865, Tilley's decision to go to the people, even at the price of being driven from office, began to seem brilliant. By throwing confederation's critics into office, New Brunswick had made them display how unprepared they were, and their alternatives to confederation began to seem threadbare and incoherent. Albert Smith and George Hatheway (who after abandoning Tilley's cabinet had joined Smith's) held views not far removed from those of Hector Langevin or Oliver Mowat. They suspected the Quebec terms because they feared the rights of the provinces had been inadequately secured against federal interference. But Robert Wilmot, Smith's government leader in the upper house, and his attorney-general, John Allen, opposed the Quebec resolutions for the opposite reason. Closer to John A. Macdonald than to their own leader, Wilmot and Allen spoke for a faction that feared the Quebec terms had not given the central government enough strength to hold the new nation together. The fiery Saint John journalist Timothy Anglin, meanwhile, had delivered much of the Irish-Catholic vote to the anti-confederate cause and could not be denied a cabinet seat, despite the discomfort he caused to patrician Anglicans like Wilmot.

Events conspired dramatically against the Smith government. By the fall of 1865, railway policies, religious antagonisms, disputes over patronage, and cabinet bickering had discredited the new government. London was emphasizing its desire to see confederation ratified, and Lieutenant-Governor Gordon, whose open dislike of the Quebec resolutions had helped undermine Tilley late in 1864, had now accepted his orders from the Colonial Office and began to harass Smith. Robert Wilmot, one of the pillars of the Smith government, was drawn into negotiations with the Canadian government over trade and came to recognize, as the Quebec delegates had, that a tightly centralized union would always be unacceptable to Lower Canada. His opposition to the Quebec resolutions faded as he abandoned legislative union as an impractical will-of-the-wisp, and he left Smith's cabinet.

In 1865, as the American civil war ended, Fenian raiders began to attack the British North American colonies as a way to punish Britain for its control of Ireland. The raids, by Irish-Americans who had learned soldiering in the Northern armies, would prove to be small, disorganized, and easily contained. But they were a boon to confederation supporters, who could preach unity in the face of external threat much more plausibly than their opponents. As Irish raiders menaced New Brunswick, a brutal smear campaign, questioning the loyalty of Irish Catholics who opposed the Quebec resolutions, drove Timothy Anglin from Smith's cabinet. Such attacks also helped persuade the leaders of New Brunswick's clerical hierarchy, who had been dubious about confederation, to affirm their loyalty by calling for approval of the Quebec plan.

When a by-election was called in York County, the region surrounding Fredericton, Charles Fisher, who had been a delegate to

Quebec and had been defeated in the general election, ran again. It was a hard-fought campaign. Tilley told John A. Macdonald it could be won – "with the expenditure of eight or ten thousand dollars." While his backers poured drinks and promised favours, Fisher made extravagant commitments, exploited Protestant bigotry against Anglin, and mocked the government's decisions. With anti-confederate funding from Halifax, Smith's supporters fought back just as hard. They, even more than Fisher, insisted that confederation was the central issue. Fisher won by a large majority. Barely six months after the New Brunswick general election, the death watch on the Smith government began.[22]

As the coalition against confederation crumbled, Tilley, confederation, and the Quebec resolutions re-occupied the moderate middle ground. Indeed, it began to seem likely that, if Smith's government did not endorse confederation, the members elected as anti-confederates just a few months earlier would put in a new cabinet that would. Smith actually agreed to endorse confederation in principle but, pushed hard by Lieutenant-Governor Gordon to accept the Quebec resolutions themselves, he resigned. Robert Wilmot formed a government, but the anti-confederates remained strong enough to defeat it and force a second general election.

The second New Brunswick election was a great confederation triumph – and a famously corrupt campaign. Thousands of dollars of "the needful" (as Tilley called it in a letter to Macdonald) flowed in from Canada to support the confederates, and thousands more came from Halifax to shore up the anti-confederates. Anyone whose vote was for sale could expect a record price. Sober analysis of the Quebec resolutions was almost drowned out by Fenian scares, accusations of disloyalty, and appeals to religious bigotry and crude self-interest. But, after a year in which confederation had been the dominant issue of New Brunswick politics, the voters endorsed it even more decisively than they had rejected it a year earlier. Having fought two elections in one year on constitutional issues, Leonard

Tilley was back in power. New Brunswick's legislature, quickly recalled for a rare summertime session, endorsed his resolution in favour of confederation thirty-one to eight. Just in case the upheavals had strengthened New Brunswick's hand at the bargaining table, however, the House approved not the Quebec resolutions, but confederation "upon such terms as will secure the rights and interests of New Brunswick."[23]

In barely a year, New Brunswick's voters had twice determined their province's confederation policy. Yet the very completeness of the pro-confederate victory in 1866 encouraged a black legend that democracy had been suborned rather than sustained. Anti-confederates insisted their enemies had bought and bullied the unwilling province into submission. Canadian and British observers, inclined to condescend to hayseed Maritimers – as if money, patronage, and corruption were unknown in their own elections – hardly bothered to contest the accusation. And historians who saw in confederation proof of the need for strong central authority would long be content to emphasize local corruption – as another argument against local autonomy.

But in mid-nineteenth-century Canada, all hard-fought elections spawned corrupt practices. Had the 1866 confederation victory been simply a question of buying votes, Tilley should have been just as able to buy the 1865 election – in which he and confederation had been routed. The issue of union mattered, too. The demonstrated inability of Tilley's rivals to form a coherent anti-confederate program probably did more to sway voters than the infamous sacks of money shipped in by John A. Macdonald.

In 1865 and 1866, Nova Scotia moved almost in lockstep with New Brunswick – but without the elections. In New Brunswick, elected members and the electorate had opposed confederation early in 1865. Members and voters had both changed their mind early in 1866. The second election proved it, but that election had only been

held because the elected members had already lost their anti-confederate passion. In Nova Scotia, the voters went unconsulted, but
the legislature, which had been unwilling to endorse confederation
in 1865, also began to have second thoughts.

Opposition remained strong, but Nova Scotian opposition to
confederation was neither total nor unconditional. Anyone intrigued
by the possibilities of railways and manufacturing saw promise in
union, and the coal and mineral regions of eastern Nova Scotia
looked forward to gaining a large national market. John Bourinot, a
conservative member from Cape Breton Island, famous in the House
for complaining of Halifax's neglect of his region, began to argue
that the island might do better in confederation than it had as part
of Nova Scotia. Even the argument from pride cut both ways. When
Tupper declared, "No intelligent man . . . can feel for a moment that,
as a Canadian, he does not occupy a far higher status than he ever
could have done as a New Brunswicker, a Prince Edward Islander,
or a Nova Scotian," he infuriated many Nova Scotians – but he
touched latent ambition in many others.[24]

Even among the "antis," opposition was not absolute. Joseph
Howe himself had often preached the benefits of colonial union –
though not on the terms proposed at Quebec – and many Nova
Scotians held out for better terms rather than no union at all. As
early as the summer of 1865, William Annand had floated the idea
of another confederation conference at which the Quebec terms
could be improved. Howe swiftly reined him in, but the idea that
the Quebec terms should be improved rather than rejected continued to float in the Nova Scotia air. As in New Brunswick, the failure
of anti-confederates to construct a plausible alternative to confederation influenced Nova Scotia opinion, and the Fenian raids provoked alarms about defence and suspicions about loyalty which the
confederates exploited skilfully.

In the spring of 1866, Charles Tupper gambled that a majority of
Nova Scotian legislators might now be ready to approve a union resolution, even against the still-hostile mood in the province. William

Miller, a liberal member from Cape Breton, who until then had condemned the Quebec terms, gave him the opportunity. Two years earlier, when the Charlottetown conference had first been proposed, Miller had declared that Maritime union should be a side issue and confederation the real objective. It was the terms negotiated at Quebec, not confederation itself, he had opposed in 1865. In the spring of 1866, his unionist convictions reasserted themselves. On April 3, Miller declared in the legislature that he would support the government if it would propose sending delegates to London to help the British government draft a confederation bill with terms more favourable than the Quebec resolutions. A week later, on April 10, Tupper staked his government on a bill that called on the British Parliament to pass "a scheme of union which will effectually ensure just provision for the rights and interests of this province."[25]

The Nova Scotia legislature began its second confederation debate. It lasted only a week, and the official record of the speeches, now a very rare volume, has been almost entirely neglected, but it was a remarkable airing of two urgent issues. Did the House believe confederation was the right answer in Nova Scotia's present circumstances? And did the House have the right to decide the issue, or did confederation have to go to the people?

The debate began with a slanging match between William Annand and Charles Tupper, in which each impugned the other's honesty and patriotism. Tupper was more skilful than Annand at this kind of parliamentary abuse. He provoked Annand into making unprovable accusations, then forced him into embarrassing withdrawals. But neither's performance was edifying. "Webster says a traitor is one who deceives, who betrays his country, and I say, taking that sense, there are men here who deserve the appellation," said Annand. "I think the honourable member is safe in making that assertion," Tupper retorted. It was other members from both sides who gradually gave the debate substance.[26]

On confederation itself, the "antis" conceded from the start that they were now a minority in the House. They also proved themselves as disunited as Albert Smith's New Brunswick government had been. Few of them bothered to support Annand's implausible proposal that, instead of joining confederation, Nova Scotia should abandon its own independent status to federate with Britain and gain a couple of seats at Westminster. "Canadians are disloyal," cried anti-confederate John Locke in a speech rich with Nova Scotian patriotism, but pro-confederates cited the frankly pro-American speeches of other anti-confederates, notably Yarmouth member William Townsend, who said, "The interests of the people do not lie in the direction of connection with Canada. . . . My people would prefer annexation to confederation." Archibald McLelan gave vigorous economic arguments for an autonomous Nova Scotia, but Tupper's cabinet colleague James McDonald was just as passionate about the economic benefits of confederation. "Give us the population of four million that union will give, strike down the hostile tariffs, . . . and you will have the market for manufactures that is now wanting. Why should not Halifax be the Boston of British North America?"[27]

On one issue there was consensus. Few speakers on either side took seriously the "better terms" proposed in the resolution. McLelan quoted George-Étienne Cartier giving his word of honour to the Canadian House that the British Parliament would vote on a confederation bill in which there were no significant changes from the Quebec terms. McLelan declared that this showed that the terms were most unlikely to be improved. But confederation supporter Adams Archibald readily agreed with him. Archibald said he was perfectly willing to vote for accepting better terms in case they somehow became available, but he said he expected none, and he still stood four-square behind the Quebec resolutions he had helped to negotiate. William Miller, who had raised the hope of "better terms," also declared union itself was the essential thing. Improvements should be made, said his seconder, Samuel Macdonell, but "union we must have!" By the end of the debate, it was evident that most members would accept the Quebec terms if they had to, and the speaker had to restrain the rambunctious pro-confederate spectators who cheered them on from the legislative gallery.[28]

The hardest-fought issue in the debate, however, was not confederation itself. It was who should decide on confederation.

The question of an appeal to the people had been around from the start. In January 1865 (when he still believed the Nova Scotia legislature would never endorse confederation), Joseph Howe had insisted that confederation could not be made legitimate "without submitting it fairly to the constituencies." Eighteen months later, he stuck to that opinion. "Let the people accept it or reject it. If they voluntarily abandon their institutions, they will sincerely support the union." Howe had a hundred objections to the Quebec resolutions, but the one that resonated most deeply was his insistence that only a general election could settle confederation in Nova Scotia.[29]

In late-twentieth-century Canada, when legislative debate had been reduced to ceremonial posturing and "elections" and "democracy" were assumed to be synonymous, it was hard to imagine that anyone would debate this point. Charles Tupper's willingness to see confederation ratified without an election has consistently been portrayed as unjustifiable and all too typical of the anti-democratic instincts of the confederation-makers.

Tupper, however, argued that it was Howe and not himself who was unorthodox. Indeed, demanding an appeal to the people against the verdict of the legislature was out of character for Howe. As Nova Scotia's premier in 1861, Howe had declared, "If Parliament were to be dissolved whenever a gentleman changed sides, or a discontented constituency petitioned, free institutions would become an endless distraction, and no man would ever dare to deliberate or run the risk of being convinced."[30]

Later that year, he had been even more explicit. "It is the undoubted principle of the British constitution that a member once returned by a constituency has to consider what he believes to be the interests of the whole country and not the simple wishes of his own constituency. He is elected a representative and not a delegate.... [His constituents] have no right . . . to expect that the royal prerogative [to hold a new election] should be used because they are dissatisfied with the choice they have made." In 1862, when the colonial secretary informed the colonies that Britain would want the colonial legislatures to approve any plan for colonial union, Premier Howe never suggested a popular mandate would be required.[31]

Tupper happily cited these views when Howe, seeing his side losing in the legislature, redoubled his demands for an appeal to the people. Indeed, Howe was being inconsistent – but he was not simply being opportunistic. Since his first newspapering efforts in the 1820s, Joseph Howe had lived by the belief that, by educating and informing the people, he would eventually see Nova Scotia reaping "a harvest of reform." In decades of writing, speaking, and travelling, he had built a remarkable rapport with Nova Scotia's people. He was not boasting when he said he had linked his "name and daily labours with the household thoughts and fireside amusements of our countrymen, aye, and countrywomen. . . . We stepped across their thresholds, mingled in their social duties, went with them to the woods . . . or the fields." Howe loved and trusted his fellow Nova Scotians and had a deep faith in their wisdom. The principles of representative government were sacred to him, but the Quebec resolutions touched the national existence of his beloved Nova Scotia. Howe could not bear to see his people's wishes unconsulted – particularly when they seemed to match his own.[32]

In the legislative debate, the anti-confederates fought desperately for an election or a plebiscite. William Annand pleaded with the pro-confederate majority in the House to consider the nine-tenths of Nova Scotians who he said were against it. "You must carry with you the sentiment of the people," he said. "Even if they are entirely wrong, you must defer to their prejudices and give them time to consider the subject calmly and deliberately." Dr. Brown of South Kings accused Tupper of stifling the people to save the rulers of the people. "We may establish what will be called a union, but will it be a union of the heart?" asked Mr. Blackwood. "The people are able to judge."[33]

Far from wilting under these charges, confederation supporters confronted them. Attorney-General William Henry was one of several who challenged the nine-tenths estimate. Many Nova Scotians objected to the Quebec resolutions, he acknowledged, but some wanted to change a few details, some wanted legislative union, and some wanted other modifications. "Nearly all," he insisted, "wish union of some shape or other." Several other members predicted public opinion was shifting to confederation, and they noted the meagre numbers of signatures on the petitions anti-confederates were presenting almost daily. Mostly, however, the pro-confederate members argued precedent and principle against their opponents' insistence that the people and not the legislature must decide. They challenged anti-confederates to support their demand with a single example from the history of representative government or British constitutionalism. "Opponents of union are not in a situation to challenge the right of this house in the exercise of its legitimate functions," said Tupper bluntly. There would be an election only if the House showed it wanted one – by rejecting the government's confederation bill.[34]

Many members proudly proclaimed the rights of parliamentary representatives. Liberal Hiram Blanchard declared that a free people settled its affairs through its deliberative assemblies. "The people were here present by their representatives," he said. Attorney-General Henry backed him up: "The constitutional doctrine prevails that the gentlemen within these walls represent the feelings of their constituents." Members, said Alexander McFarlane, were "untrammeled by pledges and free to exercise an independent judgment on the question." Several members from both sides declared they had come to exercise a representative's duty to make up their own minds. To say they should do otherwise, said James McDonald, was to strike at "one of the highest privileges of this legislature."[35]

These arguments prevailed. Stewart Campbell's motion to postpone a decision until the people had voted was soundly defeated. After hours of passionate appeals, the House passed Tupper's

better-terms resolution on April 18, at two-thirty in the morning,
with thirty-one in favour and nineteen opposed. Four of Tupper's
conservatives remained opposed, but Archibald and four other
reformers supported confederation. Confederation had its ratification in Nova Scotia. A year later, when the final text of the British
North America Act was published, and it was clear no "better terms"
had been offered, the anti-confederates made one last attempt to have
confederation put to the people. With growing confidence, the House
voted it down with a two-thirds majority on the confederation side.

In April 1866 and again in March 1867, Nova Scotia ratified confederation because a substantial majority of its elected representatives wanted it so. Had they all been bought?

Anti-confederates insisted they had been. They launched a
furious assault against the "thirty-one traitors" who had sold their
country "at black midnight," and their accusation would long endure.
William Miller, who did receive a Senate appointment in 1867 (along
with Robert Dickey, John Bourinot, and other crucial vote-chang-
ers), sued the *Morning Chronicle* in 1874 over the allegation that he
had sold his vote. Even Tupper's respectful 1916 biographer declared,
"it is not necessary to dwell upon the methods by which Dr. Tupper
got a majority, [or] to affirm that all these influences were addressed
solely to the judgment and conscience of the men with whom he
was dealing." Many historians of confederation have readily
assumed that, given the endemic corruption of Maritime politics,
bribery must have determined the outcome.[36]

Closer analysis, however, has demolished the notion that confederation was ratified in Nova Scotia simply by bribery. Money and
promises were important in elections, but corruption was not the
basis of Maritime politics in the 1860s. Whatever side they were on,
politicians hoped to be remembered if their side won, but, on an
issue as divisive as confederation, no one could predict the winning
side at the time Miller and the others decided the need for union
overrode their dislike of the Quebec terms. Resistance to – and

support for – the confederation plan in Atlantic Canada was rooted in both principles and practicalities. "No external pressure," wrote the Maritime historian Phillip Buckner in an influential 1990 re-examination of the issue, "could have compelled the Maritimes to join confederation if, ultimately, they had not been convinced that it was in their own interests to do so." It seems fair to conclude that the Nova Scotia legislature ratified confederation in Nova Scotia because most of its members believed it was the right decision and that it was their right and duty to decide.[37]

Their answer was orthodox by all the rules of parliamentary representation. The pro-confederates stood on solid ground when they insisted they were following the legitimate working of representative government under a parliamentary constitution. John A. Macdonald had said it eloquently in the Canadian House, in arguing down an election proposal from ultra-tory John Hillyard Cameron, "If we do not represent the people of Canada, we have no right to be here. But if we do represent them, we have a right to see for them, to think for them, to act for them; we have the right to go to the foot of the throne and declare that we believe it to be for the peace, order, and good government of Canada to form of these provinces one empire, presenting an unbroken and undaunted front to every foe, and if we do not think we have this right, we are unworthy of the commission we have received from the people of Canada."[38]

To an uncomprehending twentieth century, where legislators bound by party discipline never made up their own minds and parliamentary debate was an empty ritual, such arguments came down like light from a dead star. But the legislators of Nova Scotia, in a parliamentary regime where the government really was responsible to a legislature capable of independent decisions, had hold of a great truth.

But Joseph Howe had hold of a great truth, too. Confederation had raised a problem without a simple answer: at what point does a representative mandate give way to the need to seek the verdict of the people? Even if it were not the doom of Nova Scotia (as one anti-confederate cried out in the House), confederation proposed a fundamental and controversial change in the province's circumstances. Whatever the justifications, Tupper had erred in treating it as if it were a problem to be managed by parliamentary debate and parliamentary guile. His eighteen months of manoeuvres towards a pro-confederate vote in the House may have had constitutional sanction, but to many Nova Scotia voters they looked like trickery more than honest representation.

Nova Scotia finally went to the polls two months after confederation, in September 1867. The results were spectacular. Tupper was the only supporter of confederation among nineteen members sent to Ottawa. In the simultaneous provincial election, anti-confederates took thirty-six of the thirty-eight seats. Nova Scotia was perhaps not quite so unanimous against confederation as those results suggested. Many races had been closely contested, and confederates held up to 40 per cent of the popular vote. But almost every single member who had argued so firmly that it was up to the legislature to decide on confederation lost his seat.

What the elections may have shown most conclusively was Nova Scotian voters' resentment at not being entrusted with the decision on confederation. With the decision kept out of their hands until it was too late to make a difference, the voters eagerly punished those who had prevented them from expressing an opinion. The members who ratified confederation in Nova Scotia discovered that they had committed the rarest act of independent legislators. They had committed political suicide for the sake of a measure in which they believed.

In the years that followed, many of the "antis" of Nova Scotia and New Brunswick accommodated themselves to confederation. "Better terms" had been the demand of many Nova Scotians, and better terms for Nova Scotia became a political necessity immediately after confederation. "There is no use crying peace when there is no peace," was Leonard Tilley's perceptive advice, and Prime Minister Macdonald finally agreed to negotiate better financial terms for Nova Scotia. In doing so, Macdonald won over Joseph Howe himself. Shelving his argument that only the mandate of a general election could legitimize the union, Howe joined the federal cabinet in 1868.

William Annand, who became premier of Nova Scotia, continued to resist confederation, even at the price of estrangement from Howe, his lifelong mentor. As Howe had pointed out, however, the anti-confederates could have paralysed Nova Scotia's government in 1867 by refusing to accept office under a lieutenant-governor appointed by Ottawa. Premier Annand was not willing to go that far. Other prominent anti-confederates made their own accommodations. Archibald McLelan went to Ottawa with Howe in 1868 and received a seat in the federal cabinet. Thomas Killam, one of the Yarmouth members who had considered annexation to the United States better than confederation, became one of many Nova Scotian anti-confederates who, like the Quebec *rouges*, eventually became provincial-rights federalists. Killam eventually became a Ottawa cabinet minister, as did his Shelburne counterpart Thomas Coffin.

But the resentment persisted. The historian Peter Waite reports the case of Nova Scotia Premier W. S. Fielding, who, when visiting London in 1892, refused to attend a dinner marking the twenty-fifth anniversary of confederation. Even Fielding was a future federal cabinet minister, but the conviction that Nova Scotians had became Canadians against their will remained deeply rooted and hard to refute. The thirty-one Nova Scotian legislators of April 18, 1866, may have been perfectly sincere, but their action was remembered, and execrated, as an effort to negate the will of the province. Charles Tupper would remain a political powerhouse for another thirty years, and he was always able to cite sound constitutional arguments for the course he had taken in 1866, but on this issue his reputation would never entirely recover. By avoiding an election, he had left a permanent scar over Nova Scotia's entry into confederation.

Leonard Tilley had not actually wanted either of New Brunswick's two confederation elections, but he had been more willing than Tupper to let the voters sort out the crisis of confederation. Tilley accepted a shattering defeat in one election and organized an even larger triumph in the second. He got little credit for his willingness to accept the verdict of the voters – New Brunswick's black legend, that Tilley bought the second election, matched Nova Scotia's black legend, that the legislature's decision to hold no elections was a crime. But in the aftermath, it was Tupper's statesmanship, not Tilley's, that was questionable. Tilley could claim that, in New Brunswick at least, the union had been negotiated by a bipartisan delegation, ratified by an independent legislature, and endorsed by the voters as well. Tupper only had two out of three.*

Historians and political scientists have consistently declared that the makers of confederation were not democrats. They can cite George-Étienne Cartier telling the Canadian legislature that the Americans had "founded federation for the purpose of carrying out democracy on this continent, but we . . . felt convinced that purely democratic institutions could not be conducive to the peace and prosperity of nations." They can cite George Brown condemning universal male suffrage as "evil" or John A. Macdonald urging the Quebec conference to lay the groundwork for "constitutional liberty *as opposed to democracy.*"[39]

These seem like damning admissions. If they meant nineteenth-century Canadian politicians were an autocratic élite who hated and feared the electorate and concocted schemes to exempt themselves from responsibility, then we should dismiss the legacy of confederation. But Cartier, who equated "democracy" to "mob rule," fought every election of his political career under conditions not far short

---

* Tupper and Tilley might point out that the Meech Lake accord and other late-twentieth-century constitutional initiatives met none of these criteria.

of universal male suffrage. He never held a safe seat and lost almost as many elections as he won. George Brown, insisting on the principle of a propertied franchise, meant one which in practice provided votes for virtually all men. When Macdonald spoke against "democracy," he usually evoked the spectre of a president elected by a simple majority and thereafter wielding despotic authority unfettered by legislative review.

The "constitutional liberty" that Macdonald, and in effect all the confederation-makers, distinguished from "democracy," was itself hardly distinguishable from what we would call parliamentary democracy. As the experience of Leonard Tilley shows, the governments of the confederation-makers were closely answerable to broadly representative and strikingly independent legislatures, whose members' seats depended on the votes of a broad, lively, and engaged electorate. To dismiss that is to dismiss parliamentary democracy itself.

Leonard Tilley may never have been so dull as he seemed. At the London conference, one flash of personality preserved for him some place in Canadian memory. When an appropriate title and motto were being sought for the new nation, Tilley, the devout evangelical, remembered a phrase that had probably popped up in his Bible-reading during the years of debate: "And he shall have dominion from sea even unto sea and from the river to the ends of the earth." Tilley's contribution of the title "dominion" was not recorded until fifty years after confederation, but the story seems to be authentic.[40]

Three months after confederation, after five years as a widower, Tilley married Alice Chipman, the daughter of a friend. They were married almost thirty years. Several of his children migrated westward in the new nation. His son Harrison Tilley became a prominent Anglican clergyman in Toronto, and his daughters migrated to Manitoba and British Columbia. Tilley himself, the reformer drifting towards the centre, became a powerful minister in John A. Macdonald's Ottawa, probably the most skilful finance minister Canada had in the nineteenth century. Still a believer in state activism, he drafted much of the "National Policy" that became

Macdonald's flagship in his later years. He ended his career in the 1890s as lieutenant-governor of New Brunswick, and Macdonald kept him in the office when he was too ill to discharge it very effectively, because the Tilleys could not live on his pension. Money had flowed generously in New Brunswick politics throughout his career, but apparently not into Leonard Tilley's pocket.

CHAPTER SEVEN

The Leadership Secrets of
John A. Macdonald

~

ROBERT DICKEY, the lawyer and businessman from Charles
Tupper's home town of Amherst, had been government leader
in Nova Scotia's upper house and a delegate to both the Charlottetown and Quebec conferences. Despite his ties to Premier Tupper,
he began to dissent from the developing consensus at Quebec. He
supported the unpopular arguments of New Brunswick's Edward
Chandler for a loose federation, in which sovereignty would be
vested in the individual provinces, and he complained that the
financial terms proposed at Quebec would bankrupt Nova Scotia.
After he came home, Dickey released a letter declaring he had "had
the misfortune to differ from my colleagues in several important
details of the scheme."[1] Since he still hoped to see union take place,
Dickey was glad to see Tupper's better-terms resolution ratified in
1866. But his apostasy had been a boon to the anti-confederate
cause, and it was not forgotten by the winners. Dickey was dropped
from the delegation Nova Scotia sent to London for the final confederation talks later that year.

Dickey did became a senator in 1867, but he nursed ambitions of becoming lieutenant-governor of Nova Scotia. The appointment was the prime minister's to give, but Sir John A. Macdonald was dubious. He brought up Dickey's disloyalty during the confederation crisis. Was Dickey really a loyal supporter and worthy of this reward?

Dickey assured the leader he was indeed a loyal party man. "I shall support you whenever I think you are right," he said.

"Anyone will support me when they think I am right," Macdonald retorted. "What I want is a man that will support me when I am *wrong*!" Dickey never did become a lieutenant-governor. Macdonald offered the office as bait to recruit one anti-confederate Nova Scotian after another.[2]

This may not be entirely a true story. Dickey is only one of the putative victims in the versions that exist. But who was the butt of Macdonald's wit hardly matters; this has always been a story about Macdonald's ruthless pragmatism in the use of men and of power. It adapts easily into a criticism of the cynical amorality of his era. Poor Dickey, who had been absolutely right about Nova Scotia's need for better terms, was first denied the opportunity to help negotiate improvements, and later punished for being right too soon.

The misfortunes of Robert Dickey offer more than a lesson in cynicism about nineteenth-century politics. They point directly to the fundamentals of political leadership in the confederation era. And leadership inevitably brings to the fore John A. Macdonald, so far a minor figure in this account of the making of confederation.

Macdonald is the only politician of his era who still conveys a personal image – so much so that it has become hard to see his peers around him. His vivid personality still half-attracts, half-appals, much as it did in his own time. (Weeks into a progressive drunk, Macdonald once horrified an election crowd by vomiting on the stage when he got up to answer his opponent – and then won them back by saying, "I don't know how it is, but every time I hear Mr. Jones speak it turns my stomach.") When Macdonald died, Wilfrid Laurier, his successor as the master of Canadian politics, declared that the life of Sir John A. Macdonald "is the history of Canada." More than a century later, that verdict, at least on the history of confederation, remains widely held.[3]

Laurier also said that "for the supreme art of governing men, Sir John Macdonald was gifted as few men in any land or any age were gifted." To get at the leadership secrets of John A. Macdonald and their place in the constitution-making of the 1860s, there is a useful guide in a late-nineteenth-century connoisseur of political leadership, the English journalist Walter Bagehot.

In the years when confederation was being made, Walter Bagehot was a supremely fortunate young man in his late thirties. He came from a family that was very much part of the educated, well-to-do "ten thousand" who were Britain's acknowledged rulers. He had been to university. He had been called to the bar but never had to practise. For several years he held the kind of position in his father's bank that was influential and well-paid but left him abundant time to write literary essays. He had run for Parliament and been not much disappointed to lose. Wonderfully connected and well-informed, he was an amused and sceptical observer of politics and finance. He was blissfully married to an MP's daughter, and in 1861 his father-in-law had secured him his dream job: editing the family's magazine, the *Economist*.

The *Economist* had been founded to preach free trade and individual responsibility. Bagehot shared that faith, but he gave it an infusion of wit and style and tough-minded political analysis. The weekly editorial "leaders" he wrote for the *Economist* for the rest of his life made the magazine what it has been ever since: literate and ruthless at once, the pragmatic adviser to people who had money and power and intended to keep them and use them effectively.

Immersed in the politics, society, and finance of London, the *Economist* naturally saw the colonies as distant and not very interesting; Bagehot could hardly help but condescend. Still, running the Empire was part of the Englishman's burden, so the *Economist* kept an eye on colonial developments. Starting in 1864, Bagehot offered his readers concise opinions on all the key developments in British North America's debates on confederation. Just weeks after the formation of the coalition at Quebec, Bagehot declared that "the latest intelligence from Canada is the most important which has reached us for some years," though he credited the initiative to a "Mr. Browne." In the following months his spelling improved. By the end of the year, the *Economist* had published four very enthusiastic Bagehot articles on the progress made at Charlottetown and Quebec and the constitution that was being proposed. "The object of the American colonists, it is clear from every clause of the resolutions, is to form a nation," he declared after perusing the Quebec resolutions in November 1864.[4]

In the months when he was taking occasional note of the confederation conferences, Bagehot was also busy writing *The English Constitution*, the book which, along with the *Economist*, preserved his fame. Published in book form in the year of confederation, *The English Constitution* was remarkably vivid for a text in political theory. In *The English Constitution* was born the aphorism that to scrutinize the working of monarchy too closely is to "let in daylight upon magic." In Queen Victoria's heyday, it cheerfully characterized the Queen and her son the Prince of Wales as "a retired widow and an unemployed youth."[5] Elsewhere Bagehot deflated a not-quite-first-rank English politician with the throwaway line, "If he were a horse, no one would buy him." Throughout, *The English Constitution* was remarkable for its clear-eyed, unsentimental look at how power and leadership were exercised in a constitutional monarchy.

The English Constitution was also remarkable for its class prejudice. Racial minorities and women were largely beneath Bagehot's gaze, but he was deeply alarmed by the prospect that Britain might grant voting rights to men of classes lower than his own. Bagehot thought himself principled in his insistence that the elected representatives of the people of Britain must continue to be chosen by "the ten thousand." "The masses of England are not fit for an elective government," he wrote in *The English Constitution*, and it was simply self-defeating to give votes to people incompetent to choose their representatives intelligently. "The working classes contribute almost nothing to our corporate public opinion and therefore the fact of their want of influence in parliament does not impair the coincidence of parliament with public opinion," said *The English Constitution*.[6]

Despite his deep hostility to votes for working people, Bagehot faintly regretted the impossibility of universal manhood suffrage in Britain. By keeping its population uneducated and in servitude, he wrote, Britain had left them too ignorant to vote. But he conceded that a literate population, one with widespread prosperity and relative social equality, could enjoy universal suffrage without disaster. This thought inspired the only reference to British North America in *The English Constitution*: "Where there is not honest poverty, where education is diffused, and political intelligence is common, it is easy for the mass of the people to elect a fair government. The idea is roughly realized in the North American colonies of England." For a moment, Bagehot had grasped that British North America had both representative government on the British model and voting rights far broader than those existing in Britain itself.[7]

Bagehot was too much an Englishman of "the ten thousand" to pursue this thought. It was impossible, really, to consider whether the English constitution might be working better in a colony than at home. Phrases from *The English Constitution* appeared in Bagehot's articles on confederation, but Canadian processes did not influence *The English Constitution*. To tease out how Bagehot's analysis of power and leadership might apply in a society of (by English standards) social equality, general education, and widespread participation in civil society – in British North America, that is – we have to read Canadian evidence into the Bagehot description.

The key to *The English Constitution* was Bagehot's dictum that all constitutions have "dignified" and "efficient" parts. "Dignified" parts could command respect and wield influence – as the monarch did, and the great aristocrats of Britain often did – but real power to govern lay with the "efficient" parts. The analyst's challenge, said Bagehot, was always to discern which was which. In *The English Constitution*, Bagehot used this device to cut through the blather about the British government. He dismissed lofty notions of Britain's "balanced" constitution of monarchy, Lords, and Commons. "A republic has insinuated itself beneath the folds of a monarchy," Bagehot declared; Britain had become a state where the people's representatives were supreme. In phrases he might have borrowed from George Brown's analysis of the Canadian Senate, Bagehot argued that, in a parliamentary government with two chambers, only the more representative one could have real power. Accordingly, the House of Lords had become "a subordinate assembly," dignified but without significant political power, and sure to be defeated in any serious confrontation with the Commons. Bagehot saw at once it would be the same with the Canadian Senate proposed in the Quebec resolutions, and he approved.[8]

That left only the House of Commons, but Bagehot was just as hard on the Commons. The Commons, he said, was "a big meeting," and everyone knows nothing ever gets done in a big meeting. Practical leadership lay with the cabinet, which put structure into the Commons's discussions and, even more, with the prime minister who dominated the cabinet. The rise of cabinet government had brought about what Bagehot called "the close union, the near complete fusion, of the executive and legislative powers" in the English constitution. Britain was "a disguised republic" whose "president" was the prime minister, said Bagehot. Under the constitution proposed by the Quebec conference, he saw, Canada would be the same.[9]

The British constitution, however, provided a control upon the prime minister and his cabinet. An elected president, like the American one, held office for a fixed term of office. Whether or not he proved right for the job, those who made him president had no power over him between elections. A prime minister, however, was a president whose electoral college was the House of Commons, and the Commons was always ready and able to throw out a prime minister at a moment's notice. In Bagehot's view, the power to make and destroy governments, not the power to make laws, was the root of the Commons's power. In *The English Constitution*, he imagined a prime minister dismissing the often-heard suggestion that the Commons had not been accomplishing much lately. It had kept *him* in office, the prime minister might say, and keeping or dismissing him was its only really important job. Without the power to sustain or to dismiss the prime minister and cabinet, said Bagehot, the House would become merely a debating society. It would join the dignified parts of the constitution, while power migrated elsewhere.

Prime-ministerial leadership was the crucial subject of *The English Constitution*. Bagehot had learned about leadership by close observation of British politics, and he illustrated his book with lively references to many British statesmen, now mostly forgotten. Neither his book nor his editorials on confederation mentioned John A. Macdonald.* But if he could have put aside his essential Englishness, Walter Bagehot might have found in Macdonald the perfect illustration for his case about leadership. What Bagehot set out in a book-length argument about parliamentary leadership, John A. Macdonald had always known in his fingertips.

For Donald Creighton, John A. Macdonald *was* confederation, Creighton left behind the widely held impression that confederation was made by Macdonald; that Cartier, Brown, various docile Maritimers, some bankers and railway magnates, and the Colonial Office all followed the lead of his visionary statesmanship. In fact, Macdonald was at first a minor figure in the making of confederation,

---

* The two men met at least once. During a dinner party in England, probably after confederation, Macdonald remarked that he thought Bagehot the best authority on the British constitution. "I am glad to hear you say that," said his left-hand neighbour, "for I am Mr Bagehot." Given what is known of both men, it is quite possible that Macdonald knew exactly who his left-hand neighbour was, and that Bagehot would have guessed that he knew.

even though he was joint leader of the government of the Province of Canada. In the spring of 1864, he opposed George Brown's federalism initiatives, standing among a handful of doubters, virtually all the rest of whom became anti-confederates. It was George-Étienne Cartier's sudden willingness to deal with Brown which brought in Macdonald. In June 1864, the parties led by Cartier and Brown were the essential elements in the confederation coalition. Macdonald, leading only a handful of Upper Canadian politicians, had to follow Cartier or be dropped from power. Walter Bagehot, watching from faraway London, had it essentially right when he wrote of the new Canadian coalition as the Cartier–Brown ministry.

Once Macdonald came in, however, he came in strongly. He had spent a decade learning how to cobble together majorities in the fractious Canadian legislature, where he personally rarely had more than a handful of loyal followers. Whatever his coolness to federalism as a political philosophy, he quickly saw that the complicated regional, ethnic, and ideological coalitions of a confederated Canada would give wonderful scope for the skills he had been honing. He could dominate the politics of a confederated Canada as he would never dominate a union of Brown's Ontario and Cartier's Quebec. First, however, he began to dominate the conferences.

Macdonald signed the guest book at Charlottetown as "cabinet maker." It was a fair self-assessment. Bagehot could have recognized in the Macdonald of the 1860s all the skills of a superb parliamentary manager. From long experience – he had first been elected in 1844, at the age of twenty-nine – Macdonald knew both the business of campaigning and the machinery of public administration. As a lawyer and attorney-general, he knew the legalities, precedents, and principles of legislative and constitutional drafting. But parliamentary leadership – putting together majorities – was personal, and personal skills were where Macdonald shone.

When David Thompson, an unrepentant old Clear Grit farmer-politician, returned to the Commons from a long illness in the 1880s, he got brief, distracted greetings from his party leaders, Edward

Blake, a fastidious Toronto barrister, and Richard Cartwright, a dour and rigid Kingston financier. "Davey, old man," cried John A. Macdonald a moment later, "I'm glad to see you back." Thompson had never in his life voted with Macdonald, but he admitted it went increasingly against the grain that his enemy was better company than his friends.[10]

Dozens of similar stories testify to Macdonald's persuasive charm. One perceptive Macdonald historian, Keith Johnson, has suggested there was a dark, cold, private soul beneath Macdonald's affable surface.[11] But if his humour and sociability were mostly on the surface, they sufficed. Joseph Rymal, another Grit rival, marvelled over Macdonald's ability to cajole his supporters in the House. "Good or bad, able or unable, weak or strong, he wraps them around his finger as you would a thread. I have seen some of them . . . denounce the measures of government and say 'Well, I can't go that!' and still I have known these gentlemen long enough to believe that they would go it, and after there was a caucus they did go it every time."[12]

A colleague put it more admiringly. "Often when council was perplexed and you had made things smooth and plain, I have thought, 'There are wheels in that man that have never been moved yet,'" said Archibald McLelan, the one-time anti-confederate from Nova Scotia who sat in Macdonald's cabinets for years.[13] For his part, Macdonald once joked that his ideal cabinet would be "all highly respectable parties whom I could send to the penitentiary if I wished." * Lacking that power, he used his persuasive powers instead.[14]

Macdonald was good on the floor of the House, too. He was not notably an orator. George Brown, who took pride in his own oratorical powers, dismissed Macdonald's prepared address in the confederation debates as "a very poor speech for such an occasion."[15]

---

* Beset by ministerial scandals late in his career, Macdonald was unamused by the opposition member who suggested his cabinet now met all his requirements – except the respectability.

Macdonald did better later in the debate, and in a crisis he could speak strongly. With his government on the line in 1873, he rallied wavering members with a passionate five-hour argument, fuelled by gin delivered in water glasses from three different supporters, each unaware of what the others were doing. But his great strength was the casually wielded authority, which, Bagehot argued, parliaments preferred over oratory. During the confederation debates, an opposition member tried to score a point by tying Macdonald to some procedure in a long-ago debate over a temperance bill. "I don't remember," confessed Macdonald. "I don't generally go for temperance bills," and in the laughter that followed, the House acknowledged his authority to ignore the challenge.[16]

It was not all laughter, however. "The great leaders of parliament . . . all have a certain firmness," Bagehot thought, and Macdonald, with a majority at his back, used it without compunction, whether in the double shuffle of 1858 or in ruthlessly closing down the confederation debate when the New Brunswick election disaster seemed likely to give the Canadian anti-confederates an opening.[17]

It was the same with smaller matters. Joseph Rymal had been a popular and respected member of Parliament for decades when Macdonald gerrymandered his seat out of existence in 1885. "Mr Speaker, I am not made of such material that I can beg for justice," declared Rymal. "I can ask you in a plain and manly way to do what is right, but I cannot fawn and be a sycophant." Macdonald was unmoved, and his majority voted Rymal's seat into oblivion.[18]

For the photography session that recorded the delegates at Charlottetown, Macdonald crouched casually at the centre of a long line of standing delegates, so the eye was drawn to him automatically. Robert Harris gave him the same central status in the Quebec painting. But despite his important role in both conferences, Macdonald was one delegate among many, and not always in the majority. He had never fought for federalism and did not conceal his conviction that "absolute power . . . must reside somewhere" (the phrase is Bagehot's and appears in The English Constitution and several times in the *Economist*'s articles on confederation, but the opinion was also Macdonald's). That view was problematical, given the necessity of a federal union. Cartier, Langevin, and the Maritimers had frequently to rein in their colleague's acknowledged preference for legislative union.

At Quebec, Macdonald argued adroitly and yielded grudgingly, but what made him indispensable was his organizing. Approval by Prince Edward Island had never been essential to confederation, and by the end of the conference George Coles was undisguisedly hostile, yet Mercy Coles's diary shows Macdonald working relentlessly on the Coles family – and charming Mercy, if not her father. To all the delegates and hangers-on, he seemed endlessly present, more sociable than Brown, more comfortable than Cartier, more at home than any of the Maritimers, more authoritative than anyone.

It seems to have been the same behind the closed doors of the conference. Macdonald did not control even his own delegation, but his skills as an organizer had free rein. Though he made several of the major formal presentations, these were probably less important than his ability to work the room and identify potential coalitions, to draft compromise texts during the recesses, and come back to coax the resisters. For Macdonald, Quebec meant the exercise of these skills in endless days at the conference table, in late nights of resolution-drafting and early-morning briefings, and even in the midst of the lavish hospitality of the conference. His Sunday-night dinner with the Coles family, at which he entertained Mercy Coles "with any amount of small talk," was almost certainly aimed at softening her father's stand on the eve of Oliver Mowat's crucial resolution on provincial powers, and Mercy noted that, at 9:00 p.m., their guest was off to another political soirée. Although Macdonald vanished into a gin bottle as soon as the confederation tour reached Ottawa, even straitlaced Mercy Coles understood.[19]

In the thirty months between Quebec and the official proclamation of confederation by Queen Victoria, Macdonald's letterbooks show him relentlessly keeping in touch even with minor players. He maintained a correspondence with Colonel Gray of Prince Edward Island even when the confederation cause was clearly hopeless there. (One letter concluded, "Pray present my best regards to those of the Prince Edward Island delegation whom you may meet, always excepting Messrs Palmer and Coles," who by then were implacably opposed to confederation. He and Gray even discussed the merits of asking Britain to legislate the Island into confederation against its will.) Macdonald did more than write letters. During the second New Brunswick election, when Leonard Tilley sent his plea for "forty or fifty thousand of the needful" to Macdonald, Macdonald arranged the cash transfer quickly and discreetly.[20]

When confederation had been ratified by the legislatures at Quebec, Fredericton, and Halifax, one more gathering of convention delegates remained to be held. The delegates moved on to London, this time to supervise the rewriting of Quebec's seventy-two resolutions into the formal language of a bill for the British Houses of Parliament. The Colonial Office had already assigned legal draftsmen, and the colonial delegates were expected merely to consult on matters of detail and nuance.

Politics had intervened, however. As we have seen, delegates from Nova Scotia and New Brunswick headed for London under instruction to try for "better terms," and by mid-1866, those from Canada also had a wish list. The Quebec resolutions had made education a provincial responsibility, but sectarian schools that had official status at the time of confederation would be able to seek federal protection against provincial moves to limit or abolish them. The Canadian legislature had failed to pass promised legislation to provide Protestant schools of Quebec the official status they sought. At the insistence of Alexander Galt, the Canadian delegation intended to insert the protection (for minority schools in both Quebec and Ontario) directly into the constitution, despite all the assurances that the Quebec terms were a treaty that could not be amended.

Lord Carnarvon, the young English politician who had just become colonial secretary, wanted nothing to do with colonial controversies. He "proposed" that the delegates should confer among themselves and "narrow their points of difference, if any, to the smallest compass, so as to leave as little as possible for my decision and arbitration." The London conference proceeded, therefore, in two stages. In December 1866, the delegates negotiated among themselves, working steadily through all seventy-two of the Quebec resolutions. Then the bill itself was drafted early in the new year.[21]

Reopening the Quebec resolutions was no easy matter. The delegates' debates at London seem to have been as fractious and free-flowing as at Quebec. Even the degree to which the delegates were free to debate was contentious. Peter Mitchell argued that New Brunswick's "better terms" resolution empowered them to reopen only the handful of matters that he considered particularly contentious. Charles Fisher, no less dedicated a confederate, retorted that he had heard forty different objections in New Brunswick. He intended to follow his own judgement.[22]

John W. Ritchie, the new Nova Scotia delegate who had replaced Robert Dickey, said plaintively that "in the legislature of Nova Scotia it was understood that all matters should be entirely open." William Howland and William McDougall of Upper Canada, however, declared the Canadian legislature had approved the Quebec resolutions and nothing else; their hands were tied, they said. Somehow, the conference permitted this exchange to be summed up with the extraordinarily vague statement that "We are quite free to discuss points as if they were open, although we may be bound to adhere to the Quebec scheme."[23]

Hector Langevin had been to both Charlottetown and Quebec and had gone on the tours afterwards. But his letters home suggest how little friendship confederation had created among the men most responsible for making it. McDougall was ambitious but lazy, Langevin wrote, Galt was impetuous and too easily swayed, and Tupper made enemies by his bluntness. Howland was second-rate, and Fisher was mediocre. Among the Maritimers, only Leonard Tilley really impressed him, though he liked McCully and expressed some respect for one or two others. The delegates attended many banquets in London, but the one really sociable moment shared by most of them came in February, when John A. Macdonald married Agnes Bernard, the sister of his long-time aide and conference secretary, Hewitt Bernard.[24]

Langevin considered himself and Cartier as ranking number two and three among the delegates, but even Cartier now struck him as unreliable. He spent too much time in London's great society, Langevin thought, leaving Langevin to cover all the details. Langevin spent the conference fearful that, while Cartier caroused, the English and the English Canadians were still plotting to turn confederation into a tightly centralized legislative union. "This has been settled," he thundered when the form of the Senate came up for debate among the colonial delegates. He wrote to his family that he had to remain constantly alert and combative to protect the interest of French Canada. "I go my own way. When someone wants to block me, I show my teeth and I bite if I have to." Langevin was determined that the bill would remain substantially unchanged from what had been negotiated at Quebec. "I have had to see it, review it, review it again, and then re-review it whenever anyone else has put their hand to it."[25]

Even in the midst of his distrust and frustration, Langevin did not doubt who was number one among the delegates. "Macdonald is a sly fox," he wrote. "He is well briefed, subtle, adroit, and popular. He is *the man* of the conference." At the London conference, there were no more neutral chairmen. The delegates unanimously agreed Macdonald should have the job. Later, as Macdonald increasingly took precedence over him, Cartier would grouse that it was only the accident of being the cabinet member with the greatest seniority that gave Macdonald the right to chair the conference, but political longevity was only one of Macdonald's qualifications. The delegates had accepted "the ablest man in the province," in Governor General Monck's phrase, as first among equals.[26]

A week into the conference, Macdonald managed to set his hotel room on fire after falling asleep while reading by candlelight, but he carried on despite his serious burns. He steered the discussions, summed up the consensus, and wrote up the resolutions with Hewitt Bernard. The colonists' meetings wound up on December 24, 1866. Macdonald formally delivered them to the Colonial Office on Christmas Day. Several significant details had been added, but the bargain struck at Quebec two years earlier remained essentially unchanged.

Drafting the bill itself proved as difficult as the negotiations among the colonial delegates. The Colonial Office staff, always dubious about federalism and seemingly oblivious to the hard-fought trade-offs the colonial politicians had made, drafted a bill that recklessly breached the Quebec agreements in order to reinforce the central power. With Langevin hotly suspicious that Macdonald was colluding with the English to further his own centralizing aims, Macdonald supervised the final tense exchanges between the delegates and the British officials. Redrafting went on through January and February of 1867. In the end, the British North America bill went to Parliament with minimal alterations in the colonials' plan.*

The pressures, deadlines, tensions, and suspicions of the London sessions were a nearly perfect environment for the exercise of Macdonald's parliamentary skills. Frederic Rogers, the deputy minister at the Colonial Office and a man not much inclined to defer to colonials, paid Macdonald a tribute that was also an acute accounting of his abilities. "Macdonald was the ruling genius and spokesman," Rogers said of the London conferences,

---

* The main change the British insisted on was a provision to further weaken the Senate by authorizing the cabinet to appoint extra senators in the event of a deadlock between Senate and House. The delegates consented, but insisted that the extra appointments must preserve the sectional balances they had established. This power was never needed until 1990, when extra senators were appointed to pass the Goods and Services Tax bill, which had been rejected by an opposition-dominated Senate.

and I was very much struck by his powers of management and adroitness. The French delegates were keenly on the watch for anything which weakened their securities; on the contrary, the Nova Scotia and New Brunswick delegates were very jealous of concessions to the *arrière* province; while one main stipulation in favour of the French was open to constitutional objections on the part of the home government. Macdonald had to argue the question with the home government on a point on which the slightest divergence from the narrow line already agreed on in Canada was watched for – here by the English, and there by the French – as eager dogs watch a rat hole; a snap on one side might have provoked a snap on the other; and put an end to all the concord. He stated and argued the case with cool, ready fluency, while at the same time you saw that every word was measured, and that while he was making for a point ahead, he was never for a moment unconscious of the rocks among which he had to steer.[27]

When the confederation bill was introduced into Parliament, Walter Bagehot declared his approval in the *Economist*. He thought the new nation should be named "Northland" or "Anglia," instead of "Canada." He wondered why a Senate was necessary at all, and he repeated his doubts about federalism. But he declared it a bill with few defects, one that served a good purpose and deserved all-party support in the British Parliament.[28]

Bagehot's enthusiastic approval reflected the views he had stated in *The English Constitution*, which was just about to be published. He saw in the British North America Act the essence of the English constitution, adapted to Canadian conditions. Indeed, his chief complaints involved attempts to include "dignified" holdovers which he thought unnecessary and ill-suited to Canada – like the monarchy.

But these were quibbles. In Bagehot's view, parliamentary government and presidential government were the pre-eminent alternatives for "government by discussion" – his phrase for the self-government of free peoples. Canadian confederation reassured him that the parliamentary system was not an historical accident unique to Britain. It could indeed be exported to other countries. North America would have more than one form of constitutional liberty from which to choose, said Bagehot, and, as a good free-trader, he was glad to see this competition of alternative modes of government. In the British North America Act, he had foreseen the twentieth-century flourishing of parliamentary government, not only in Britain's settler colonies, but in nations as diverse as India, Ireland, Israel, Jamaica, and Japan.[29]

John A. Macdonald once said that, until confederation, he never knew what it was to govern. Before then, he had held power for a decade, but always insecurely, and usually as a dependent partner. Despite being so late to convert to confederation, he became its earliest and greatest beneficiary, for it launched his remarkable career as a parliamentary prime minister. After the London conference, he was the inevitable choice to form the new nation's first government, and the Crown further marked his pre-eminence with a knighthood – to the fury of Cartier and several other coalition partners, who received lesser honours or none at all.

Canadian politics after 1867 provided a wonderful opportunity for Macdonald's skills as a parliamentary politician. George Brown had left the Canadian coalition in mid-1866 and was eager to restore party politics as soon as possible. But Macdonald, with the levers of power in hand, was steps ahead of him, using the coalition to draw potential rivals into his orbit. Conservative allies like Cartier and Tupper moved readily into national politics, but Macdonald also convinced many of the reformers who had helped define confederation that they had a duty to help run the new country. Nova Scotia's Adams Archibald, New Brunswick's Leonard Tilley, and Ontario's William McDougall helped ensure that Macdonald's "Liberal–

Conservative" party would dominate the first federal Parliament. Brown was left trying to reassemble a reform coalition from disgruntled anti-confederates in Quebec and the Maritimes. In the first federal election, Brown lost to a coalition candidate.

In 1868, Macdonald made perhaps the most extraordinary recruit to his coalition. Joseph Howe was not only a bitter anti-confederate, but also a lifelong reformer and a stern political moralist. When he admitted sadly that there was no future in opposing confederation, it was Tilley of New Brunswick who saw a deal could be made, but it was Macdonald who nailed it down. He happily offered federal funds to Nova Scotia, and in exchange persuaded Howe to join his cabinet. Howe, who had long been seeking a larger stage on which to test his skills, now found it in Ottawa politics, not in the Imperial civil service at London. By recruiting Howe, Macdonald tore the heart out of anti-confederate opposition in Nova Scotia, and strengthened his own party in the process. His Liberal–Conservatives, almost wiped out there in the anti-confederate sweep in 1867, would themselves sweep Nova Scotia in the 1872 election.

Macdonald was proving himself superbly adept at what Bagehot understood as the essential business of a parliamentary leader – putting together parliamentary majorities from the materials at hand, however unlikely. During the confederation debates, Christopher Dunkin had predicted that the great diversity of the new nation would create difficulties in assembling a cabinet backed by a coherent majority. "That cleverest of gentlemen who shall have done this for two or three years running," he said sarcastically, "had better be sent home to teach Lords Palmerston and Derby their political alphabet. The task will be infinitely more difficult than the task these English statesmen find it none too easy to undertake." Cartier bobbed up to say he foresaw no difficulty, but it was Macdonald, not Cartier, who surmounted the very real difficulties for a quarter-century. The first time, he seems to have done it while drunk. On June 23, 1867, a week before the first Canadian cabinet was to take office, Alexander Galt wrote to his wife that Macdonald was "in a constant state of partial intoxication" and the coalition was about to break up. But it did not, and Galt accepted office as minister of finance.[30]

Beneath the recruiting of cabinet colleagues and parliamentary allies, something deeper was going on. Even as he worked to assemble and maintain parliamentary majorities in the way Bagehot would have approved, Macdonald was seeking to build a party system that would free him from endlessly having to coax, cajole, and bully allies and rivals into line behind him. Bagehot could have identified what Macdonald's intention was. In *The English Constitution*, Bagehot described one great threat to parliamentary government. A prime minister could, he feared, became so powerful that he did not have to worry about his parliamentary support. Bagehot illustrated the danger with funny stories of one prime minister describing loyal and naive new backbenchers as "the finest brute votes in Europe," and another leader, confident his caucus would follow him, saying blandly about the problems in a bill he had just introduced: "This is a bad case, an indefensible case. We must apply our majority." But the problem was serious. Instead of being under perpetual review, Bagehot reasoned, a prime minister who was able to dictate to his caucus would be a president, beyond all control for years at a time.[31]

Bagehot saw that, if MPs became more loyal to their party than to their constituents and simply voted as their leader told them to, the Commons would be merely a talking shop. This was one of the reasons he feared universal suffrage. "I can think of nothing more corrupting or worse for a set of poor ignorant people than that two combinations of well-taught and rich men should constantly offer to defer to their decision and compete for the office of executing it." Party caucuses were essential to organize the "big meeting" of parliamentary politics, but Bagehot feared that, if the parties grew too powerful, Parliament would abruptly shift from the efficient to the merely dignified side of the English constitution. There would remain no check on prime ministerial authority.[32]

Powerful parties were only a remote threat to the gentlemanly politics of Bagehot's England of "the ten thousand." Once again, Bagehot
might have seen the future in the colonies, for John A. Macdonald was
already far ahead of the English theorist.

Macdonald excelled at cabinet-making and the construction of
parliamentary caucuses, however temporary and fragile, but presiding over such caucuses was always risky and demanding. There
was always the danger that a Robert Dickey would suddenly decide
his leader was wrong and refuse to vote with him. In fact, a sudden
collapse in parliamentary support had been the almost inevitable
fate of British North American leaders before confederation. The
fight over confederation itself had caused secure majorities to evap-
orate beneath both Charles Tupper and Leonard Tilley in 1865. A
year later, anti-confederates William Annand and Albert Smith
found themselves similarly abandoned. In both Prince Edward
Island and Newfoundland, backbenchers had instructed their governments not to proceed with confederation, and both governments had meekly submitted. Even in 1866, when Leonard Tilley
urged that a hint of Canadian openness to "better terms" would help
him in his struggle to regain power in New Brunswick, Macdonald
and Cartier could not oblige. The backbenchers of Canada East,
said Macdonald, would desert to a man if their leaders deviated
from the deal struck at the Quebec conference. The loyalty of
Quebec's *bleus* had long been exceptional in Canadian politics, yet
Hector Langevin had been terrified that the backbenchers would
desert Cartier if Quebec's public opinion, particularly clerical
opinion, turned against confederation.

It was little different after confederation. In 1873, it was
Macdonald's turn to suffer the defection of a secure majority. After
a hard fight against a fast-rising Liberal Party, Macdonald and his
party had won a fifty-seat majority in the 1872 federal elections.
Then the newspapers published Macdonald's secret telegrams ("I
must have another ten thousand"), which revealed the victory had
been greased by huge cash transfusions Macdonald had received

from the financiers who were to get the contract for the transcontinental railway. The "Pacific scandal" erupted.

With a majority, a late-twentieth-century Macdonald would be immune to parliamentary rebuke, and some unelected ethics commissioner would have to tell him to resign. In 1873, however, governments answered to the House of Commons. Conservative backbenchers, disgusted by the revelations or simply fearful of their constituents' wrath, turned into "loose fish" as the debate raged, and the loose fish soon shoaled towards the opposition. The House decided John A. and his government had become a liability and turned them out of office less than a year after the general election.

When he was tossed from the prime minister's office, Macdonald avoided being dumped by what remained of his own caucus. To general astonishment, the disgraced leader of 1873 led his party back to power in the 1878 federal election. He would not be defeated again. From 1878 to his death in 1891, even as he was growing into the grand old leader of Canadian politics, Macdonald worked incessantly to reduce his vulnerability to the kind of parliamentary rebuke he had suffered in 1873. He did that by building a disciplined and obedient political party, and he did *that* mostly by patronage.

"In the distribution of government patronage, we carry out the true constitutional principle: whenever an office is vacant it belongs to the party supporting the government," Macdonald said unapologetically.[33] As prime minister, he supervised the appointment of station-masters, customs officers, and postal clerks, and he never considered this time wasted. He wanted men in every riding who could be trusted to support the party because they owed it for some office or appointment. He called this kind of politics "the long game." "Depend on it, the long game is the true one," he declared. His franchise bill of 1885 authorized him to appoint a federal revising officer – a loyal party member appointed by patronage – to supervise federal elections in each riding. Not only could he gerrymander the Liberal Joseph Rymal out of the House, but he could also threaten independent-minded backbenchers of his own party. When the bill went through, Macdonald called it "the greatest triumph of my life."[34]

Macdonald was not the only one seeking such triumphs. His old nemesis Oliver Mowat, the Christian statesman, employed the same tools to build a Liberal Party machine in Ontario. "In Ontario there was an ethical line drawn between patronage and corruption," writes S. J. R. Noel, the historian of Mowat's party machine, and Mowat walked the line with a clear conscience. Like Macdonald, Mowat insisted there could be no impropriety in patronage, so long as the appointees were competent. With the help of William Preston, a professional organizer with the wonderful nickname "Hug-the-Machine," Mowat made dozens of Liberal supporters into Ontario government inspectors, agents, trustees, and even rain-gaugers. Faced with temperance demands to control alcohol, Mowat readily agreed that all taverns should be inspected and licensed. The temperance movement was pleased, but so was the party, for every licence inspector appointed was a loyal Grit.[35]

As the parties grew stronger, few candidates could hope any longer to be elected without the support of these loyal party workers and the party machine. The price of that support was loyalty. Soon, says historian Noel, Mowat "had no need to bargain in the lobbies of the legislature with capricious independents and local patrons who would never lend more than their conditional or nominal support to any leader."[36]

Yet even with their machines primed and their caucuses tamed, leaders like Mowat and Macdonald did not enjoy unchallenged authority. Party leadership could still be removed at a moment's notice. In 1880, Alexander Mackenzie, former prime minister and leader of the Liberal opposition in Ottawa, was abruptly replaced when his backbenchers decided they preferred Edward Blake to lead them. In 1896, the Conservative cabinet forced the resignation of Prime Minister Mackenzie Bowell – "a weak, vain, decent old mediocrity," in historian Peter Waite's phrase, which seems to be the kindest thing anyone has said about him – in the hope that Charles Tupper could save them from Wilfrid Laurier's Liberals. But the era of independent members who could topple a government or unseat a leader was waning. Far-sighted leaders were using the party machines to drain the pool of loose fish.

Disciplined party organizations flexed their muscles in all democratic societies late in the nineteenth century. In Britain, Liberal leader William Gladstone invented "the platform" and began to run national campaigns focused on the leader. Soon the British Labour Party demolished the cosy, gentlemanly politics of "the ten thousand" through national campaigns aimed at the masses of working-class voters who had finally been enfranchised. (Walter Bagehot, who died in 1877, was spared from seeing it.) In Canada, Macdonald's "National Policy" platform also directed attention away from local candidates to the party and its leader. It was after Macdonald's death, however, that Canada became unique among parliamentary democracies in the steps it took to reduce the ability of backbenchers to influence their leaders.

In 1919, the Liberal Party, split by the conscription crisis of 1917 and left leaderless by the death of Wilfrid Laurier, turned a policy conference it had planned into a leadership convention. William Lyon Mackenzie King wrapped himself in the mantle of Laurier, won the race, and became the first Canadian party leader chosen by a party convention rather than by the parliamentary caucus. The party hailed the convention that chose Mackenzie King as a great advance over the older method, and every other party followed its example. Since 1919, federal and provincial parties in Canada have chosen their leaders in mass party gatherings.*

---

* It is an odd – and unstudied – coincidence that the power of leadership selection was removed from MPs within a year of women achieving the right to vote and to participate in selecting MPs. Despite their newly won right to vote, women did not participate in the Liberal leadership convention of 1919. Conventions remained deeply hostile to female participation as late as 1976, when (according to her biographer) gender prejudice was a key factor that undermined Flora MacDonald's campaign for the leadership of the Progressive Conservative Party.

Canadians have celebrated leadership conventions as a way to let the people participate directly in government, and the selection process has expanded steadily. Instead of being gatherings of a few hundred, dominated by the party brass, conventions came to involve thousands of delegates choosing among candidates who spent millions of dollars on elaborate media campaigns. In the 1980s, the parties began to abandon conventions themselves in favour of even more broadly based processes, in which a hundred thousand or more party members could cast leadership ballots.

Canadian politicians and analysts have always identified mass membership participation in the choice of party leaders as a triumph of democracy. The cost, barely noticed, was the abrupt loss of what little influence elected members of Parliament still had over their leaders. Mackenzie King understood his new authority perfectly. He never sent his cabinet colleagues to the penitentiary, but he sometimes kept their signed resignation letters on file, and he used one when his defence minister tried to stand up to him in the conscription crisis of 1944. King emphasized to his caucus as often as necessary that, since it could not challenge his leadership, it could not challenge his policies. He represented the party and was answerable to it, not to them, and he controlled his MPs ruthlessly.

Being "answerable" to the party was no great burden to King; the Liberal Party did not meet again in convention until he chose to retire in 1948. King had made "Parliament will decide" his maxim, and he trotted it out whenever he wished to avoid a decision. He knew that, so long as his party won the general elections, Parliament would decide what he told it to. Since the other parties still acted as if Parliament was the essential forum, King's Liberal Party enjoyed remarkable success for a generation. Macdonald would have admired, and envied.

King actually had substantial parliamentary skills and might have prospered as a party leader answerable to caucus. John Diefenbaker was the first Canadian to become a party leader and a prime minister on the strength of a "grass-roots" leadership campaign. Sweeping to the leadership of his party and then the country on the strength of his personal appeal to voters. Diefenbaker soon demonstrated his inability to work within the machinery of parliamentary government. Since his cabinet and caucus had no authority to challenge him, Diefenbaker's party was thrown into years of turmoil when he refused to relinquish the party leadership, even in defeat.

Still, the principle that Canadian party leaders should be immune to parliamentary control survived. In 1988, when the opposition Liberal caucus members in Ottawa had the same kind of dissatisfaction with their leader as their ancestors had felt with Alexander Mackenzie in 1880, a majority of them signed a declaration that John Turner must resign. Unlike Mackenzie, however, Turner could defy the members of Parliament. Claiming "democratic legitimacy," because he had been chosen by a leadership convention, Turner obliged the dissident majority to recant. Turner led his party into the 1988 election and resigned only after the party's defeat.

The independence of Canadian party leaders has been most spectacularly underlined in provincial, rather than national, politics. William Vander Zalm, elected premier of British Columbia soon after winning a leadership convention in 1986, ran an erratic one-man government that alienated many of his cabinet and caucus members, few of whom had wanted him as leader. As he became mired in scandals in 1991 and fell precipitously in the polls, virtually all wanted rid of him. All accepted, however, that Vander Zalm was not answerable to them. They dutifully supported him in office until a conflict-of-interest commissioner (an unelected civil servant personally appointed by the premier) told Vander Zalm he must go. Almost all his party's elected members lost their seats in the election that followed.

By the late twentieth century, it had become understood in Canadian politics that backbenchers were responsible to their leaders, rather than vice versa, even when blind allegiance ensured their imminent defeat. This faith in the leader's unlimited authority was as strong in new "grass-roots" parties as in established ones, and it was accepted in regional blocs as well as national parties. Even the occasional proposals to "strengthen" Parliament, usually by encouraging party leaders to "allow" more "free" votes on matters of limited importance to them, confirmed the absolute power of leaders over their followers' votes. By the time Pierre Trudeau joked that members of Parliament were nobodies fifty yards from the House of Commons, it was unclear why he would invoke the fifty-yard rule.* In the name of participatory democracy, the elected representatives of the Canadian people had become the only individuals in the country without any political opinions of their own.

When general elections in Canada cost $100 million, almost all of it funnelled through the political parties (heavily subsidized by taxpayers), virtually no one could be elected except on the parties' terms, and most proposals to change the system, through proportional representation and "recall" initiatives, for instance, were aimed at weakening individual members even more. In other countries with parliamentary governments, the power of political parties – and their leaders – had also expanded greatly. But from Australia to Japan, and almost everywhere else that the parliamentary system endured, elected representatives still retained a veto over party leadership and party policy.

Bob Hawke launched his career as the most successful prime minister of recent Australian history in 1983 when the Australian Labour Party caucus, worried about its electoral chances, dumped its leader and chose Hawke in a hastily convened meeting on the day the Conservative government called a federal election. Hawke went on to win the election and to dominate Australian politics for a decade. In 1992, however, the caucus that had chosen him decided on the eve of another election that Hawke, the sitting prime minister, had

---

* In *The English Constitution*, Bagehot quoted the comment of a friend elected to a genuinely powerful parliament: "I got into Parliament and before I had taken my seat I had become somebody."[37]

become a liability. Leading the challenge to Hawke was Paul Keating, a rival who had left Hawke's cabinet to contest the leadership from the backbenches. Even though Australia was much less regionally diverse than Canada, Hawke and Keating fought their battle by seeking support from the powerful regional blocs within the Labour Party caucus. Keating won. He replaced Hawke as party leader and prime minister, and defied the polls by leading Labour to an upset majority victory.

In New Zealand, it was policy struggles that fuelled leadership battles. In the 1980s, David Lange's opposition to nuclear testing in the South Pacific made him perhaps the only world-renowned prime minister New Zealand ever had. But as New Zealand's deficit worsened, Lange and his finance minister became embroiled in economic policy disputes. Unable to hold his caucus's support on a matter of fundamental party policy, Lange was bounced from the party leadership and the prime ministership.

The most famous beneficiary *and* victim of caucus control over parliamentary leadership was British Prime Minister Margaret Thatcher. As a woman and as a politician with a combative personality and strong policy views, Thatcher was the kind of candidate who could never have won a leadership convention. Caucus colleagues identified her leadership potential, and their support enabled her to depose an incumbent leader and go on to lead the British Conservative Party to three consecutive election victories. Then, while Thatcher was still at the peak of her influence as a world leader, her caucus dumped her as swiftly and ruthlessly as it had chosen her. By then, the British Labour Party had moved to the Canadian system of letting the party at large select party leaders. Its leader, Neil Kinnock, was described by veteran British political commentator Peter Jenkins as the kind of leader "who could not conceivably have come to the fore" except by leadership convention.[38] Against him, Thatcher's replacement, John Major, won an upset victory.

The crisis that had provoked Britain's Conservative Party caucus to depose a sitting prime minister was a deeply unpopular new tax, the "poll tax." Prime Minister Thatcher had been determined to implement it in defiance of the public mood, even though most of her backbenchers feared it would make their re-election impossible. Deposing Thatcher enabled the backbenchers to kill the poll tax, and enough of them survived the ensuing election to keep the Conservatives in power. Their aim was saving their seats, that is, but the result was that a prime minister with a majority government had been prevented from implementing an unpopular policy.

Almost simultaneously, the Canadian prime minister, Brian Mulroney, introduced his own unpopular taxation measure, the Goods and Services Tax. It, too, helped provoke a disastrous slide in party popularity, but Mulroney's backbenchers understood they had no right to interfere in either policy issues or party leadership. They dutifully voted to impose the new tax. Mulroney retired at a time of his own choosing. His hapless backbenchers, obliged to defend the new tax under a new leader chosen by a leadership convention, suffered annihilation in the 1993 election.

John A. Macdonald was joking – and understood to be joking – when he told Robert Dickey he wanted backbenchers who would support him even when they thought he was wrong. Macdonald would have enjoyed such support, and he worked diligently to bring about a rough approximation of it. But he never lived in an era of absolute party leaders. He was a brilliant parliamentary leader because his prime ministership was always subject, not only to ratification at general elections, but also to constant, critical, informed parliamentary review of a kind his late-twentieth-century successors never had to fear. That is, Macdonald as prime minister was responsible to a parliamentary majority – rather than it being responsible to him.

This reflection on parliamentary leadership in a book about the making of confederation in the 1860s has seemed worthwhile because the changed nature of leadership has constitutional significance.

Despite the late-twentieth-century consensus that confederation was imposed by an undemocratic and anti-democratic élite, confederation in the 1860s was not a prime ministerial measure. It was not a party measure. It was not a cabinet measure. It was, above all, a legislative measure.

In order to woo sceptical, independent-minded legislators, confederation's advocates in 1864 had been obliged to recruit bipartisan delegations. These delegations engaged in heated debates on the way to a consensus they thought might win the support of their legislative colleagues, even though several of the delegates, as well as most of the excluded political factions, continued to dissent. The confederation proposals that emerged at the conferences were vigorously tested in all the legislatures, in debates that were listened to because every legislator was potentially a recruit to either side. "Loose fish" did triumph over party leaders, at least temporarily, in all four Atlantic provinces. They did not in either Canada West or Canada East, but they could have if confederation had not satisfied them, and leaders like Hector Langevin feared that they might.

The ratification of confederation in British North America between 1864 and 1867 was a deeply imperfect process. An electoral system that excluded women for their gender and men for their lack of property was far too narrowly based. Substantial, politically active minorities, such as the Acadians of New Brunswick and the Catholics of several provinces, were shockingly under-represented in the process. Aboriginal nations and racial minorities such as black and Chinese Canadians were almost completely disenfranchised. All parties applied crude and gamy techniques of persuasion to legislators and voters alike, and the system provided few opportunities for redress. No one spoke of a charter of rights.

Nevertheless, amidst the heated battles, the furious allegations, and the deep-rooted opposition that confederation provoked during the 1860s, the Canadian constitution that came into effect on July 1, 1867, had been judged – and finally endorsed – by legislatures of elected representatives who maintained substantial independence from, and ultimately a veto upon, the governments that were responsible to them. Doubts, resentments, and even deep opposition remained. But the process by which the new constitution had been negotiated and ratified had conferred on it a legitimacy that was celebrated by its supporters, acknowledged grudgingly by opponents, and – above all – generally accepted by the Canadian population that would begin to govern itself under it.

Superficially, constitution-makers had things much easier in the 1980s and 1990s. To produce the British North America Act for five small colonies with barely three-and-a-half-million people in the 1860s, thirty-six mutually hostile and politically diverse delegates had to engage in weeks of intense negotiation, and their draft agreement was subjected to two years of vigorous, open-ended, and unpredictable legislative debate. By comparison, the Meech Lake accord of 1987, drafted by lawyers and bureaucrats, required barely a day of discussion by the first ministers – the famous "eleven white men in a room." Slated for ratification by docile legislatures almost entirely subservient to executive control, it was derailed almost by accident. The patriation round of 1981 had been similarly exclusive, and Quebec in particular never accepted the legitimacy of the process, which produced what came to be known as "the Trudeau constitution." The process leading to the Charlottetown accord of 1992 included more public comment, but its final terms were once more a matter of executive decree. The 1992 referendum, in which voters were invited either to ratify the accord or be held liable for the destruction of the country, reflected the widespread belief that "democracy" and "direct democracy" were the same thing – and Parliament largely irrelevant. Though it ignited passionate debate among Canadians, the referendum was a very limited substitute for genuinely representative scrutiny of the terms of the deal.

In the late twentieth century, Canada continued to govern itself through parliamentary forms. But the long quest for more "direct" participation in government had – paradoxically – conferred enormous power upon first ministers. It was not that the politicians sought to be dictators. They submitted to leadership conventions, fought election campaigns, occasionally held referendums, and followed the polls devoutly. But they and their advisors made constitutions in a vacuum, because the only ongoing, effective control upon them – control by legislatures – had largely ceased to operate. Parliament no longer provided a forum in which elected representatives could test and potentially reject executive initiatives. Except for the election-night tallying of which party leader controlled the most seats and would become prime minister, a seat in the Commons had become largely ceremonial. Dignity was not a word much associated with late-twentieth-century Canadian parliaments and parliamentarians, but Walter Bagehot would have said that they had indeed shifted from the efficient to the dignified side of the constitution.

Would John A. Macdonald, that connoisseur of power, have envied the vast freedom conferred upon his successors as prime ministers and premiers? Perhaps not. Macdonald, like all the confederation-makers, had undergone his apprenticeship to politics in the moment when "responsible government" was shiny, fresh, and new. He wielded executive power ruthlessly when he could, and he always sought to maximize it. But in his day, elected legislators had only recently wrested power from unelected, arbitrary executives. They guarded their new responsibility jealously, and they used it both to make or unmake governments and to veto or ratify policies. No policy could achieve legitimacy without their consent. In nineteenth-century Canada, the great convenience of ruling by executive decree was understood to be cancelled out by its lack of legitimacy – as Oliver Mowat demonstrated to Macdonald so convincingly in the fight over the power of disallowance. By the late twentieth century, that understanding had largely been lost.

The wrenching and potentially disastrous inability of the Canadian political system to reform the British North America Act in the late twentieth century has long seemed to be a challenge to draft the right "deal." Assessed from the perspective of the 1860s, it seems more precisely a problem of how to assess and legitimize deals, a problem of parliamentary government.

CHAPTER EIGHT

Nation and Crown

~

THOMAS D'ARCY McGee, who turned forty in 1865, was a small, ugly, charming Irish-Catholic journalist with a complicated past. He had been an Irish rebel who recanted, a patriotic American who grew disillusioned, an anti-clerical who had made his peace with the Catholic Church, a reformer who had gone over to John A. Macdonald, and a teetotaller given to alcoholic binges. (Macdonald once instructed him he would have to quit drinking; the cabinet did not have room for two drunks.) In 1857 he had settled in Montreal, launched a newspaper, and got himself into the legislature. His constituents, Montreal's Irish, were a narrow and not always secure power base, but McGee was funny, quick-witted, and a natural orator. He soon became popular in the House, and a prominent, more than a powerful, figure in Canadian affairs.

McGee was barely off the train from Boston in 1857 when he began advocating federal union, westward expansion, and the nurturing of a national literature for Canada. "A new nationality" became his platform and slogan. McGee had good reason to seek a nation. He despaired of Ireland, was an alien in Britain, and resented

American intolerance of foreigners and Catholics. He was also a journalist, but unlike George Brown, the millionaire publisher of the *Globe*, or Edward Whelan, who was at least solidly established in his Charlottetown newspaper, McGee always scrambled to make a living. The national vision became a valuable stock in trade.

McGee travelled widely in British North America. With help from railway barons who had their own reasons to encourage such visions, he organized intercolonial good-will trips for politicians and public figures. By 1865, he had been to Atlantic Canada seven or eight times, when many Canadians were still asking him, "What kind of people are they?" Though he had never gone west of Canada West, McGee even outlined a plan for a separate province to be set aside for the native nations on the plains of the far North-West. He had begun to imagine a new country where none existed.

It was a vision upon which he launched many articles and speeches. Amid the tension of the confederation debate in the Parliament of the united Canadas early in 1865, McGee was the first speaker to make the House laugh. It was a feat he achieved consistently in that speech and throughout his public career, but he was just as adept at rolling, patriotic oratory. "I see in the not remote distance," he declared in 1860, when there was no serious prospect of British North American union, "one great nationality bound, like the shield of Achilles, by the blue rim of ocean. . . . I see within the ground of that shield the peaks of the western mountains and the crests of the eastern waves." In the confederation debate, he celebrated the beauty of the Canadian land, rejoiced that confederation would elevate "the provincial mind" to nobler contests, and welcomed the advent of "a new and vigorous nationality."[1]

McGee's passionate Canadianism – "not French-Canadian, not British-Canadian, not Irish-Canadian; patriotism rejects the prefix" – disquieted listeners for whom the prefixes defined patriotism. But "a new nationality" had gone into the language. McGee modestly disclaimed sole credit for the phrase (It's always the same, he told the House: "Two people hit upon the same thought, but Shakespeare made use of it first"), but it popped up in many celebratory speeches during the 1860s. Anticipation of a "new nationality" was even written into the Throne Speech that Governor General Lord Monck read to the legislature at Quebec on the eve of the great debate on the Quebec resolutions – inspiring the *rouges*' clever amendment, proclaiming that they were too loyal to want such a thing.

Bleu supporters of the coalition defeated Dorion's amendment, and their unanimity was an early indication that they would not be swayed by attacks on the Quebec resolutions, but they did not much like doing it. McGee defended his phrase, and Macdonald made a point of using "the expression which was sneered at the other evening." But George-Étienne Cartier was careful to say that confederation would create "a political nationality," and he went on to stress that "the idea of unity of races was utopian – it was impossible. Distinctions of this kind would always appear. . . . In our own federation we should have Catholic and Protestant, French, English, Irish and Scotch, and each by his efforts and his success would increase the prosperity and glory of the new confederacy."[2]

Cartier was glad to escape from awkward questions of nationality to the safer ground of monarchy. He celebrated the benefits of monarchical rule and French Canada's love of monarchy. "If they had their institutions, their language, and their religion intact today, it was precisely because of their adherence to the British Crown," he said. Confederation had been made, he said, "with a view of perpetuating the monarchical element. . . . the monarchical principle would form the leading feature." In the Nova Scotia legislature, Charles Tupper said something similar, covering his declaration that the colonies should "advance to a more national position" with assurances that confederation would bind the new nation to the British Crown "by a more indissoluble tie than ever before existed."[3]

McGee, for all his celebration of the Canadian land and the Canadian nationality, took the same stand. "We need in these provinces, we can bear, a large infusion of authority," he said, and he wound up his speech in direct address to Queen Victoria: "Whatsoever charter, in the wisdom of Your Majesty and of your Parliament you give us, we shall loyally obey and fulfill it as long as it is the pleasure of Your Majesty and your successors to maintain the connection between Great Britain and these colonies." Such frankly deferential talk was as common in confederation speeches as talk of the new nationality.[4]

It too had its pitfalls. Confronted with it, Dorion smoothly shifted his line of attack to declare that confederation's advocates were reactionary tories, who "think the hands of the Crown should be strengthened and the influence of the people, if possible, diminished, and this constitution is a specimen of their handiwork." A Halifax newspaper put the same thought more vividly after the Charlottetown conference. When the delegates let their secrets out of the bag, said the *Acadian Recorder*, their constitution would prove to be "a real sleek constitutional, monarchical, unrepublican, aristocratic cat."[5]

This view of confederation – something imposed on cringing colonial Canadians by the reactionary local agents of Imperial dictate – became part of the late-twentieth-century consensus, much more than the confederation-makers' talk of a new nationality. The political scientist Peter Russell opened his survey of Canadian constitutional history, *Constitutional Odyssey*, by quoting a piously deferential Canadian declaration that confederation would "not profess to be derived from the people but would be the constitution provided by the imperial parliament." Taking the statement at face value, Russell identified the 1867 constitution as an Imperial and monarchical imposition. It could not be considered a legitimate beginning for a sovereign community, Russell concluded. Like many theorists and politicians, he declared this failing made the work of the original constitution-makers irrelevant, deserving of the neglect lavished upon it.[6]

Walter Bagehot, who sometimes enjoyed playing the plain journalist taking the mickey out of rarefied theorists, might have enjoyed seizing on lines like these. In parliamentary government, Bagehot had insisted, monarchy was always part of the "dignified," that is, ceremonial side of the constitution. Beneath the trappings of monarchy and aristocracy, which could mislead even the wisest scholars, political power in mid-nineteenth-century Britain, and even more in British North America, was securely in the hands of the representatives of the people. The confederation-makers knew that worshipful addresses to Victoria lent dignity to their business, but they also knew power lay elsewhere. Britain and British North America were disguised republics – in disguise certainly, but certainly republics, if republic meant a government derived from the people.

Bagehot understood as soon as he looked at the Quebec resolutions that the Senate and the governor general were going to be largely powerless in the new Canadian confederation. Dignified for ceremonial purposes they might be, but real power would rest securely in a Canadian House of Commons, elected to represent the Canadian people on a franchise as wide as any then existing in the world. The role of the monarchy was even more illusory. Bagehot did not take seriously the confederation-makers' florid assertions of loyalty and devotion.

In *The English Constitution*, Bagehot had argued that, although the monarchy was integral to British society and tradition, it was not essential to parliamentary government itself. In his confederation editorials, which welcomed the rise of an independent nationality in Canada, he doubted whether Canada needed a monarchy at all. He even suggested that the confederation-makers were not entirely sincere in proposing one. "We are not quite certain this extra and, so to speak, ostentatious display of loyalty was not intended to remove objections which might have been entertained at home," he said of the monarchical clauses of the Quebec resolutions.[7]

Bagehot was wrong to suspect the confederation-makers were insincere about the monarchy. But he would certainly have been right to mock the idea that confederation had been made by Imperial dictate. As late as 1841, Britain had imposed a made-in-London constitution on the mostly unwilling colonists of Upper and Lower

Canada. But in 1862, with responsible government firmly established, the colonial minister informed the colonies that, if they worked out a plan of union, Parliament would pass it. When the colonies took up the offer in 1864, the constitution that emerged was indeed what McGee called it: "a scheme not suggested by others, or imposed upon us, but one the work of ourselves, the creation of our intellect and of our own free, unbiased, and untrammelled will." By "us," he meant the legislatures representing the people of British North America.[8]

The confederation deal hammered out by the British North Americans in conference had appalled most of the British colonial officials involved with it. Lacking parliamentary experience, lieutenant-governors like Gordon of New Brunswick and MacDonell of Nova Scotia never fully grasped the compromises that had produced the Quebec resolutions. When the Colonial Office requested clause-by-clause comments on the resolutions, they responded with contemptuous disapproval, demanding an assertion of central power on virtually every point. Officials in London were frequently just as obtuse about the political realities that made federal union a necessity. Expecting deference, not direction, from colonials, they largely ignored the elaborate division of powers worked out in the Quebec resolutions when they began to draft a text for the British North America bill.[9]

Fortunately, British politicians were more realistic. Colonial Office functionaries could still imagine they were administering an empire in North America, but British politicians understood that trying to intervene in Canadian domestic politics meant responsibility without power. Even on a constitutional measure that required action by the British Parliament, they avoided any policy commitment that was not endorsed by the colonial legislatures themselves. The British government formally accepted the Quebec plan for confederation, not merely as advice, but as "the deliberate judgment of those best qualified to decide upon the subject." Bagehot approved. "It is not, that we know of, the duty of Parliament to see that its colonial allies choose constitutions such as Englishmen approve," he said of the Quebec resolutions (though in this case, he did approve and thought Parliament also would).[10]

When Britain's Liberal government collapsed in mid-1866, the outgoing colonial minister, Edward Cardwell, left two questions for his successor. First, could they draft a confederation bill that would get through Parliament quietly, without partisan division? More important, if the staff could draft such a bill, would the provinces accept the text? "This is of cardinal importance," emphasized Cardwell about the second point. His Conservative successor, the thirty-five-year-old aristocrat Lord Carnarvon, agreed. Like his officials, he thought power in the new state ought to be centralized at Ottawa as much as possible. But he understood changes in that direction were possible "only with the acquiescence of the delegates . . . this must depend upon them." Both ministers overruled their advisers to endorse the colonials' choices. When Governor MacDonell of Nova Scotia proved intransigent, he was transferred to Hong Kong, glad to be off to a colony where he could actually wield power. Gordon of New Brunswick held his job only by shelving his doubts about confederation.[11]

George Brown, who went to Britain after the Quebec conference to sound out British reaction, wrote back to John A. Macdonald that the British government might criticize a few details of the seventy-two resolutions, but only for the sake of appearances. "I do not doubt that if we insist on it, they will put through the scheme just as we ask it." Canadian politicians of the 1860s may have been more polite than Pierre Trudeau, who suggested that, since his patriation package had been ratified in Canada, the British Parliament should hold its nose and pass it. But British and Canadian politicians agreed in the 1860s that the political relationship was much the same.[12]

The bill drafted early in 1867 sailed through the Lords and Commons. Britain had been looking forward to British North American union for years, and there was no party division over its terms. This proved fortunate, since the British government was close to collapse in bitter debates about expanding the franchise, and no contentious measure could have passed. Lord Carnarvon, indeed, resigned from cabinet early in March 1867 to protest a bill that would give British men voting rights approaching those long enjoyed by men in British North America, but a new minister shepherded his confederation bill through to the final vote on March 12. Queen Victoria granted the royal assent to the British North America Act on March 29, 1867.

The confederation bill passed so speedily that some of its makers were discomfited. They noticed that even a measure concerning dog licences, introduced in the Commons after second reading of the British North America Act, provoked livelier debate. Macdonald later complained that confederation was treated like "a private bill uniting two or three English parishes," but he would not have tolerated changes to his bill, and British MPs were unlikely to waste time simply dignifying the passage of a bill when their only function was to approve it.[13]

Parliament's refusal to heed the Nova Scotian anti-confederates permanently disillusioned Joseph Howe about British Imperial guardianship of small colonies like his, and his associate William Garvie fumed about the measure being rushed through with lazy contempt. But even sympathetic British politicians agreed that the British Parliament had, as Carnarvon said, no business considering private petitions asking it to overrule the Nova Scotia legislature. In any case, most Britons thought they were creating a union in which Howe's dissidents were an insignificant minority. Bagehot dismissed Nova Scotian opposition with the cool disdain of someone at the centre of a centralized state. Nova Scotia's dissidents, he said, "must perforce give way. For purposes like these, the four provinces . . . must be taken to be one, and in that view the federation has been voted in . . . by 3,800,000 to 200,000. No plebiscitum has ever been more free or more decisive." The discontented Nova Scotians, he said, "must now content themselves like the discontented Scotch, by using the new resources the loss of their isolation will assure them."

Successful Canadian politicians, already learning about regional sensitivities in a federal state, would have been unlikely to express such a view so bluntly.*

British leaders accepted that they would be obliged to protect British North America if it were threatened, but they were ready to consider granting Canada outright independence if the colonists insisted on it. The confederation-makers, however, were so absolutely sincere in desiring both a monarchy and continued ties to Britain that British observers were struck by the "excessive timidity" with which British North America advanced toward its inevitable independence. Political independence and the "new nationality" somehow lived in harmony with monarchical deference.

They did so because the politicians who negotiated the Quebec resolutions were determined to preserve the pomp and dignity of a constitution modelled on Britain's – and equally determined that having one would not fetter their actions. Bagehot's distinction between the dignified and efficient aspects of parliamentary government had not entered the vocabulary of politics in 1864, but the concept was no mystery to the seasoned parliamentarians who gathered at Quebec. Once they established that the efficient (that is, the power-wielding) parts of confederation were securely in parliamentary hands, they could see nothing but benefits in the dignified aspects Britain could provide in abundance. They were eager to remain loyal subjects of Queen Victoria's Empire, even when there was no pressure on them to remain, even when some in Britain thought they should be striking out on their own.

The confederation-makers of the 1860s had many reasons to avoid challenging the new nation's place in the old Empire, and also one hard, realistic, positive reason to embrace the Empire. In the

---

* Ontario's Richard Cartwright once complained of having to listen to the demands of "half a dozen small provinces" – when Canada had only seven provinces. But that attitude helps suggest why Cartwright was never very successful, beyond Ontario at least.

1860s, Canada needed Britain, needed it much more than Britain needed Canada. Canadian development depended on British capital, often supported by British government guarantees. Canadian exports depended on access to British markets, assisted by Britain's maternal attitude. Above all, Canada was a small nation sharing a large continent with a huge neighbour, and that meant it needed to shelter under both the military force and the diplomatic influence that only Britain could provide.

D'Arcy McGee caught this sense in his confederation speech. There had always been a desire among the Americans for expansion, he said, "and the inexorable law of democratic existence" in the United States seemed to require appeasing that desire. "They coveted Florida, and seized it; they coveted Louisiana, and purchased it; they coveted Texas, and stole it, and then they picked a quarrel with Mexico, which ended by their getting California. They sometimes pretend to despise these colonies as prizes beneath their ambition; but had we not had the strong arm of England over us, we should not now have had a separate existence." If you seek reasons for confederation under the Crown, he had said earlier, look to the embattled valleys of Virginia, "and you will find reasons as thick as blackberries."[14]

Confederation should have given McGee scope to develop his entwined themes of nation and Empire. Though he was elected to the first House of Commons, he preferred the power of the pen over an uncertain future in politics, and Macdonald promised him a civil-service sinecure from which he could write on Canadian history and literature. But McGee's insistence, even in Ireland itself, that the Irish must abandon republican violence in favour of a constitutional solution modelled on Canada's, had made enemies. Ten months after confederation, Irish terrorists stalked him as he left a late-night session of Parliament and shot him dead at the door of his rooming house on Sparks Street. McGee's death, coming just months after that of Ned Whelan, the other gifted writer among the makers of confederation, ended the likelihood that any of them would write a substantial account of it from the inside.

The Fenian raids into British North America during 1866 had strengthened McGee's argument that the Canadian nation needed the British Empire to resist the American threat. Confederation's propagandists had exploited the raids to the hilt. But the American threat went far beyond the comic-opera Fenian attacks or even the more disquieting, but still unlikely, danger of an American invasion. In the Quebec resolutions, the confederation-makers had proclaimed their ambition to annex the North-West, incorporate British Columbia, and build a transcontinental nation. To become practical possibilities, all those ambitions required American acquiescence and British support.

Just two years after confederation, it was British military muscle that would enable Canada to put armed force behind its negotiations with Louis Riel and the provisional government of Red River over Manitoba's entry into confederation. W. L. Morton, the most geopolitically sensitive of confederation's historians, long ago identified the bargain being made when Britain withdrew its Canadian garrisons in 1871. Britain was using confederation to disclaim a military presence in North America, confirming that it – and Canada – would not challenge American pre-eminence on the continent. On those terms, the Americans accepted the existence of a transcontinental Canada. It was a subtle enough bargain, with British disengagement as a bargaining chip to offer in exchange for American agreement not to seek the whole continent. Canada's unilateral abandonment of the British alliance would not have strengthened its position in negotiation with its neighbour.

If Canada had somehow been cut loose from Britain's Empire in 1867, it might indeed have survived. With good fortune and American restraint, it might even have achieved its westward expansion. Bagehot breezily concluded in 1867 that, if Canada became wholly independent, merely twenty years of growth would render it able to stand on its own feet, impervious to any American military threat. With or without British support, capital would have come, export markets would have been found. Canada would have developed foreign policies, armed forces, and other attributes of sovereignty merely at a more accelerated pace than it actually did.

But Canadian leaders had to contemplate those twenty years. No Canadian leader was willing to ask Britain to cut ties that would have been cut upon request. In the 1860s, Canada wanted the symbols of monarchy and Empire not least because it urgently needed the benefits of alliance with the most powerful state in the world. In 1864, when he was arguing that the colonies must unite to defend themselves better, George-Étienne Cartier said it was a good question whether Britain would fight to help Canada, and a few years later a British statesman doubted whether the colonials would ever fight for Britain in a European war. In fact, the British did accept that, if Canada needed protection, national honour would compel a British response, even at the risk of a nightmare war with the United States. By 1918, sixty thousand Canadian war graves proved the commitment cut both ways, but in the 1860s, Canada needed that alliance far more than Britain did.

There was no debate about monarchy and Empire in the 1860s, because there were almost no voices arguing against them. Financially, economically, politically, culturally, militarily, London was the capital of the world in the mid-nineteenth century, even more than Washington and New York were in the late twentieth. Even Antoine-Aimé Dorion and George-Étienne Cartier could speak unselfconsciously of "home" when they spoke of England. Joseph Howe in his anti-confederate phase did his best to suggest Nova Scotians were choosing between "London under the dominion of John Bull" and "Ottawa under the dominion of Jack Frost," but the confederation-makers assiduously avoided forcing such a choice. Instead, Charles Tupper cited the Maritime provinces' chronic lack of influence in London to prove that "if these comparatively small countries are to have any future whatever in connection with the Crown of England, it must be found in a consolidation of all British North America." [15]

The alliance with Britain, so tangible, so "efficient," in the 1860s, had by the mid-twentieth century dwindled to nothing but dignified traditions. There had been a moment around 1900 when English-Canadian "Imperial federationists" aspired to share in running the British Empire, but Britain's long decline from Imperial might gradually took away most of the benefits the Imperial alliance had offered Canada in 1860 or 1900. Canada and Britain had clearly grown into foreign countries. Incorporating another country's monarchy in its constitution was vastly more anomalous in the 1990s than it had been in the 1860s.

As Walter Bagehot grasped, and the experience of many nations has shown, parliamentary democracy thrives without monarchy. In Canada, an elected governor general, holding the same limited powers as the appointed one, would be more legitimate both in the exercise of those powers in a constitutional emergency and as a Canadian symbol around which the meaning of Canadian nationality could continue to be debated. The inability of modern constitutional negotiators to discuss the head of state surely indicated their inability to respond to Canada's actual situation. A constitutional process that imitated the 1860s by including representatives of all shades of political opinion and by giving them time to debate the issues would surely find that issue arising, among many others. A constitutional process that debated such issues would gain legitimacy whatever it decided.

The monarchy helped the confederation-makers to bypass potentially awkward issues of the "nationality" of the societies being joined by the British North America Act. Nationalism was one of the defining concepts of the nineteenth century, but allegiance to monarchy allowed McGee to boast of a nation even as Cartier and Langevin emphasized that confederation did not require a single tribal nationality. Allegiance, however, was sharply separated from the exercise of sovereign power. Before and after 1867, the confederation-makers consistently identified the legislatures elected by the people as the legitimate source of political authority. Cartier carefully called that "political nationality," and no threat to the French-Canadian nation he represented, but McGee could still frame the question of national allegiance in terms that resonated with men from whom "manliness" was always a vital touchstone. "For what do good men fight?" he asked the legislature. "When I hear our young men say as proudly 'our federation' or 'our country' or 'our kingdom,' as the young men of other countries do, speaking of their own, then I shall have less apprehension for the result of whatever trials the future may have in store for us." [16]

On the eve of July 1, 1867, George Brown sat in the *Globe* offices in Toronto, back in his favourite role, writing for the newspaper. They were finishing the Dominion Day edition, and Brown wanted the front page for a long article. Maurice Careless captured the scene in his biography. He evoked Brown scribbling relentlessly through the hot night, sweating and gulping down pitchers of water and steadily handing out pages for the typesetters. He continued to write as the harassed night foreman warned that the mail train that would deliver the paper to eastern Ontario would soon be leaving. But the deadline for the eastern mail was missed, and then for the western mail, too. Then "Mr. Brown, all the mails are lost," but Brown kept demanding a little more time. He ignored the pealing church bells at midnight, and he ignored the roar of artillery at dawn. Early in the morning, celebrating crowds gathered on King Street for a copy of the historic edition, and Brown was still writing. Finally, about seven in the morning, Brown declared, "There's the last of it." He handed over the final sheet of a nine-thousand-word history of confederation and went home to bed. [17]

Careless's evocation of the article's creation is wonderful, but Brown's article was really rather dull. Loaded down with a conventional recital of history back to John Cabot, and with reams of unlikely economic statistics, this account by one of the insiders said almost nothing insightful about the way confederation was actually made. Even in its time, it must have been neglected in favour of the *Globe*'s descriptions of how Toronto would celebrate July first: the fireworks, the bonfires, the parades, the boat excursions, the roasting on Church Street of an immense ox purchased by public subscription from a Yorkville farmer, "the new farce 'Dominion Day'" opening at the Royal Lyceum, even the grand balloon ascension hoped for at Queen's Park ("if arrangements can be consummated with parties in New York"). Brown's only really vivid line in the whole historical article was his opening, in which he offered that stirring and ambiguous phrase, "We hail the birthday of a new nationality."

Brown's true voice, the roar of the passionate politician, rang out more truly in the accompanying editorial. With the first federal election to be held later that summer, he warned with ungrammatical passion that "the only danger that threatens us is lest the same men who have so long misgoverned us, should continue to misgovern us still."

These same men were just about to remove Brown from active politics. A year before, he had left the coalition government he had helped create in 1864. Brown had plunged back into partisan politics, intending to make his Ontario reformers the core of a pan-Canadian Liberal Party to sweep John A. Macdonald permanently from office. Macdonald, however, had already drawn many of Brown's natural allies into his own coalition. Brown was no longer exactly "the impossible man," but John A. Macdonald was making it impossible for him to hold on to political power. The Liberals would be badly defeated in the summer elections of 1867, and Brown himself would lose to a Conservative, Thomas Gibbs, who drew many reform votes to the confederation candidate. Brown never sat in the Canadian House of Commons he had done so much to bring into being. He would only go to Ottawa when a later Liberal leader appointed him to the Senate, which Brown had helped to ensure would never wield serious political power.

Brown was not too sorry to be out. He preferred journalism to politics and crusades over intrigues. If political success required honing the political adroitness that John A. Macdonald had, it was a price Brown was not willing, and probably unable, to pay.

When Brown and Macdonald were both dead, a wrangle continued among their partisans as to which was the true father of confederation. "Some inspired historians of Canada insist on referring to Macdonald as the father of confederation. He, who tried to prevent it until the last ring of the bell. To George Brown and to George Brown alone belongs the title," insisted W. T. R. Preston, Oliver Mowat's indispensable "Hug-the-Machine," in his 1927 memoir *My Generation of Politicians and Politics*.[18]

The "inspired" historian who provoked Preston to sarcasm may have been Macdonald's first biographer, Sir Joseph Pope. As a ten-year-old, Pope had watched his father, William Henry Pope, organizing the Charlottetown conference. He grew up to be John A.'s personal secretary and keeper of the Macdonald flame. In *The Memoirs of John A. Macdonald*, which he published upon Macdonald's death, Pope dismissed Brown as a merely sectional leader. Smugly, he quoted Macdonald's patronizing view of his rival: "He deserves the credit of joining with me; he and his party gave me that assistance in Parliament that enabled us to carry confederation."[19]

This battle to identify a single hero in the confederation wars was renewed by two Toronto history professors in the 1950s. Donald Creighton relentlessly championed John A. Macdonald ("The day was his, if it was anybody's," was Creighton's take on July 1, 1867) and Maurice Careless insisted there was also a place for George Brown, "the real initiator of confederation." Later, there were ghostly echoes of the search for a father in the debates of the 1980s that set "the Trudeau constitution" against "the Mulroney deal."

Concerning the 1860s, however, the quest for a father has always been misguided. The brilliance of the 1860s process was the way it permitted a George Brown to make a fundamental contribution to constitution-making, even as it kept him from executive authority. The confederation process let Brown, and much-less-prominent delegates, and even ordinary representatives like those who changed their minds in Nova Scotia and New Brunswick, assert their aims and contribute their ideas without ever achieving unrivalled power. This was the success of a parliamentary process rather than a leader-driven, quasi-presidential one.

A clue to the success of the confederation-makers was inadvertently given in 1865 by one of their most incisive critics. Tearing the Quebec resolutions apart in the legislature at Quebec, Christopher Dunkin seized on some damaging statement made in New Brunswick by George Hatheway, "one of the gentlemen who took part in the negotiations."

"Mr. Hatheway was not here at all," shouted D'Arcy McGee across the floor.

Dunkin was unabashed. "I acknowledge I have not burdened my memory with an exact list of the thirty-three gentlemen who took part in the conference," he said.[20]

Far from being an insult to them or a comment on Canadians' amnesiac attitude to history, the anonymity, even in their own time, of most of the makers of confederation suggests a crucial ingredient of the constitutional achievement of the 1860s. The constitution-making of the 1860s drew in relatively minor figures from almost every political faction, several of whom dissented from the agreement their meetings reached. Their agreement was then reviewed by rather independent legislatures – four out of five of which at first declined to endorse it. The confederation-makers would have done well to have been more broadly representative, and their confederation might have been received more warmly had they seated even more political factions around the table. Still, their achievement should not be minimized.

In the 1990s, it was impossible for a regional or sectional representative, whether from the West, from Quebec, or from any class or ethnic bloc, to influence constitutional matters without becoming a first minister – or perhaps the head of a separate state. Yet a constitution for the twenty-first century would probably require, not eleven first ministers, but several times the thirty-six delegates of the 1860s in order to match the degree of inclusiveness they achieved. The efficient secret of Canada's parliamentary government in the 1860s was its ability to incorporate in constitution-making even those it kept from power. It was an idea the 1860s were lucky to have and the 1990s desperately lacked.

POSTSCRIPT

If We Had a Parliamentary Democracy . . .

~

I DID NOT THINK I was nostalgic for the 1860s. But I finished this book about the making of confederation in the spring of 1997, when a federal election campaign was dominating the news. Against that spectacle, I could not help envying some aspects of the politics of British North America in the era of confederation.

During the campaign leading to the election of June 2, 1997, television coverage focused almost exclusively on the party leaders. They jetted about the country, seeking photogenic backdrops against which to strike poses and to deliver the sound bites by which advertising managers hoped to gain a point or two in the polls. I was glad when it was over.

In the west Toronto constituency where I live, the winner was a first-time candidate, a Liberal. She seemed able and energetic and well-meaning, as, indeed, did many candidates around the country. But, like all the other candidates in all the parties, she offered nothing but blind support of her leader. Though we had made her a member of Parliament and a member of the government caucus, it seemed understood that she could do nothing to represent us, or even to assert her own convictions. Should the re-elected government decide to bulldoze a square mile at the centre of our constituency to build a nuclear waste disposal facility, her duty would be to tell us that it might be unfortunate but it had to be done. Should she resist that assignment, she would suffer the fate of the member for a neighbouring riding, John Nunziata, expelled from his caucus and his party for voting against a party measure. Nunziata won re-election on June 2, defeating an official candidate personally designated by the party leader. But as an "independent," Nunziata would be as unable to influence policy as he had been as a docile member of caucus. The government's majority was small (and had been won with only 35 per cent of the vote), but unconditional support from its backbenchers would keep the government beyond control of Parliament and the voters for another four years.

After the election, many Canadians seemed to find it difficult to credit that in these ways one of the world's great democracies chose among leaders who seemed little more than media images. Indeed, the election seemed to have strengthened many Canadians' loathing for the whole political and constitutional tradition of their country. In the weeks after the election, demands for fundamental change, even for the immediate creation of "the republic of Canada," floated through opinion columns and talk shows.

These pleas all started from the assumption that parliamentary democracy was the root of the problem. As ex-MP James Gillies put it in his post-election plea for establishing an American-style republic, a system "designed for a small, relatively non-industrialized unitary state" may have been appropriate in the élitist and anti-democratic day of confederation, but was simply out of date in modern, sophisticated times like ours. In the summer of 1997, that kind of contempt for the Canadian political tradition was a rarely challenged proposition.[1]

In those circumstances, I wondered if it was simply perverse to be offering a book that gave close and often respectful attention to the ways responsible government and parliamentary democracy had

made possible the constitution-making of the 1860s. Yet the 1860s
suggest powerfully that the problem of the 1990s lies less with parliamentary government than with the fact that it has largely ceased
to function in Canada. When the election was over, what seemed
missing from Canadian politics was that dead, and dismissed, and
derided concept from Victorian textbooks, responsible government.

In the middle of the nineteenth century, responsible government
meant that the survival of the prime minister and his cabinet depended, day by day, on the verdict of a vigilant Parliament. Members of
Parliament were chosen by, close to, and dependent on (for those
times) a broadly based and well-informed electorate. Contemplating
the results of the election of 1997, I found myself wishing we lived
under conditions more like those.

If parliamentary democracy functioned in Canada, the future of
Prime Minister Jean Chrétien would depend on the Liberal Party
caucus. It was widely expected after the 1997 election that Chrétien
would not lead his party in the next election. But it was also understood that his retirement would come entirely at his own choice and
he would determine the timing. Neither the Liberal caucus, nor the
party at large, nor the voting public, would wield any notable
influence on the decision. In a functioning parliamentary democracy, however, Prime Minister Chrétien's leadership – and the choice
of his successor – would lie in the hands of the caucus of elected
parliamentarians. They would assess it constantly – according to
their own political calculations, according to the interests of their
constituents, perhaps even according to the needs of the country. The
same would apply to the leadership of Mr. Manning, M. Duceppe,
and all the other party leaders. If the 301 men and women whom
Canadians elected in June 1997 recovered authority over their
leaders, they would also recover power over the making and changing of party policy.

No constitutional amendment, not even a legislative act, would
be required to return a prime minister's tenure in office to the control
of the parliamentary majority, or to make all the party leaders

answerable to their caucuses. It would simply require an act of moral courage and a little organizing on the part of the backbenchers.

Compared to calls for spectacular transformations – for proportional representation, referendums, an elected Senate, a Republic of Canada – mere parliamentary democracy seems a very modest, unambitious, and anti-utopian notion. It offers, however, the great advantage of being possible. To restore parliamentary authority, no sweeping constitutional amendments and no radical legislative initiatives would be needed. The starting point would be a change of mind. At the beginning, all that would be required would be an act of will by elected members of Parliament, a decision to shoulder once more the fundamental responsibility of representatives in a parliamentary assembly – the making and breaking of governments.

This book has been about constitutional deal-making in a parliamentary system. And it may be in the constitutional sphere that parliamentary government offers the most intriguing possibilities. No sovereign Parliament could possibly permit the astonishingly autocratic (and consistently unsuccessful) constitution-making that our first ministers have engaged in for twenty-five years. Parliaments that actually controlled governments would certainly insist on participating in the making of a new constitution.

"Responsible government," more or less as the confederation-makers of the 1860s understood it – but under the universal suffrage that prevails today – has been the least "thinkable" of all the political options Canadians have canvassed during the 1990s. It would, however, be relatively easy to reach. If it did not save the country, it would at least offer a political scene more lively, more interesting, *less demeaning* to all concerned than the present spectacle.

– July 1997

NOTE ON SOURCES

In the endnotes, I have cited sources for direct quotations in the book.

I began this book by reading the standard histories of confederation, most notably Peter Waite's *The Life and Times of Confederation* (1962), Donald Creighton's *The Road to Confederation* (1964), and W. L. Morton's *The Critical Years: The Union of British North America, 1857-73* (1964), as well as the two-volume biographies *John A. Macdonald* by Creighton (1952, 1955) and *Brown of the Globe* by J. M. S. Careless (1959, 1963). I was also helped and influenced by the interviews several historians granted me for my radio documentary "Historians on Confederation," broadcast on CBC-Radio "Ideas" on November 28 and 29, 1991. One of those scholars, Ged Martin, has since published one of the few substantial recent works on confederation, *Britain and the Origins of Canadian Confederation, 1837-67* (1995). Throughout, I relied constantly on many volumes of the indispensable *Dictionary of Canadian Biography*.

"George Brown and Impossibility" relies heavily on Careless's *Brown of the Globe*, though I was also influenced by S. J. R. Noel's view of the union in *Patrons, Clients, Brokers: Ontario Society and Politics, 1791-1896* (1990).

For "Charles Tupper Goes to Charlottetown," I found no really good study of Tupper. Scholars have not produced a solid collection of the confederation documents, and for the proceedings of the Charlottetown conference, I relied on G. P. Browne's compilation for undergraduate use, *Documents on the Confederation of British North America* (1969).

"Ned Whelan and Edmund Burke on the Ramparts of Quebec" relies on Whelan's writings and items from Burke's *Writings and Speeches*, as cited in the notes. Conor Cruise O'Brien's *The Great Melody* (1992) shaped my sense of Burke, although the great hole in that book is Burke on Britain and its constitution. This chapter also owes much to Ian Ross Robertson's fine book *The Tenant League of Prince Edward Island, 1864-67* (1996).

For "Under the Confederation Windows," I relied on Browne's *Documents* for conference minutes and notes. My sense of Mowat's role was influenced by several works by Paul Romney cited in the notes and by Robert C. Vipond, *Liberty and Community: Canadian Federalism and the Failure of the Constitution* (1991). Creighton's *Road* led me to Mercy Ann Coles, whose diary remains unpublished.

"If Brother André Went to Parliament Hill" relies on Andrée Desilets's biography *Hector Langevin, un père de la confédération canadienne* (1969), Jean-Paul Bernard's *Les Rouges* (1971), *The French-Canadian Idea of Confederation* (1982) by Arthur Silver, *Quebec: A History, 1867-1929* (1983) by Paul-André Linteau, René Durocher, and Jean-Claude Robert, and Brian Young's biography *George-Étienne Cartier: Montreal Bourgeois* (1981). In *Le Québec et la confédération: un choix libre?* (1992), Marcel Bellavance argues against the legitimacy of the confederation process in Quebec. All the quotations from the Canadian legislative debates are from *Parliamentary Debates on the Subject of the Confederation* ("the Confederation Debates"), published in 1865 and again in 1951.

Like all post-1990 writing on the Maritimes and confederation, "Leonard Tilley and the Voters" has been influenced by Phillip Buckner's ground-clearing essay "The Maritimes and Confederation: A Reassessment," in *The Canadian Historical Review* (1990). I also drew on Carl Wallace's dissertation, "Sir Leonard Tilley: A Political Biography" (1972). Michel Brisebois of the National Library of Canada and the inter-library loan staff of the University of Saskatchewan

Library helped me locate the rather important and remarkably inaccessible *Debates of the Nova Scotia House of Assembly* for 1865, 1866, and 1867.

Considering "The Leadership Secrets of John A. Macdonald," I was surprised by how little attention has been paid to the *Economist*'s articles on confederation, which I read in conjunction with Walter Bagehot's *The English Constitution*. Beyond the standard sources and several compilations of Macdonald anecdotes, I relied on Gordon Stewart, *The Origins of Canadian Politics* (1986), on the party-building process. For the comparison of leadership processes in other parliamentary states, I relied on interviews I did for my documentary "Leadership Conventions" (CBC-Radio "Ideas," February 1, 1993). One of the interviewees, William Hague, became leader of the British Conservative Party in 1997. Professor John C. Courteney was also most helpful.

NOTES

Chapter One: *"George Brown and Impossibility"*

1. *Brown of the Globe* was published by Macmillan of Canada in 1959 (Vol. I: *The Voice of Upper Canada 1818-1859*) and 1963 (Vol. II: *Statesman of Confederation 1860-1880*). Dundurn Press republished both volumes in an attractive paperback set in 1989.
2. *Globe*, March 23, 1850.
3. *Globe*, March 23, 1850.
4. *Globe*, March 23, 1850.
5. *Globe*, March 23, 1850.
6. William G. Ormsby, "Francis Hincks," in *Dictionary of Canadian Biography*, XI, 413.
7. Careless, *Brown of the Globe*, Vol. I, pp. 288-304 analyses Brown's disillusion and the *Globe*'s editorials, particularly at pp. 289 and 302.
8. Tom Flanagan, *Waiting for the Wave: The Reform Party and Preston Manning* (Toronto: Stoddart, 1995), p. 22.
9. Careless, *Brown of the Globe*, Vol. I, pp. 311-22 on the Reform convention.
10. S. J. R. Noel, *Patrons, Clients, Brokers: Ontario Society and Politics, 1791-1896* (Toronto: University of Toronto Press, 1990), p. 174.

Chapter Two: "Charles Tupper Goes to Charlottetown"

1. There are character sketches of Tupper in Sandra Gwyn, *The Private Capital* (Toronto: McClelland & Stewart, 1984) p. 63; and A. H. Colquhoun, *The Fathers of Confederation* (Toronto: 1916), pp. 45-6.
2. Peter Waite, *The Man From Halifax: Sir John Thompson, Prime Minister* (Toronto: University of Toronto Press, 1985), pp. 211-13.
3. Donald Creighton, *The Road to Confederation* (Toronto: Macmillan of Canada, 1964) p. 5.
4. Donald Creighton, *Road to Confederation*, p. 23.
5. John Hamilton Gray, *Confederation, or the Political and Parliamentary History of Canada from the Conference at Quebec* (Toronto: Copp Clark, 1872), p. 29.
6. Creighton, *Road to Confederation*, p. 6.
7. Ged Martin, *Britain and the Origins of Canadian Confederation, 1837-67* (Vancouver: University of British Columbia Press, 1995), p. 5.
8. J. Murray Beck, *Joseph Howe* Vol. II: *The Briton Becomes Canadian*, 1848-73 (Montreal: McGill-Queen's University Press, 1983), p. 182.
9. McCully's *Morning Chronicle* of August 4, 1864, quoted in Peter Waite, *The Life and Times of Confederation* (Toronto: University of Toronto Press, 1962), p. 61.
10. Eric Sager and Gerald Panting, *Maritime Capital: The Shipping Industry in Atlantic Canada, 1820-1914* (Montreal: McGill-Queen's University Press, 1990), p. 178.
11. Gray's remark of April 12, 1864, quoted in Creighton, *Road to Confederation*, p. 34.
12. Duke of Newcastle to Lieutenant-Governor Mulgrave, July 6, 1862, in G. P. Browne, *Documents on the Confederation of British North America* (Toronto: McClelland & Stewart, 1969), pp. 30-1.
13. Careless, *Brown of the Globe*, Vol. II (Toronto: Dundurn Press, 1989), p. 153.

14. Peter Waite, "Comment," in *Canadian Historical Review* 61 #1 (March 1990), p. 34.

15. Waite, *Life and Times*, pp. 73-85; Careless, *Brown of the Globe*, Vol. II, p. 153.

16. Saint John *Morning Telegraph*, September 1864, quoted in Waite, *Life and Times*, p. 76.

17. Careless, *Brown of the Globe*, Vol. I, p. 319 and Vol. II, pp. 167-8.

18. Browne, *Documents*, pp. 32-49, are the source of all Charlottetown conference statements and resolutions quoted here, unless otherwise noted.

19. Careless, *Brown of the Globe*, Vol. II, p. 156.

20. Careless, *Brown of the Globe*, Vol. II, p. 155.

21. Waite, *Life and Times*, p. 78; Careless, *Brown of the Globe*, Vol. II, p. 155.

22. Careless, *Brown of the Globe*, Vol. II, p. 156.

Chapter Three: "Ned Whelan and Edmund Burke on the Ramparts of Quebec"

1. Whelan's speech of April 1850, in Peter McCourt, *Biographical Sketch of the Hon Edward Whelan together with a Compilation of Speeches* (Montreal: 1888; Canadian Inventory of Historic Manuscripts #26184, 1982), p. 124; Francis Bolger, *Prince Edward Island and Confederation* (Charlottetown: St. Dunstan's University Press, 1964), p. 42.

2. Edward Whelan, *The Union of the British Provinces* (Charlottetown: 1865), p. 109.

3. Peter Waite, "Edward Whelan Reports from the Quebec Conference," *Canadian Historical Review* 42 (1961), pp. 23-45.

4. Donald Creighton, *The Road to Confederation* (Toronto: Macmillan of Canada, 1964) p. 141-2.

5. Peter Russell, *Constitutional Odyssey: Can Canadians Be a Sovereign People?* (Toronto: University of Toronto Press), p. 32;

George Woodcock, "Confederation as a World Example," in Keith Banting and Richard Simeon, eds., *And No One Cheered: Federalism, Democracy and the Constitution Act* (Toronto: Methuen, 1983), pp. 333-47.

6. McCourt, *Biographical Sketch*, p. 262 ff., Whelan's speech "Eloquence as an Art," January 29, 1864.

7. D. C. Harvey, "The Centenary of Edward Whelan," in G. A. Rawlyk, ed., *Historical Essays on the Atlantic Provinces* (Toronto: McClelland & Stewart, 1971), pp. 207-28.

8. Edmund Burke, *Reflections on the Revolution in France* (London: Penguin, 1968), pp. 169-70.

9. Conor Cruise O'Brien, *The Great Melody* (London: Minerva Books, 1993), p. 311.

10. Edmund Burke, "Speech on the Economical Reform," in *Writings and Speeches*, Vol. II (London: 1889), p. 112.

11. Burke, "Speech on the Economical Reform," p. 112.

12. O'Brien, *The Great Melody*, p. 94.

13. "Thoughts on the Causes of the Present Discontents," in Paul Langford, ed., *Writings and Speeches of Edmund Burke*, Vol. II (Oxford: Clarendon Press, 1981), pp. 251-322, at p. 308.

14. O'Brien, *The Great Melody*, pp. 208-9.

15. "Thoughts on the Causes," p. 279.

16. John Beverley Robinson, *Canada and The Canada Bill* (London: 1839).

17. Burke's speech on the Constitutional Act, May 6, 1791, in William Cobbett, ed., *The Parliamentary Register*, Vol. 29 (London: Debrett, 1791) p. 379.

18. Speech to the Electors of Bristol, 1774, quoted in O'Brien, *The Great Melody*, p. 75.

19. Quoted in O'Brien, *The Great Melody*, pp. 184-5.

20. Whelan's speech on increased representation, 1856, in McCourt, *Biographical Sketch*, p. 130.

21. G. P. Browne, ed., *Documents on the Confederation of British North America* (Toronto: McClelland & Stewart, 1969), pp. 153-65.

22. Allan Greer and Ian Radforth, eds., *Colonial Leviathan: State Formation in Mid-Nineteenth Century Canada* (Toronto: University of Toronto Press, 1992), p. 13.

23. Edmund Burke, "Thoughts and Details on Scarcity" (November 1795) in *Works*, VII (London: Rivington, 1826), p. 373 ff.

24. Harvey, "The Centenary of Edward Whelan"; Ian Ross Robertson, "Edward Whelan," in *Dictionary of Canadian Biography* IX (Toronto: University of Toronto Press, 1976), pp. 828-35.

25. Ian Ross Robertson, *The Tenant League of Prince Edward Island, 1864-67: Leasehold Tenure in the New World* (Toronto: University of Toronto Press, 1996).

26. Whelan's speech on the lieutenant-governor's address, 1856, and Whelan's speech on the visit of the Prince of Wales, 1860, in McCourt, *Biographical Sketch*, pp. 92, 178, respectively.

27. Whelan's speech on the visit of the Prince of Wales, 1860, in McCourt, *Biographical Sketch*, p. 178.

28. Whelan's article of May 30, 1864, in *The Examiner*, quoted in Robertson, *The Tenant League*, p. 70.

29. Whelan's article of May 30, 1864.

30. Speech of J. H. Gray, September 8, 1864, in Edward Whelan, ed., *The Union of the British Provinces* (Charlottetown: 1865, reprinted 1965), p. 13; Creighton, *Road to Confederation*, p. 22. Bolger, *Prince Edward Island and Confederation*, pp. 59-61.

31. Robertson, "Edward Whelan," p. 831.

32. *The Protestant* (Charlottetown), quoted in Bolger, *Prince Edward Island and Confederation*, p. 61.

33. Whelan's speech of May 7, 1866, in McCourt, *Biographical Sketch*, p. 216; Waite, "Edward Whelan Reports from the Quebec Conference," p. 26.

34. Harvey, "The Centenary of Edward Whelan," p. 227.

35. Dufferin's letter to Macdonald quoted in Bolger, *Prince Edward Island and Confederation*, p. 292.

36. Whelan's speech at Montreal, October 29, 1864, in Whelan, *Union*

of the British North American Provinces, p. 109; Whelan's speech of May 7, 1866, in McCourt, *Biographical Sketch*, p. 216.

37. Waite, "Edward Whelan Reports from the Quebec Conference," pp. 37-8.

Chapter Four: "Under the Confederation Windows"

1. Mercy Ann Coles, "Diary," National Archives of Canada, MG24 B66.

2. Frances Monck, *My Canadian Leaves: An Account of a Visit to Canada in 1864-5* (London: 1891).

3. Peter Waite, ed., "Edward Whelan Reports from the Quebec Conference," *Canadian Historical Review* 42 (1961), pp. 23-45.

4. Whelan's speech of October 29, 1864, in Edward Whelan, *The Union of the British Provinces* (Charlottetown: 1865), p. 109.

5. Waite, ed., "Edward Whelan Reports," p. 40.

6. Details of the conference are from the reports and minutes collected in G. P. Browne, ed., *Documents on Confederation of British North America* (Toronto: McClelland & Stewart, 1969), pp. 55-165.

7. Moncrieff Williamson, *Island Painter: The Life of Robert Harris, 1849-1919* (Charlottetown: Ragweed Press, 1983).

8. Browne, ed., *Documents*, September 29, 1859, pp. 29-30.

9. Peter Waite, *The Life and Times of Confederation* (Toronto: University of Toronto Press, 1962), p. 94.

10. Peter Waite, ed., "Edward Whelan Reports," p. 35.

11. Browne, ed., *Documents*, p. 138.

12. Canada, *Parliamentary Debates on Confederation of the British North American Provinces* (Quebec: 1865), p. 495.

13. Browne, ed., *Documents*, p. 98.

14. Jeffrey L. McNairn, "Publius of the North: Tory Republicanism and the American Constitution in Upper Canada, 1848-54," *Canadian Historical Review* 77 (1996), pp. 504-37.

15. J. S. Mill, *Utilitarianism, On Liberty and Considerations on Representative Government* (London: J. M. Dent and Sons, 1972), p. 354.

16. Brown's Toronto speech of November 3, 1864, quoted in Whelan, *Union of the British Provinces*, p. 193.

17. *Confederation Debates*, p. 171.

18. Browne, ed., *Documents*, p. 108.

19. A. Margaret Evans, *Sir Oliver Mowat* (Toronto: University of Toronto Press, 1992) p. 17.

20. Evans, *Sir Oliver Mowat*, p. 155.

21. Evans, *Sir Oliver Mowat*, p. 162.

22. Donald Creighton, *Canada's First Century* (Toronto: Macmillan, 1970), p. 46.

23. Browne, ed., *Documents*, pp. 55-93, Minutes of the Quebec Conference; Donald Creighton, *The Road to Confederation* (Toronto: Macmillan of Canada, 1964), pp. 162-7.

24. The first Creighton quotation is from *Canada's First Century*, p. 49, the second from *Road to Confederation*, p. 174.

25. Browne, ed., *Documents*, p. 123.

26. Ibid., p. 123-5.

27. Tilley: Browne, ed., *Documents*, pp. 77-8; Brown: *Globe* of August 30, 1864, quoted in Evans, *Sir Oliver Mowat*, p. 145.

28. J. Keith Johnson, "John A. Macdonald," in J. M. S. Careless, ed., *The Pre-Confederation Premiers of Ontario* (Toronto: University of Toronto Press, 1985), pp. 197-245; James Young, *Public Men and Public Life in Canada* (Toronto: 1912), p. 225.

29. Charles R. W. Biggar, *Sir Oliver Mowat: A Biographical Sketch* (Toronto: Warwick Bros. and Rutter, 1905), p. 132.

30. Paul Romney, "Oliver Mowat," in *Dictionary of Canadian Biography* XIII (Toronto: University of Toronto Press, 1994), p. 729.

31. Phrase "miniature responsible government" from Creighton, *Road to Confederation*, p. 164.

32. Speech on the lieutenant-governor's speech, 1856, in Peter McCourt, *Biographical Sketch of the Hon Edward Whelan together*

with a Compilation of Speeches (Montreal: 1888; Canadian Inventory of Historic Manuscripts #26184, 1982), p. 92.

33. *Confederation Debates*, p. 500.
34. Robert C. Vipond, *Liberty and Community: Canadian Federalism and the Failure of the Constitution* (Albany: State University of New York Press, 1991), p. 26.
35. Vipond, *Liberty and Community*, p. 5.
36. Evans, *Sir Oliver Mowat*, p. 154.
37. Ibid., p. 155.
38. Vipond, *Liberty and Community*, pp. 78-82.
39. Evans, *Sir Oliver Mowat*, p. 161.
40. Ibid., pp. 178-9.
41. J. M. S. Careless, *Brown of the Globe*, Vol. II (Toronto: Dundurn Press, 1989), p. 171.
42. Whelan, *Union of the British Provinces*, p. 214.
43. Browne, ed., *Documents*, Document 19, July 6, 1862.
44. Mercy Coles, "Diary."

Chapter Five: "If Brother André Went to Parliament Hill"

1. Henri-Paul Bergeron, *Brother André: The Wonder Man of Mount Royal* (Montreal and Paris: Fides, 1958).
2. Speeches of Henri Joly, Cartier, and Dunkin in Canada, *Parliamentary Debates on Confederation of the British North American Provinces* (Quebec: 1865), pp. 358, 1,015, and 498-9, respectively.
3. Brian Young, *George-Étienne Cartier, Montreal Bourgeois* (Montreal: McGill-Queen's University Press, 1981).
4. Allan Greer, *The Patriots and the People: The Rebellion of 1837 in Rural Lower Canada* (Toronto: University of Toronto Press, 1993), particularly Chapter Nine.
5. Andrée Desilets, "Étienne-Paschal Taché," in *Dictionary of Canadian Biography* IX (Toronto: University of Toronto Press, 1976), pp. 774-9.

6. *Confederation Debates*, pp. 59-60.

7. J. M. S. Careless, *Brown of the Globe*, Vol. II (Toronto: Dundurn Press, 1989), p. 171; Peter Waite, ed., "Edward Whelan Reports from the Quebec Conference," *Canadian Historical Review* 42 (1961), p. 43.

8. Careless, *Brown of the Globe*, Vol. II, p. 120.

9. Canada, *Confederation Debates*, p. 9.

10. Canada, *Confederation Debates*, p. 500.

11. Canada, *Confederation Debates*, pp. 61, 614.

12. Louis Archambault, December 23, 1864, quoted in Andrée Desilets, *Hector Langevin, un père de la confédération canadienne* (Québec: Presses de l'Université Laval, 1969), p. 140.

13. *Confederation Debates*, p. 251.

14. *Confederation Debates*, pp. 655, 354.

15. Jean-Paul Bernard, *Les Rouges: Libéralisme, nationalisme, et anti-cléricalisme au milieu du XIXe siècle* (Québec: Presses de l'Université Laval, 1971), p. 253.

16. *Confederation Debates*, pp. 585-626.

17. *Confederation Debates*, p. 250.

18. Desilets, *Hector Langevin*, p. 150.

19. Desilets, *Hector Langevin*, particularly p. 130.

20. Desilets, *Hector Langevin*, p. 171; *Confederation Debates*, pp. 362-92.

21. *Confederation Debates*, p. 386.

22. *Confederation Debates*, p. 255.

23. *Confederation Debates*, pp. 387 (Langevin), 10 (Taché).

24. *Confederation Debates*, pp. 391-2.

25. *Confederation Debates*, pp. 15, 31.

26. Msgr. Charles Cazeau, quoted in Desilets, *Hector Langevin*, p. 123.

27. Waite, *The Life and Times of Confederation*, p. 156.

28. *Le Pays* of June 4, 1867, quoted in Bernard, *Les Rouges*, p. 292.

29. Evans, *Sir Oliver Mowat*, p. 327.

Chapter Six: "Leonard Tilley and the Voters"

1. Carl M. Wallace, "Sir Leonard Tilley: A Political Biography" (unpublished Ph.D. dissertation, University of Alberta, 1972).
2. Wallace, "Sir Leonard Tilley," p. 86.
3. Wallace, "Sir Leonard Tilley," p. 110, expressing Tilley's opinion in 1860; J. H. Gray, *Confederation* (Toronto: Copp Clark, 1872), p. 151.
4. Tupper to Macdonald, January 4, 1865, and Macdonald to Colonel J. H. Gray, March 24, 1865, in John A. Macdonald Papers, Vol. 51, National Archives of Canada, MG24 A.
5. Wallace, "Sir Leonard Tilley," p. 203.
6. Macdonald to Colonel J. H. Gray, March 24, 1865, in Macdonald Papers, Vol. 51, NAC, MG24 A.
7. W. L. Morton, "The Extension of the Franchise in Canada: A Study in Democratic Nationalism," Canadian Historical Association *Annual Report* 1943 (Ottawa, 1943), pp. 72-81; John Garner, *The Franchise and Politics in British North America* (Toronto: University of Toronto Press, 1969), p. 3.
8. Garner, *The Franchise and Politics*, p. 28.
9. Quoted by Gail Campbell in "Disenchanted but Not Quiescent: Women Petitioners in New Brunswick in the Mid-19th Century," in Janet Guildford and Suzanne Morton, *Separate Spheres: Women's Worlds in the 19th-Century Maritimes* (Fredericton: Acadiensis Press, 1994), p. 63.
10. Donald Creighton, *The Road to Confederation* (Toronto: Macmillan of Canada, 1964), p. 229; Tilley to Macdonald, February 1, 1865, Macdonald Papers, Vol. 51., p. 19,970, NAC, MG24 A.
11. Wallace, "Sir Leonard Tilley," p. 28.
12. Peter Waite, *The Life and Times of Confederation* (Toronto: University of Toronto Press, 1962) p. 240.
13. Gray to Macdonald, March 13, 1865, Macdonald Papers, Vol. 51, p. 19978.

14. Gray to MacDonald, March 13, 1865.

15. Nova Scotia, *Debates and Proceedings of the House of Assembly, 1866* (Halifax: 1866), p. 278.

16. Draft of Botheration Letter, Joseph Howe Papers, Vol. 26-1, p. 143, NAC, MG24 B29.

17. J. Murray Beck, ed., *Joseph Howe: Voice of Nova Scotia* (Toronto: McClelland & Stewart, 1964), p. 168.

18. Tupper to Macdonald, January 4, 1865, Macdonald Papers, Vol. 51, p. 19930, NAC, MG24 A.

19. Tupper to Macdonell, May 10, 1865, Macdonald Papers, Vol. 51, p. 90,030, NAC, MG24 A.

20. Nova Scotia *Debates* 1865, p. 203.

21. Tupper to Macdonald, April 9, 1865, Macdonald Papers, Vol. 51, p. 90,030, NAC, MG24 A.

22. Creighton, *Road to Confederation*, p. 319.

23. Waite, *Life and Times of Confederation*, p. 275.

24. Phillip Buckner, "Charles Tupper," in *Dictionary of Canadian Biography* XIV (forthcoming).

25. April 10, 1866, in Nova Scotia *Debates* 1866, p. 211.

26. April 13, 1866, in Nova Scotia *Debates* 1866, p. 233.

27. Nova Scotia *Debates* 1866, pp. 241-4 (Locke), 246 (Townsend), 276-83 (McLelan), 269-76 (Macdonald).

28. Nova Scotia *Debates* 1866, pp. 185-9 (Miller), 190 (Macdonell).

29. Beck, ed., *Joseph Howe*, p. 179.

30. Howe's statement of January 29, 1861, quoted in Nova Scotia, *Journals of the House of Assembly*, 1866, Appendix 10, April 26, 1866.

31. Howe's statement of March 30, 1861, quoted in Nova Scotia, *Journals* 1866, Appendix 10.

32. Beck, ed., *Joseph Howe*, p. 101.

33. Nova Scotia *Debates* 1866, pp. 190 (Annand), 293 (Brown), 287 (Blackwood).

34. Nova Scotia *Debates* 1866, pp. 247-54 (Henry), 211-22 (Tupper).

35. Nova Scotia *Debates* 1866, pp. 244-6 (Blanchard), 247-54 (Henry), 283-4 (McFarlane), 269-76 (Macdonald).

36. J. W. Longley, *Sir Charles Tupper* (Toronto: Morang, Makers of Canada Series, 1916), p. 79.

37. Phillip Buckner, "The Maritimes and Confederation: A Reassessment," *Canadian Historical Review* 61 (1990), pp. 1-45.

38. Canada, *Parliamentary Debates on Confederation of the British North American Provinces* (Quebec: 1865), p. 1007.

39. *Confederation Debates*, p. 59 (Cartier); G. P. Browne, *Documents on Confederation of British North America* (Toronto: McClelland & Stewart, 1969), p. 95 (Macdonald).

40. Tilley story, noted in 1917, is recorded in George S. Holmsted Papers, NAC, MG27 II H6.

Chapter Seven: "The Leadership Secrets of John A. Macdonald"

1. Canada, *Parliamentary Debates on Confederation of the British North American Provinces* (Quebec: 1865), p. 946, quoting Dickey's letter of December 5, 1864.

2. E. B. Biggar, *An Anecdotal Life of John A. Macdonald* (Montreal: Lovell and Co., 1891) p. 116-7.

3. Joseph Pope, *The Memoirs of Sir John A. Macdonald* (Toronto: Musson, 1927), p. 780-3.

4. The *Economist's* major articles on confederation in 1864 appeared on July 16 (Vol. 22, p. 892), August 27 (Vol. 22, p. 1080), October 15 (Vol. 22, p. 1279), and November 26 (Vol. 22, p. 1455).

5. Walter Bagehot, *The English Constitution* (London: 1867). I used the 1963 Fontana edition, edited and introduced by Richard Crossman, in which these quotations appear on pp. 84 and 102.

6. Bagehot, *The English Constitution*, p. 98.

7. Bagehot, *The English Constitution*, p. 245.

8. Bagehot, *The English Constitution*, p. 94.

9. Bagehot, *The English Constitution*, p. 156.

10. Biggar, *Anecdotes*, pp. 190-1.

11. J. K. Johnson, "John A. Macdonald," in J. M. S. Careless, *The Pre-Confederation Premiers of Ontario* (Toronto: University of Toronto Press, 1985).

12. Biggar, *Anecdotes*, p. 131.

13. Donald Creighton, *John A. Macdonald*, Vol. II: *The Old Statesman* (Toronto: Macmillan of Canada, 1955), p. 522.

14. Richard Cartwright, *Reminiscences* (Toronto: Wm. Briggs), p. 304.

15. Donald Creighton, *The Road to Confederation* (Toronto: Macmillan of Canada, 1964), p. 236.

16. *Confederation Debates*, p. 1007.

17. Bagehot, *The English Constitution*, p. 152.

18. Biggar, *Anecdotes*, p. 134.

19. Mercy Ann Coles, "Diary," National Archives of Canada, MG24 B66.

20. Macdonald to Gray, March 24, 1865, John A. Macdonald Papers, Vol. 51, NAC, MG24 A.

21. Carnarvon to Monck, August 10, 1866, in G. P. Browne, ed., *Documents on Confederation of British North America* (Toronto: McClelland & Stewart, 1969), p. 193.

22. Quotations from the London debates are drawn from the minutes kept by Macdonald's secretary, Hewitt Bernard, and published in Browne, ed., *Documents*, p. 195ff.

23. Browne, ed., *Documents*, p. 214.

24. Langevin's letter to his brother Edmond, quoted in Andrée Desilets, *Hector Langevin, un père de la confédération canadienne* (Québec: Presses de l'Université Laval, 1969), p. 159.

25. Desilets, *Hector Langevin*, p. 164.

26. Desilets, *Hector Langevin*, p. 159; Creighton, *Road to Confederation*, p. 408.

27. Creighton, *Road to Confederation*, p. 420.

28. *Economist*, Vol. 23, February 23, 1867, p. 203.

29. *Economist*, Vol. 23, April 22, 1865, p. 463, and September 9, 1865, p. 1086.

30. Dunkin quoted in *Confederation Debates*, p. 498; Galt quoted in H. B. Timothy, *The Galts: A Canadian Odyssey* (Toronto: McClelland & Stewart, 1984), p. 108.

31. Bagehot, *The English Constitution*, p. 159.

32. Bagehot, *The English Constitution*, p. 277.

33. Gordon T. Stewart, *The Origins of Canadian Politics* (Vancouver: University of British Columbia Press, 1986), p. 67.

34. Stewart, *Origins of Canadian Politics*, p. 70.

35. S. J. R. Noel, *Patrons, Clients, Brokers: Ontario Society and Politics, 1791-1896* (Toronto: University of Toronto Press, 1990), p. 286.

36. Noel, *Patrons, Clients, Brokers*, p. 285.

37. Bagehot, *English Constitution*, p. 94.

38. Peter Jenkins, "Article," *Independent*, April 10, 1992.

Chapter Eight: "Nation and Crown"

1. Canada, *Parliamentary Debates on Confederation of the British North American Provinces* (Quebec: 1865), p. 125-46.

2. *Confederation Debates*, p. 60.

3. *Confederation Debates*, p. 59; Nova Scotia, *Debates and Proceedings of the House of Assembly 1865* (Halifax: 1865), p. 207-10.

4. *Confederation Debates*, p. 146.

5. Dorion: *Confederation Debates*, p. 255; *Acadian Recorder* (Halifax), September 12, 1864, quoted in Phillip Buckner, "The Maritimes and Confederation: A Reassessment," in *Canadian Historical Review* 61 #1 (March 1990), p. 25.

6. Peter Russell, *Constitutional Odyssey: Can Canadians Be a Sovereign People?* (Toronto: University of Toronto Press) p. 3.

7. *Economist*, Vol. 2, October 15, 1864, p. 1279.

8. *Confederation Debates*, p. 146.

9. G. P. Browne, ed., *Documents on Confederation of British North America* (Toronto: McClelland & Stewart, 1969), pp. 185-9, Observations and Notes on the Quebec Resolutions, July 24, 1866; pp. 247-62, Initial draft of the BNA Act, January 23, 1867.

10. Browne, ed., *Documents*, p. 169; *Economist*, Vol. 22, November 26, 1864, p. 1455.

11. Browne, ed., *Documents*, p. 180.

12. Joseph Pope, *The Memoirs of Sir John A. Macdonald* (Toronto: Musson, 1927), p. 289.

13. The quotation and much of the detail here are from Ged Martin, *Britain and the Origins of Canadian Confederation, 1837-67* (Vancouver: UBC Press), pp. 284-90.

14. *Confederation Debates*, p. 132; Peter Waite, *The Life and Times of Confederation* (Toronto: University of Toronto Press, 1962), p. 28.

15. Waite, *Life and Times of Confederation*, p. 194; Nova Scotia *Debates* 1865, p. 211.

16. *Confederation Debates*, p. 145.

17. *Globe*, July 1, 1867; Careless, *Brown of the Globe*, Vol. II, p. 251-3.

18. W. T. R. Preston, *My Generation of Politicians and Politics* (Toronto: Rose Publishing, 1927), p. 18.

19. Pope, *Memoirs of Sir John A. Macdonald*, p. 274.

20. *Confederation Debates*, p. 541.

Postscript: *If We Had a Parliamentary Democracy . . .*

1. James Gillies, "Thinking the Unthinkable: The Republic of Canada," *Globe and Mail*, June 28, 1997, p. D9.

INDEX